The Art of
Astonishment

The Art of Astonishment

Reflections on Gifts and Grace

Alice Brittan

BLOOMSBURY ACADEMIC
NEW YORK · LONDON · OXFORD · NEW DELHI · SYDNEY

BLOOMSBURY ACADEMIC
Bloomsbury Publishing Inc
1385 Broadway, New York, NY 10018, USA
50 Bedford Square, London, WC1B 3DP, UK
29 Earlsfort Terrace, Dublin 2, Ireland

BLOOMSBURY, BLOOMSBURY ACADEMIC and the Diana logo are
trademarks of Bloomsbury Publishing Plc

First published in the United States of America 2022

For legal purposes the Acknowledgments on pp. ix–x constitute
an extension of this copyright page.

Cover design: Eleanor Rose
Cover image: Detail of the feathers on the wing of a
Roman Sculpture © Eukeni Uriarte / iStock / Getty Images Plus

A catalog record for this book is available from the Library of Congress.

ISBN: HB: 978-1-5013-8357-1
         PB: 978-1-5013-8356-4
       ePDF: 978-1-5013-8359-5
      eBook: 978-1-5013-8358-8

Typeset by Integra Software Services Pvt. Ltd.

To find out more about our authors and books visit www.bloomsbury.com
and sign up for our newsletters.

For my parents, and my daughters.

CONTENTS

ILLUSTRATIONS

ACKNOWLEDGMENTS

When I lose my way in a book, I always turn to the pages where the author gives thanks. To be honest, this strategy doesn't help much if the problem is that I don't understand what I'm reading. Here the solution is to brew a strong pot of tea (if it's daylight and I'm getting lazy) or pour a glass of wine (if it's nighttime and I'm trying too hard), and issue a plea to my own powers of concentration. But rereading the acknowledgments helps a great deal if the problem is that I've stopped caring about the book in my hands. No matter how plainly written or briefly stated, any homage to the people who make writing possible reminds me that the book I'm holding was created by someone with mentors, colleagues, friends, family, perhaps a partner or children—in short, a rich and busy life. This reminder helps me to glimpse a particular mind at work in the words that lost my interest and to adjust my own gait to the way that mind walks around an idea. Before I express my gratitude to the people whose attention keeps me going, I send a greeting to *you,* along with the hope that these acknowledgments will serve to energize you as you make your way through this book. I'd brew your tea or pour your wine if I could. Instead, I offer these thanksgiving pages.

Fragments of this book began as conference talks given in Toronto, Vancouver, Ottawa, Halifax, Montreal, Boston, Princeton, and Providence, and in helpful conversations with participants and seminar organizers. Over the years, friends and colleagues read sections of the manuscript or made valuable suggestions, including Carrie Dawson, Bernie Rhie, Jeremy Braddock, Erin Wunker, Alyda Faber, Rohan Maitzen, Michael Clune, and Simon Couper. Rita Barnard has been a support for many years, and so have my colleagues in the English Department at Dalhousie University, particularly Christy Luckyj, Lyn Bennett, and Shao-Pin Luo. My students always change my reading habits and stretch my thinking, and I thank them all, especially Brandi Estey-Burtt. I also thank the anonymous readers who offered insightful feedback when this book was at the manuscript stage; although I could not accommodate all their recommendations, I hope they will sense their influence here and feel that their time was well spent. Mistakes, omissions, idiocies: these are all mine.

This book is as indebted to my family, friends, and neighbors as to my professional life as a scholar. Who would I be, how would I know to prepare the ground, without all of you? These bonds, no matter how difficult, teach me what stories are for: they show us how to live as generously as we can. There are too many people to list here, but I should make special mention of the Sandlers, the Brotmans, the Wright-Rainham clan, Bob Bean, and Barbara Lounder. The first and best storytellers of my life are my parents, Cora and Eric, and my sisters, Francesca, Jennifer, Suzannah, and Kelly, a sister in spirit. My patient husband Ilan Sandler cohabited with this book for a long time, and so did my beloved daughters, Ava and Eloise. They came to me like a gift, against all expectation, and returned me to the very roots of storytelling. I hope this book keeps faith with what I've learned there.

Introduction: Astonishment

The theory of the gift is a theory of human solidarity.
MARY DOUGLAS[1]

There was once a young man named Philippe Petit who spent his days riding through the streets of Paris on a unicycle and giving impromptu performances on a tightrope stretched between two lamp posts. When he saw the police coming, he stashed his juggling balls, pocketed the change in his hat, and quickly cycled away on one wheel. Petit was a kind of circus performer, but his big top was the city and his audience was the accidental passerby. One day he was leafing through a magazine when he came across a story about two enormous towers that were soon to be built side by side in New York City. "They are making those towers especially for me!" he thought. Soon Petit began to gain a reputation for his extraordinary feats of guerrilla tightrope. With the help of a small crew of conspirators, he strung a wire between two pinnacles of Notre Dame Cathedral and walked across it. Then he flew to Australia with a few of the same friends, set up a cable between two pylons of the Sydney Harbour Bridge, and walked across that. Even as Petit was strolling through the air in Paris and Sydney, he was preparing for the Twin Towers in New York and making plans for how he would smuggle himself, a team of assistants, and several hundred pounds of steel cable onto the rooftop without being caught by construction crews or security staff. He succeeded, and early in the morning of August 7, 1974, he walked out into the space between the two towers of the World Trade Center and spent forty-five minutes dancing, jumping, running, and kneeling on his high wire. When the police arrived to recall him to the safety of the rooftop, Petit laughed and saluted the clouds.[2]

"Why did you do it?" asked members of the press when Philippe Petit came down to earth. He thought this a uniquely American question. No one in France had asked him why he played his trick on Notre Dame. How could there be a reason other than mischief and joy? The mischief is obvious enough, but the joyousness of Petit's performance is what most impressed onlookers. He didn't scuttle from one building to another; he danced. He behaved as though the Twin Towers really had been built so that he could create the kind of astonishment that comes from watching an unprotected human body move across the sky as though it belonged there and had simply folded its wings away, like an angel or a bird in repose. Throngs of people greeted Petit when he was released from police custody, and although none of the film footage or photographs captured the presence of Hermes, I am sure that he was there to claim the Frenchman as a brother. Their fraternity begins with their airborne natures, but it's deepened by the way Petit broke the law and then walked out into a state of pure mortality, returning to the temple of trade with the casualness of someone who does business with death every day.

Hermes is a messenger, a go-between, a tightrope where no one expects to find one, and he appears in the pages of this book with the same tact that characterizes his appearances in the ancient myths and epics, where he flies in to facilitate contact among people and places that would prefer to ignore each other and then exits without trying to steal the scene.[3] Lewis Hyde places him within the trickster tradition, and writes that his job is to "disturb the established categories of truth and property and, by doing so, open the road to possible new worlds."[4] From the moment of his mythic birth, as described in the Homeric *Hymn to Hermes*, the mischievous son of Zeus and Maia is busy with the task of changing the way wealth and ideas circulate, all with a chuckle rather than a scowl. He kills a turtle and from its shell invents the first lyre, steals fifty cows from Apollo and artfully conceals their tracks as well as his own, lies to Apollo's face when accused of being a cattle rustler, and in the end sings and plays his lyre so winningly that instead of being vengeful, Apollo is charmed by his precocious half-brother. So charmed that he trades gifts with the little miscreant—the lyre for the cattle whip and the golden wand—and then observes that their father Zeus has given Hermes "the honor of initiating deeds of exchange trade among men."[5] Hermes takes this honor seriously, while always managing to give the impression that he might at any moment break into the foxtrot or perform a grand jété.

Lies and misdirection are the lures by which Hermes gets his older brother's attention, but what the boy really wants is some of Apollo's power. "Why do we live in a damp cave rather than on Mount Olympus?" Hermes asks his mother. "Why do mortals not sacrifice and pray to us, as to the other gods?" "You may be content with leftovers and half-portions, but I am not," he sniffs. The gifts that conclude the *Hymn* are mere prelude to the realization of Hermes's larger ambition, which is to gain some dignity and a better place in the economy. To do this he steals cattle but then carefully performs a ritual sacrifice and engages in a conventional gift exchange. No anarchist, he. This blend of obedience and misbehavior characterizes Hermes's entire portfolio as a god. He blesses the shopkeeper as well as the thief, applauds the public storyteller and the person who speaks in parables, establishes thresholds but encourages trespass, and in the end escorts spirits to the House of the Dead, although he alone is also empowered to lead you back to life should fate or your own heroic effort ordain a reprieve. (This doesn't happen very often.) No one else can carry cargo back and forth across that dark frontier.[6] This book isn't about Hermes, although his name comes up more than once, as do the epics in which he plays a brief but important role. If scholars are allowed muses, then I claim the god of astonishment as mine.

It may seem strange to introduce essays about grace with a discussion of two outlaws, particularly because many people think of grace as a merciful gift bestowed by God or an accident of the stars. "There go I but for the grace of God," people say, even people who don't believe in God. Then again, "grace is not so poor a thing that it cannot present itself in any number of ways," as Marilynne Robinson writes.[7] The ways that I write about in this book tend to be rooted in (or routed through) humanity rather than a divinity, although over the years I have come to believe that firm distinctions between the two are beyond my capacity to identify, much less to enforce, and to understand that this is not an unusual problem to have, or perhaps a problem at all. When Robinson describes housekeeping as "precisely sacramental," she implies that it is unwise to insist upon the difference between worship and washing the dishes, or any of the other tasks by which people care for one another with whatever resources are to hand.[8] There was a time when I thought it was important to keep matters of faith and housework separate, and believed that they represented two entirely different registers of being, but I am no longer sure about this. It is the nature of the gift to move from one domain to another, often changing form while in transit. Considerable agility is required in the effort to track it, mixed with an equal part of humility.

We sometimes talk about grace as though it were a dainty mille-feuille nestled among hearty wholegrains, a dreamy moment before the gavel descends, or a crocheted doily on the conference table where the deals are brokered. We imagine a decorative filigree on a load-bearing beam: a striking refinement of physical or expressive beauty that is pleasurable to encounter, to be sure, but certainly not fundamental to the basic support of anyone's existence or to the beliefs and practices that hold us together or drive us apart. For example, the other day I was in a parking garage whose owner had posted two signs on the payment kiosk. The first read, "No grace period will be given after your ticket is issued." The second read, "We appreciate your tips." There is a confusion here, and it extends well beyond one parking lot in New York City. My husband left some money in the tip box, although he later told me that he regretted it, not because he is unkind or unaware that parking lot attendants generally do not make the rules or profit by them, but because if transfers of grace are foreclosed at the outset it is hard not to feel that gratitude is anything but a transaction or a triviality. This is not the way grace has been understood historically. For millennia, it has been recognized as essential to the vitality of inner life, as well as to the large-scale shifts in perspective and legislation that improve the way we live together. It is real food, real justice, real work, and real life; fundamental, not ornamental.

The theologian Stanislas Breton placed a gift at the center of the world and all that happens in it, a gratuity on a scale grander than anyone can imagine. "The world is all that happens by an initial, gratuitous gift," he writes.[9] He anchored this belief in Paul's epistles, but Breton was a Marxist political philosopher as well as a theologian, and he believed that Paul's letters were as valuable for secular thinkers as they are for the faithful or the historian. The idea of grace that is at the center of Paul's contribution to the invention of Christianity has nothing to do with moral or physical exceptionalism, but with the limits of being, where we become most vulnerable to violence but also available to transformation. Even when God vanishes from our thinking, this idea of the gift remains indispensable. In part this is because it is notoriously difficult to disentangle gods and gifts, as the inhabitants of Lystra learned when they mistook Paul for Hermes. This story is told in chapter fourteen of Acts of the Apostles, and it takes place shortly after Saul of Tarsus is blinded on the road to Damascus by a radiant cloud of light in which he hears the voice of Jesus. After his conversion and change of name, Paul becomes an evangelist, and one day finds himself in the town of Lystra, where he preaches the gospel and tells a crippled man to get up and walk. The man jumps to his feet, at which point amazed onlookers are seized by the belief that Paul is Hermes come down to earth. "Paul they called Hermes because he was the chief speaker," and presumably because he has a knack for restoring life to dead limbs.[10] Paul is not flattered by the comparison, and he tries to explain that he is a man like any other, and that his power comes from the living God, not from any of the geriatric Greco-Roman deities, who must now be called down from the heavens and retired from duty. The episode ends badly, in confusion and outrage. As usual, Paul narrowly escapes with his life.

Some 2000 years later, the theologian and former Archbishop of Canterbury, Rowan Williams, calls the Christian God "a movement of gift."[11] This definition might have helped to bridge the distance between Paul and the people of Lystra, who recognized a miracle when they saw one, but felt no need to change their minds about who was responsible for it. Like Marilynne Robinson, Williams suggests that it is impossible to know where the divine might become visible at any moment or how it is reliably to be distinguished from gifts that seem to come from non-celestial sources.

Williams's God is on the go, not quarantined in a room called "The Sacred" that one can choose to enter or to avoid. Nor did the earlier Greeks consider gifts to be exclusive to either religious ritual or places of worship. Thanks to Hermes, they could appear any time a person went for a walk, spoke to a stranger, told a story, sang a song, looked at a piece of art, conducted business, or commemorated the dead. In short, almost anywhere.

"Every subject is initiated on the basis of a charisma," writes the philosopher Alain Badiou.[12] He too believes that the epistles have something to offer a secular understanding of selfhood and social power. What is charisma? The Pauline word derives from Greek *charis*, or grace, which was a pre-monetary social system in which material gifts were used to create lasting bonds, even with strangers and enemies. Thus charisma is a sudden access of grace. No one can anticipate or demand this rush of life, but oh how we hunger for it. As Paul tried to explain to the Romans, Corinthians, Galatians, Thessalonians, and anyone else who wanted to understand the relationship between divine grace and Mosaic Law in the decades immediately following Jesus's death, "neither circumcision counts for anything, nor uncircumcision, but being a new creature."[13] Throughout his letters Paul claims that divine grace founds but also bends sacred law, and thereby changes what it means to comply with the Jewish rules of religious observance, including circumcision. More broadly, he claims that grace makes you feel newly alive—a new creature. So do charismatic people and works of art, which seem to release courage for the taking, dislodge dead perspectives, and open confinements of all sorts.

It was just such an experience that led me to begin to think about grace in the first place, and it happened at a time in my life when I was exhausted to the core. I am a person whose body is prone to collapse, whose mind occasionally short circuits. All the fuses blow, and everything goes dark. One afternoon, at the end of a particularly grueling year, I found myself with forty-five minutes in which to rest before I needed to pick up my two daughters from preschool, who required and deserved a great deal of my nonexistent energy. I decided to spend those minutes drinking a strong cup of tea and reading the introduction to Lewis Hyde's *The Gift*, which had been sitting unopened on my bedside table for months. As I read Hyde's remarkable book, my fatigue lifted for a moment. I had already been studying the gift for several years at this point, the topic was certainly not new to me, and I knew that the surge of lightness I felt was produced by something more than the subject matter alone. That something more is grace. Even in its most modest forms, it helps us to get out of bed and take care of the people we love.

Whenever people pull the ancient histories of astonishment into the present tense, they credit grace with the renewal of the self and of the social contract. In fact, this desire for more equitable social and economic relationships is just what motivated the anthropologist Marcel Mauss to begin his foundational research on the gift more than a century ago. His purpose was not simply to study "The Form and Reason for Exchange in Archaic Societies," although this is the slightly misleading subtitle to his classic *Essai sur le Don*. Mauss's larger and more pressing aim was to understand the form and reason for exchange in his own society and in Europe more generally. His anthropological analysis of the gift as a "total system" or social phenomenon—one that links people with their neighbors as well as with strangers, the gods, the earth, and the dead—was intended to challenge liberal utilitarianism, a political philosophy in which the circulation of wealth has nothing to do with the enrichment of human solidarity or with respect for the planet and the invisible forces within and around it. Writing a new foreword to Mauss's essay in 1990, the anthropologist Mary Douglas predicted that new forms of economic utilitarianism might encourage people to think carefully about the gift again, and she was right.[14] Across disciplines and fields of endeavor, it is increasingly clear that what is made in one generation is given to the next, and if that inheritance includes life itself, it also includes the destructive practices and beliefs that have led to climate collapse, the global refugee crisis, dehumanizing economic disparities, systemic racism, and all the forms of vanity and greed that jeopardize our survival on this irreplaceable planet. To think about the gift in the twenty-first century is always to think about what is given: to seek to protect it or, when necessary, to try to change it for the better.

The editors of the South African anti-apartheid literary magazine *Staffrider* opened their first issue, in March 1978, with the following editorial statement:

> A staffrider is, let's face it, a *skelm* [rascal] of sorts. Like Hermes or Mercury—the messenger of the gods in classical mythology—he is almost certainly as light-fingered as he is fleet-footed. A skilful entertainer, a bringer of messages, a useful person but ... slightly disreputable. Our censors may not like him, but they should consider putting up with him. A whole new literature is knocking at the door, and if our society is to change without falling apart it needs all the messages it can get—the bad as well as the good.[15]

As writer and editor Mothobi Mutloatse explained, a staffrider is "somebody who rides 'staff' on the fast, dangerous and overcrowded trains that come in from the townships to the city, hanging on to the sides of the coaches, climbing on the roof, harassing the passengers," saving the price of a train ticket but also flaunting the trespass that in a small way attacked the rigidity of apartheid itself.[16] The editorial policy outlined in the magazine's first issue stated that its goal was to "encourage and give strength to a new literature based on communities, and to establish important lines of communication between these writers, their communities, and the general public."[17] This goal made the apartheid government nervous, and one month after its first issue *Staffrider* was banned for sedition by South Africa's Censorship Board.[18] No one involved with the magazine could have been surprised. Staffriders are illegal, and the idea of opening up lines of communication between the white public and the black townships, where most of the magazine's contributors and readers lived, ran counter to every technique of racial segregation practiced by the ruling National Party. *Staffrider* tried to open a road in just the way that Hermes favors: by connecting those who have been given a great deal of power and are eager to preserve it with those who have very little and are desperate for change. Riding or writing "staff" is as life-threatening as a high-wire walk between the Twin Towers, or a plan for social advancement that involves ridiculing Apollo, but without this danger there can be no *hermaion*, or gift-of-Hermes: the shock that explodes the established hierarchy.[19] Astonishment is kin to wonder, but not quite its twin.

An abusive political system will accelerate the drive for change, but the need for grace pervades every life. Many people feel that who they are at any time is an intolerable constraint on the variety and vastness of who they are capable of being, and although the experience of injustice is sure to amplify and focus this feeling, there is no social structure, however benevolent, that can eliminate it. No one ever loses the need to be reminded of their inner affluence. In a late essay titled "Altered States," the neurologist Oliver Sacks writes, to "live on a day-to-day basis is insufficient for human beings; we need to transcend, transport, escape" or we lose hope and "the sense of a future."[20] One of the more destructive manifestations of this need is the misuse of hallucinogens and opiates that Sacks goes on to describe. One of the simplest manifestations of it is the impulse that pulls people's eyes toward windows and doors, including the cell phones and screens to which we have all become addicted. "I need to escape into another reality for a while," says my daughter wearily as she picks up her phone and pulls on her headphones. "I don't just want to read my book," says her older sister, "I want to live *inside* it." It is no accident that this impulse toward anything that is not here, not this, and not me animates so much of the literature written for children.

When I began to imagine this book, my children were so young that I still read aloud to them every day, often for hours at a stretch. We never tired of fairy tales. We were not ready for bed. In those years it occurred to me that for people like us, people who do not practice a religion or a faith, the stories of childhood are amniotic. They offer original food that I hope will nourish my children all their lives, telling them where to look for help when their courage fails. Like my own mother, I welcomed my daughters to this world by showing them the exits: the dark woods, the rabbit hole, the cyclone, the wardrobe, the secret garden, the wrinkle in time, the chocolate factory, the wild things, the train platform, the subtle knife. And like most children, mine believed that these exits could be found behind the couch, in the backyard, under the sidewalk—anywhere at all. Sometimes they took this literally, as children do. I remember the summer evening when I found their beds empty and stood, paralyzed by terror, until I heard shrieks of laughter through an open window and looked out to see that they had crept downstairs to frolic outside by moonlight, their little bodies wild with glee. I have never seen such exuberance. After that night we installed locks at the top of the exterior doors because it is not safe for unaccompanied toddlers to roam the neighborhood at any hour. Years later, we have begun to use those locks again because one of my daughters walks in her sleep, as I did at her age. Recently I heard her footsteps in the middle of the night and jumped out of bed to follow her downstairs, where I found that she had flung open the back door and was standing at the threshold, eyes wide open yet fast asleep, staring expectantly into the dark.

Generations of storytellers have decided that one of the most important things we can teach children is that to be here they need to plant one foot somewhere else. At every opportunity they need to step into the dark, despite the startling and often frightening visions that appear there. Take young Conrad Cornelius o'Donald o'Dell, of Dr. Seuss's *On Beyond Zebra!*, who masters his ABC's only to be informed by his more adventurous friend, "*My* alphabet starts where *your* alphabet ends!" "Explore!" his friend urges, "Like Columbus! / Discover new letters!" as well as new orthographies and the marvelous, never-before-seen creatures that they were invented to describe.[21] Do you really want to be the kind of lad who stops at the Z? No, which is why children's books are filled with cunning little doors and passageways that lead to secret realms filled with even more hiding places, many of which come as a surprise even to the people who live there and might be expected to know their way around. Jadis, the White Witch of Narnia, is undone by old laws of love and sacrifice that she had forgotten about, and so is Lord Voldemort, who never imagines that a mother's kiss could awaken primordial sorcery more powerful than anything he has mastered. Just as physical space is deceptive, and often far roomier than outward appearances suggest, moral codes are more supple than they look. There is always magic outside of magic, and laws older and stranger than the ones currently in use.

Notice that the Cat in the Hat enters and exits through the very same door that the children's mother uses, yet as she is walking up her front path she cannot see him rushing in and out of her house with his tidy-up machine.[22] The Cat crosses the same threshold as everyone else, but he comes from and vanishes back into a kingdom of his own. That kingdom offers an escape from a rainy day, but also refreshes the mind so that it can once again pay attention to familiar things. Journeys to or visitors from other worlds always seem to make children more appreciative and better behaved. I suspect that Sally and her brother are very happy to see their mother when the Cat leaves, just as the villagers in Gabriel García Márquez's children's story, "The Handsomest Drowned Man in the World," enter a "maze of fantasy" that makes them love each other, and even strangers from distant villages, as much as they love the charismatic corpse that washes up on their shoreline.[23] Only the lesser children's writers trivialize this love by attempting to turn it into a lesson plan. Nevertheless, even the most fantastical stories eventually send children home, where they must learn to love the everyday. When Dorothy Gale tearfully swears that she'll never again dream of visiting somewhere over the rainbow, we know that she's wrong, and that although her grown-up experience of elsewhere and otherwise will not involve high-stepping with Munchkins, it will be Munchkin-*like* to the degree that it carries her beyond her horizon and then convinces her, for a time, that there is no place like home and no one dearer than friends and family. Dorothy has no idea how much more difficult this process will become as she grows older. Surely this is why we work so hard to preserve our children's trust in dreams, especially in times of difficulty.

Walking around my neighborhood during the first wave of the coronavirus pandemic of 2020, I noticed a sudden profusion of fairy houses. Have you ever seen one? Children attach a tiny door to the base of a tree trunk and then decorate the surrounding area with brightly colored figurines and little shiny things, presumably belonging to the fairy family who lives there. Some of these houses are quite elaborate.

FIGURE 0.1 *Fairy House. Photo credit: Ilan Sandler.*

I could see that frazzled parents were trying to occupy their small children during the months of lockdown, and I wondered, are we beckoning the fairies into our world or begging them to grant us asylum in theirs? Naturally, adults understand grace differently from children, which is why there is a limit to my desire to think about fairies and Munchkins. I promise to refer to them only intermittently in the pages that follow, although I confess upfront to a total lack of restraint when it comes to elves. Perhaps this is not the moment to mention the angels.

* * *

Anne Carson writes, "people need / acts of attention from one another."[24] No one who has lived through a plague can doubt the truth of this statement. Yet there is ample evidence to suggest that people are not very good at attending to one another, and any number of reasons why. In the Iron Age of Ovid's *The Metamorphoses*, which in many respects sounds suspiciously like our own, errors of attention have such violent consequences that people are routinely hounded out of their own skins, but no one can simply decide to shut their eyes or stay at home, because the "damned desire of having" keeps everyone on the move.[25] The very first metamorphosis is the one that fells, hollows, and shapes trees into the boats that carry their makers to places no one has ever seen before, and they immediately lay claim to what they find. Exploration introduces the idea of private property—the ground itself, once free to everyone, is "stepped off by surveyors" and mined for gold—but at the same time individuality becomes increasingly unstable.[26] When bodies leave home they begin to brush up against and merge with one another, animals, and the gods in new ways, moving morally and spatially out of bounds and melting distinctions between things, much as a boat turns a human being into a temporary amphibian and lets him live a little while on the surface of an element where he does not belong. Exchanging native earth for water, the citizens of the Iron Age travel to the unfinished edges of who they are, often colliding with strangers, and sometimes losing themselves in the process. After Ovid, writers from Franz Kafka to Frantz Fanon have described people who are exiled from humanity because they are regarded with contemptuous or utilitarian intent, or because they are not regarded at all. Those who are not known cannot "merge with any reality," wrote Bruno Schulz a few years before he was murdered by the Nazis, and are therefore "condemned to float eternally on the periphery of life, in half-real regions, on the margins of existence."[27] Decades later, living under Soviet censorship and surveillance, Milan Kundera described the unbearable lightness of being that causes people to "soar into the heights, take leave of the earth" and become "only half real."[28]

Over the last few decades, scholars in the humanities have often credited acts of generous attention with the ability to prevent people from becoming animals or monsters or objects. The study of empathy and cosmopolitanism tested the premise that we are capable of considering one another without violence or empty piety. Like the Greek cosmopolitan, grace is an idea that has thrived for several millennia, including at the center of the Abrahamic faiths. Although we cannot know when it is working quietly in people's hearts, gift thinking tends to bloom when political and economic systems fail, and when laws no longer protect against exclusion and abuse. Paul's gospel of the gift, which promised to unite men and women of all religions and nationalities, was in part a response to the brutality of Roman rule, which led to his execution for sedition, to the Jewish War of 66–73 CE, and to the starvation or slaughter of almost all of Jerusalem's inhabitants.[29] As France fell to the Nazis in the summer of 1940, Simone Weil wrote an essay about the siege of another walled city, Troy. In the *Iliad,* she saw an earlier version of the charisma that becomes so important to Paul and to the Greek Bible. She called it "the grace of war."[30] A decade later, with Europe still in ruins, Mauss's *The Gift* was published in book form for the first time. Then and now, the gift is where the mind goes to build a door out of a way of life that is falling apart.

Each chapter of this book is about one of those doors. They are marked "Grace," "Charity," "Secrets," "Shame," "Patience," and "Rest." The early chapters focus on the things we do to prepare the ground for grace. The later ones are about the times when we no longer know what to do. Chapter 1, "Grace," begins with an imaginary meeting between two aristocratic strangers on a quiet road outside of Athens, two generations before the Trojan War. Both men travel with an entourage, and all are heavily armed. I won't tell you what happens next, because that would ruin the surprise. I can tell you that years later, in the pages of Homer's *Iliad*, their grandsons Diomedes and Glaucus meet on opposing sides of the battlefield at Troy. When they discover that their grandfathers once crossed paths, they throw their weapons down and promise never to try to kill one another, even though the kings they serve are at war. The bond that unites Diomedes and Glaucus—and their grandfathers before them—is part of the system called *charis,* which was essential to governance, diplomacy, and social life in pre-monetary Greece, although it does not vanish after the invention of money in the sixth and fifth centuries BCE. This chapter explores the persistence of gift thinking across a wide range of stories and moments in history, from Paul Celan's Bremen Prize acceptance speech to Paul's epistles, from Abolitionism to Karl Ove's Knausgaard's *My Struggle,* and any number of fairy tales.

Please don't get the wrong idea about Chapter 2. It's called "Charity," but you don't need to call your accountant or consult the tax code to read it. In fact, the word charity derives from *charis*; it is a form of grace that entails caring for others even if they don't seem to deserve it and may not be willing to return your generosity. When the early modern scholar William

Tyndale undertook the first translation of the Bible into English, working directly from Greek, he used the word love rather than charity precisely in order to restore emotional depth to the act of giving, especially to the deprived and outcast. The South African Nobel Laureate J. M. Coetzee has always been particularly interested in unrewarded love of this kind, and his novels are at the center of this chapter, as is my experience of teaching those novels to hundreds of students over the last twenty years. Like Marilynne Robinson, Coetzee's work considers the social force of charity as well as the range of forms it is capable of taking, some of which are very shocking. Unlike Robinson, Coetzee does not anchor that force in the divine, although he is deeply attentive to angels and messiahs (and demons too). His writing explores the old idea that the cruelest forms of systemic violence are redressed not by efforts of will or acts of imagination, but by an uncalculated outpouring of kindness. Both during and after apartheid, he places charity and *caritas*—loving care—at the heart of real societal change: not empathy, not intellect, and not even legislation, but the "holes in the heart" through which our strangest impulses and deepest needs are expressed.[31]

After reading Elena Ferrante's novel *The Days of Abandonment*, the Pulitzer Prize-winning writer Jhumpa Lahiri decided to fulfill a lifelong dream: she moved her family to Rome and gave up the English language for Italian. Lahiri describes this process in a collection of essays called *In Other Words*, written in Italian and translated into English by Ann Goldstein, who also translated all of Ferrante's novels. Why does an internationally celebrated writer choose to verbally incapacitate herself so that she has to write in what she calls "a state of complete bewilderment"—a state of astonishment?[32] This is a central question for Chapter 3, "Secrets," which is about a need that is expressed in various ways by many artists: to shed what they know in order to access a secret part of the self. The conviction that the singular voice is inherently emancipatory, not just for the person in retreat but for everyone who is able to listen in, animates Lahiri's transformation, as well as all of Ferrante's novels, especially the Neapolitan Quartet. It also created a turning point in my family history. When my father moved to London to apply to art school, his eccentric landlady offered him reduced rent on one condition: they would meet every Sunday to discuss a novel of her choice, beginning with *The Idiot*. To say that my father was not a reader at this stage in his life is to be guilty of understatement. He had a police record, but no library card. His landlady was Francesca Mary Wilson, the humanitarian activist and writer, who for over a decade listened to my father's inexpert thoughts on Russian and American literature as though he were George Steiner. I end this chapter by considering the value of this kind of amateurism, and the pressure it places on the scholarly expertise I have spent my life acquiring, and would now like to suspend so that I too can write in a state of complete bewilderment.

A few years ago, I saw a homeless white man in New York City who was sitting on the sidewalk in front of a handmade sign that read, "Unemployed, Sad, Embarrassed, Ashamed." This sign is the point of departure for Chapter 4, "Shame," as is the following observation of Simone Weil's: "He who has absolutely no belongings of any kind around which social consideration crystallizes does not exist."[33] Weil was writing at the end of the Depression and the beginning of the refugee and humanitarian crises created by the Spanish Civil War and the Second World War: she knew what it meant to be penniless, homeless, and bereft. This chapter is about the anger and shame that people feel when they fall out of the economy, and about the resources that might bring them back to life, from the creation of a Basic Income Grant (or Universal Basic Income) to asylum and citizenship for refugees. I begin with my own family's financial collapse, and the neighborhood I grew up in, which was zoned for demolition because its residents were considered criminal trash. Drawing on an array of stories and situations, from Greta Gerwig's debut film *Lady Bird* to my grandmother's beauty salons, I write about how invisible people try to feel consequential. The anthropologist James Ferguson argues that "asocial inequality"—total civic invisibility— is one of the global emergencies of the twenty-first century.[34] Many agree, including the authors of novels about the contemporary refugee crisis, including Jenny Erpenbeck, Mohsin Hamid, and NoViolet Bulawayo. Like other thinkers across disciplines, these writers turn to traditions of charity and gift that are not based on guilt or moral obligation, and do not calculate human value exclusively in relation to GDP.

Does anyone know how to rest anymore? Does anyone know what it means to be patient? I claim no natural authority here. I come from a line of women who died standing up, and of men who worked all day and then said yes to the night shift. My final chapters are about people who are waiting for painful situations to change, and because they have exhausted the avenues for action, their only choice is to be patient or to give in to despair. Lewis Hyde famously argues that "the gift moves toward the empty place."[35] In "Patience" and "Rest" I explore a different possibility, which is that sometimes the gift comes *from* the empty place: from grief, desolation, and helplessness. My cast of characters includes Odysseus and Aeneas, who are both sent to the underworld at a time of paralysis, Martha and Mary, standing before the tomb of their brother Lazarus, and the thirty-three Chilean miners who in 2010 survived sixty-nine days trapped in darkness at the bottom of a collapsed mineshaft because they believed that God was watching over them. These are people who learned how to bide their time. However, I am equally alert to situations when the empty place is just empty, like the Holocaust Void in Daniel Libeskind's Jewish Museum in Berlin. Thus my cast of characters also includes Euripides's Hekabe, Queen of Troy, who after the Trojan defeat takes vengeance by murdering blameless children, and my dangerous grandfathers, whose misery brutalized and bankrupted their families. In these final chapters, I am particularly interested in astonishing responses to acts of depravity, both literary and lived. Twenty-four years after her daughter's unsolved murder, my mother-in-law won an award for her exceptional record as a volunteer with refugees, new immigrants, and the homeless. My parents have a similarly hyperbolic impulse to give. These are people who bear their suffering not passively but patiently, in the ancient belief that what is empty slowly comes back to life again. I am not very good at this kind of patience, and I write about that too.

The experiences that emerge from states of exhaustion can reveal our hidden fidelities more vividly than any others, and I suspect that is why Hermes is in charge of the dead. There is often a subtractive capacity inherent in gifts, the feeling of a burden lifted or a pain eased, and this is especially true of the gifts that appear when everything has been taken away, so that a person stands alone in a state of absolute vulnerability. This is why the images of Philippe Petit walking between the Twin Towers are so arresting. We call these kinds of acts "death-defying," but what they really defy is any local notion of how one can or should live. Like a staffrider, a man on a high wire makes death his closest ally, not an enemy to be taunted and bested. He defies a limited vision of life, reaching his hand into the darkness in order to reimagine what it is possible to be. This is the wisdom of Hermes and his many successors. It is also the story of this book.

* * *

Hermes is usually associated with the winged cap and sandals, but I always think of him as the most manual of the gods. What qualifies him to reign over the ethereal, over the air itself, is this commitment to tangible things. He understands that you have to gut the turtle before you can invent the lyre, just as he understands that a poem or song vitalizes material endeavors. Hermes is a spirit guide because he can always be trusted to discover a path from here to there, however sneaky and sinuous, and because he can be relied upon to beckon the wilderness that pulses outside. He can usher life out of the world and then create the doorways and windows that let the darkness back in, not as a ghost or an echo, not as grief or melancholy, but as the source of all gifts and every grace.

1

Grace

Long before the fall of Troy, two aristocratic strangers meet on a lonely road outside of Athens. If either one of them puts on a show of hostility the encounter could escalate into a full-scale war between their families, with bloodshed and conflict lasting for several generations. With this in mind, one of the men puts down his weapons, calls off his guard, and stands in front of his potential killer. He hopes that instead of being rushed with a sword he will be offered a gift, which he will accept and reciprocate with gratitude. In this scenario we have to imagine that he has packed wisely and is prepared to hoist a handsome object out of his luggage or from somewhere about his person, an object whose intricate handwork and precious materials will match or slightly exceed the excellence of whatever he has been given. If this is not the case, then he might invite the other man back to his home, offer him a meal and whatever provisions he needs, hear the chronicle of his life, and then give him a beautiful piece of leather or metal work. With this exchange, the strangers become *xenia,* or ritualized friends, and forge a familial alliance that deliberately imitates the inherited kinship ties that unite one generation to another. Anyone who refuses to press his own wrist to the other's opened vein invites death.[2]

Years later, the two men's grandsons are fighting on opposite sides of the Trojan War. The practices of *charis* that brought the strangers together have fallen apart, and not for the obvious reason that the *Iliad* takes place in a war zone. Even in battle, a man with a sword at his throat might be spared if he can afford to pay a royal ransom and his enemy is feeling gracious; if not, the defeated soldier has the minimal right to expect that his dead body will be returned unmutilated to his camp to be mourned and buried with appropriate reverence. Beginning with King Agamemnon, who in the opening scene of Homer's epic publically disgraces his most powerful warrior, Achilles, leader of the Myrmidons, these traditions of battlefield mercy are abandoned. The conquered are refused ransom and the dead are denied burial. In this moral chaos, a ferocious Greek hero named Diomedes encounters a Trojan named Glaucus in the no-man's-land between the armies. "Who are you my fine friend?" calls Diomedes, not in a spirit of conviviality but to make sure that Glaucus is mortal.[3] No reasonable man wants to pit his strength against the gods, who have a terrifying habit of masquerading as human beings in order to advance their own complicated projects of retribution and glory. When he hears Glaucus's family history, Diomedes realizes that their grandfathers were *xenia*. Moreover, he knows exactly what gifts they exchanged: my "kinsman offered a gleaming sword-belt, rich red," and yours gave "a cup, two-handled, solid gold," he says.[4] Diomedes is so confident in the durability of this friendship that he raises his spear and drives it into the ground, "deep down in the earth that feeds us all."[5] Given the circumstances, this is a fairly rash act.

Fortunately for Diomedes, the bond holds. "Splendid," he says to Glaucus, "you are my friend, / my guest from the days of our grandfathers long ago!"[6] He leaps from his chariot, clasps Glaucus's hand, and proposes that the two men renew the pact that has bound their houses for three generations, despite the battle raging in the distance:

> Come, let us keep clear of each other's spears,
> even there in the thick of battle. Look,
> plenty of Trojans there for me to kill,
> your famous allies too, any soldier the god
> will bring in range or I can run to ground.
> And plenty of Argives too—kill them if you can.
> But let's trade armor. The men must know our claim:
> we are sworn friends from our fathers' days till now![7]

Men who give up their armor in the *Iliad* are usually dead or soon to die, like Patroclus and Hector, who both come to grief dressed as Achilles. Diomedes and Glaucus give up their armor not to prove a conquest but to show that each man's life is dependent on the garment that once protected the other. This act of grace awakens loyalties deeper and older than the oaths they have sworn to their warring kings, almost as deep as the earth that feeds us all.

* * *

Grace is one of those elusive ideas that tends to run faster than we can catch it. It is the nature of grace to run away, because it is a kind of life outside of visible life. Paradoxes are handy for trapping slippery thoughts like this, so I'll begin with two. Both are embedded in Anne Carson's idea that grace is a coin, which sounds like an error rather than an insight, because gifts and money have long been understood to be antithetical. This wasn't quite the case in the sixth and fifth centuries BCE when modern money was invented in Athens. During this period of transition, grace and coins weren't friends, but they weren't exactly enemies either. They lived alongside one another like irascible neighbors. True, they were competing ways of organizing the circulation of goods and social bonds, and in the end money won. But on the streets and in the marketplace they had to cooperate with each other for many years, as the gift slowly and haphazardly yielded to a new way of distributing wealth and attention.[8]

In *Economy of the Unlost*, her comparative study of Paul Celan and Simonides of Keos, Anne Carson studies what it was like to be a poet-for-hire in a changing world that mixed money and gifts unpredictably. As a poet and scholar of aesthetics in the fifth century BCE, Simonides needed to make sense of how grace and coins interacted so that he could judge when he was or wasn't being properly paid, and also so that he could understand how money altered the way imagination worked and expressed itself in language. Although he was famously stingy and avaricious, and wrote several poems complaining about cheapskates who didn't know what a poem was worth, he was also alarmed by money, because the practice of exchanging a handful of coins for an inventive arrangement of words seemed to deny the purpose of such arrangements of words, as Simonides understood it. Carson writes that he "spent his literary as well as his historical life exerting a counterpressure to the claims of the merely visible world," mainly by trying to expand its contents.[9] To this end he is said to have added a new note to the lyre, four letters to the Greek alphabet, and several decades to his own life by refusing the draught of hemlock that the men of hardscrabble Keos were obliged to drink when they reached the age of sixty in order to ensure that the younger generations had enough to eat.

Having refused to disappear, Simonides devoted himself to helping others do the same. He became celebrated for his war memorials and funeral songs, wrote more epitaphs than any other poet of his era, and developed a mnemonic system after all the guests at a dinner party he was attending were crushed by a collapsing roof, an event that considerably intensified his preoccupation with evanescence. Carson describes all of these forms of increase and preservation as an "economy of the unlost," and argues that it "always involves gratuity"—something extra and unaccounted for.[10] Hence, for Simonides, the conflict between poetry, which summons the forgotten and unseen, and money, which can be counted up and used to pay for that summons as though it were a bale of hay. No tip required.

Simonides's distress leads to the second paradox in Carson's claim: a coin with more than two sides. In Simonides's view, money lacked the exorbitance that was central to *charis*, which was the fulcrum of a social system that called for generosity and surprise. Born at the crossroads between the "material and moral," grace allowed for the creation of the political alliances on which ancient diplomacy and governance depended, as we know from Diomedes and Glaucus, as well as their grandfathers.[11] Bonnie MacLachlan writes, *charis* "broke down the barriers that confined the self," and in this unguarded condition it was possible to become friends with a stranger or enemy.[12] However, grace was not just for averting military or political crisis; it was also a daily practice of honoring the dark matter in people and things. The mere presence of another person was enough to demand this acknowledgement, often including the exchange of gifts that were tokens of loyalty. So was the mysterious energy contained in works of art, even if it was only silently acknowledged in the mind. One of the many surprising links that Carson makes between Simonides and Paul Celan, the Romanian-Jewish poet and Holocaust survivor, concerns this interior response. It is called thinking.

Celan was at least as haunted as Simonides was, and as alert to a poem's capacity to expose a bond between reader and writer, no matter how distant from one another they appear to be. In 1958, he accepted the Bremen Prize for German literature with a speech that famously begins with the following statement: "The words 'denken' and 'danken', to think and to thank, have the same root in our language." He goes on to observe that this shared root reveals thought and gratitude to be etymologically connected with one another, as well as with the German words for memory, devotion, and contemplation. "Allow me," he says to his audience in Bremen, "to thank you from there."[13] This gratitude is as far from conventional politeness as Celan's poetry is from conventional language.

Even in English, we *give* thanks just as we give thought to a question or a problem. In both cases, giving is also a demand made of oneself. Gratitude worthy of the name is not a rote response or a verbal formula any more than thinking is. The full extent of these demands is clear in Celan's address to the people of Bremen, who rewarded him for poems in which he was engaged in the excruciating process of contemplating the murdered Jews of Europe, including his parents, who vanished from their home at the beginning of the war and were never seen or heard of again. In return, Celan stands before German men and women who were at the very least complicit in this genocide and tells them that what they admire in his poetry was shaped by a Hassidic culture that has been "dropped from history." That is a euphemism. Writing after the orchestrated slaughter of European Jewry, Celan imagines that his poems are like a "letter in a bottle thrown out to sea" in the attempt to reach "something open, inhabitable, an approachable you."[14] His Bremen Prize speech suggests that his letters have managed to reach the very people whose nation is responsible for his grief, and that when they thank one another, Jewish poet and German readers in turn, they are also thinking together. In this moment, they are joined imaginatively and metaphysically by the gratuity that they acknowledge in one another. Considering the context, this is an extraordinary union.

For Simonides, two and a half millennia earlier, the act of exchanging coins for poems threatens to untie the knot that binds thinking and thanking, at least for the person making the purchase, and perhaps for the poet as well. How can he express gratuity if people are no longer willing to receive it with the gratuitous part of themselves? Years ago, my father found himself asking this question when he was awarded a commission to paint a minor diplomat and his family. This was in the mid-1970s, when we still lived in London. About a year after the portrait was finished, the diplomat wrote to say that he had gotten divorced, and that his wife was so angry with him that she cut the painting in two and took half with her. The man had paid for a whole painting but now had only half of one, so surely my father would refund half his fee? At the time, our family's primary residence was a van, so no, the money would not be returned. "I told you so," Simonides would say. This is what happens when the relationship between artist and patron is reduced to a bill of sale. No glad surfeit is offered to the poet or to the poem, which contains news of the invisible that should cast the sufficiency of any payment into doubt, and a great deal else besides. It is possible that a customer could experience this surfeit without offering a bonus on top of the agreed upon fee, but this strikes Simonides as a bad bargain as well as a threat to the transfers of grace that allow him to do his job. It's also possible that the customer could demand a rebate because his ex-wife picked up a pair of scissors and then walked away with half of what he paid for, but as far as I know this did not cross Simonides's mind. Even a brilliant thinker can't cover all the angles.

Celan did not share Simonides's concerns about money, although he did believe in transfers of grace. He writes that a poem expresses a "unique, mortal soul," which does not mean that the poet works entirely alone. Poems are "gifts to the attentive," and they require attention itself to operate differently.[15] Other people can help with this, if only by attending to works of art. *Charis* helped by focusing everyone's attention on the givenness that glows in people and objects, and this attentiveness did not end in the fifth century BCE, despite the invention of modern coinage. Marveling at the surrealist paintings of Edgar Jené, Celan writes, "my hearing has wandered into my fingertips and learns to see; my heart, now that it lives behind my forehead, tastes the laws of a new, unceasing, free motion." If, like the people who conferred the Bremen Prize, we are grateful to those who help us to discover ears in our fingertips and taste buds on our hearts, it is because we need to sense what Celan called "words and figures" hidden in the "remotest regions of the spirit."[16] It is undeniable that Celan's need was more desperate than most.

The idea that grace reveals hidden connections among lives, no matter how far apart or antagonistic they appear to be, is not confined to artists or to pre-monetary Greece. One of the central arguments made in Marcel Mauss's *The Gift* is that there are continuities between exchange in ancient societies—in the Greek, Roman, Babylonian, and Indo-European traditions—and in the early twentieth-century indigenous cultures of Oceania and the American Northwest. He argues that in both archaic and contemporary indigenous gift cultures, "things are mixed up with spirits" and are "living beings," which means that "by giving one is giving *oneself*" and by receiving one shapes the life of another.[17] To give a gift is to say, "With this object I put my life and the life of my people in your hands." To return one is to reply, "I acknowledge your life and that of your community, and with this object I invite you to collaborate with mine," much as Diomedes and Glaucus did when they threw down their weapons in the middle of a particularly brutal war and then traded the warrior's most intimate possession. In their case, the community in question is very small—two families. Nevertheless, it prevents these men from killing each other in a situation where killing is what is required of them. In Mauss's analysis, as in Homer's epic, people who break the rules of gift exchange always court death, ostracism, or enslavement, because what is actually being traded is nothing less than an invitation to participate in social life.[18]

There's no need to pretend that this invitation is perfectly altruistic or devoid of strategy. These are human beings we're talking about. Thanks to Zeus, who muddles Glaucus's senses, he trades his golden armor for Diomedes's bronze, "the worth of a hundred oxen just for nine."[19] Diomedes does not see fit to mention his friend's mistake. He reduces the number of his Trojan enemies by one and profits nicely in the process, although this is not entirely his fault, because he is the collateral beneficiary of Zeus's private agenda, which is determined by pressures that neither Glaucus nor Diomedes know anything about. Their god-tainted exchange echoes the crisis of *charis* that precipitates the epic itself, which involves two captive women with very similar names: Briseis and Chryseis. Briseis is the most valuable prize Agamemnon gives Achilles for valor in battle, and Chryseis is the woman he claims for himself, until Apollo insists that she be returned to her father, who just happens to be a priest of Apollo. Enraged by this conflict of interest, Agamemnon determines that if he has to surrender his prize, he will take Achilles's in her place. Naturally, Achilles protests this reversal, but Agamemnon says, "What if you are a great soldier? That's just a gift of god."[20] In other words, you can take no credit for your military prowess and therefore deserve no special reward. Agamemnon drives this argument home by promising to reclaim Briseis "so you can learn just how much greater I am than you."[21] He will spend the rest of his life regretting this idiotic boast.

From one perspective, Agamemnon is right. Achilles is the son of Thetis, a water nymph who has the ear of the gods, and at her request he is armored by Hephaestus, immortal smithy to the Olympians. Even among epic heroes, Achilles is exceptional. He is made of water and armed by fire, he strikes bargains with deities and negotiates the terms of his own fate. However, none of this means that he should not be rewarded for his excellence, as Agamemnon learns very quickly when Achilles withdraws from battle and the Greeks are threatened with defeat. Agamemnon is king of kings, leader of all the Greek warlords camped outside the ramparts of Troy, but it is not within his power to understand why fortune and talent move as they do, or to measure where divine will ends and human achievement begins.

In his first book about the gift, called *Given Time*, Jacques Derrida claims that Mauss is insufficiently concerned by the fact that gifts are often snarled up with obligation and prestige, as they are in the *Iliad*. This is because Derrida wants to imagine a pure gift that acts on people without anyone needing to feel grateful for it.[22] Agamemnon would have appreciated this line of thought, and for this very reason I am suspicious of it. It is true that the need to give thanks is one of the ways in which gifts become demands, but it is also one of the ways in which gifts reveal bonds that extend in many directions, some of them invisible to the naked eye. Unlike Derrida, writing in the early 1990s, Mauss was not interested in the possibility of a free gift that no one knows they have received or feels called to respond to, and neither am I. He was interested in the possibility that even in the early twentieth century, elements of gift thinking might survive in Europe to reveal urgently needed strands of human solidarity. In the conclusion to *The Gift*, he writes, "The system that we propose to call the system of 'total services', from clan to clan—the system in which individuals and groups exchange everything with one another—constitutes the most ancient system of economy and law .... Now, that is exactly the kind of law, in due proportion, towards which we would like to see our own societies moving." He was heartened to find residual traces of that ancient law in folk traditions and fairy tales, including "The Sleeping Beauty."[23]

I too often find it helpful to think alongside children's stories, as you will have noticed. Perhaps this is because whatever their theme or subject matter, stories for children expose the passionate heart at the center of an idea. Sometimes I reflect on the fact that nearly a century apart, Walter Benjamin and the Swiss philosopher Jean-Luc Nancy both chose to deliver lectures for children, much as Professors Lewis and Tolkien wrote novels for young readers.[24] The ostensible purpose of these lectures was to educate the very young, but there is a great clarity that comes from the necessity of speaking so that a child can understand not only what is being said but why it needs to be said at all, which can only be because an idea responds to our deepest needs. If a child cannot hear an idea's beating heart and feel it within her own chest then she will not care about it, and neither will anyone who is not in the beleaguered business of being a scholar in the humanities. When I am exhausted or in pain I return to the best stories written for children, and I do this because they restore some fullness I've lost. They don't offer arguments or make appeals to intellect; they slip hope straight into my bloodstream, like the medicine I need. These stories make me feel that stones and animals, trees and furniture, wind and rain are filled with life that touches mine by routes that I cannot see, and even when that life is not wholly benevolent it dispels the illusion that I am on my own in this world with my tiny scrap of intelligence and this alarming little body.

Like any good children's story, "Sleeping Beauty" is an excellent way to think about how gifts expose the mutual involvement of living things. It begins as many fairy tales do: with a couple that has long been unable to conceive a child.[25] If this is a common starting place, it is because infertility lays bare our desire to feel connected to the movement of life at any cost. When the child is born we discover that the costs are higher than we imagined. We pay them, whether we like it or not. One day the queen in "Sleeping Beauty" is told by a frog that she will finally give birth to a daughter, and when the child is born the king holds a feast for all the wise women in the kingdom so that they will come to give presents to the infant, named Rosamond. There are thirteen of these women, but the king only has twelve golden plates, so he decides to leave one of the women off the guest list. Needless to say, this is the wrong choice (why not buy or borrow another plate?) and the spurned woman issues her curse: at the age of fifteen, the girl will prick her finger on a spindle and die. This fate is softened by the twelfth wise woman, who commutes the death sentence to a century of sleep. As predicted, at the age of fifteen Rosamond pricks her finger, everyone in and around the castle falls into a deep slumber, and an impenetrable hedge of thorns grows to enclose the kingdom. After a hundred years, the thorns turn to flowers, a prince enters the castle and … but you know about the kiss. I'll come back to that in the next chapter. Right now I'm more interested in the curse and the hedge of thorns.

First of all, there is a strong sense that Rosamond herself is a gift given to the king and queen, although it's not clear by whom. Presumably the frog is just a messenger, but his prophecy suggests that someone (or something) is helping to bring the child into existence, and although the tale gives us no reason to believe that the wise women have anything to do with the pregnancy, the feast is nonetheless an occasion to give general thanks as well as to solicit further gifts to protect Rosamond in the future. In this sense, the wise women stand in for every beneficent and fertile force that might have brought the child into being, and the king's failure to give full and proper thanks to these women, and through them to all that is wise in the world, calls down the curse, which brings life to a halt and seals the castle so that no one can disturb its paralysis. Those who try—brave princes, all—are caught in the hedge and die there, horribly spitted on the thorns. Their bodies are a reminder that until the curse ends and the hedge flowers, the kingdom is closed to everyone.

Insofar as anything is clear in fairy tales, it is clear in "Sleeping Beauty" that gifts are linked to the perpetuation of individual as well as collective life. It is impossible to say exactly where that life comes from, so although it is foolish of the king to slight one of the wise women, it is also understandable. Who can say how the frog, the women, and the king and queen work together to produce a child? No one, and that's the point. Gifts reveal presence, and in the primal landscape of fairy tales they are often depicted *as* presence—as children who emerge from a vast network of influences, most of which are invisible to their parents. Like Rosamond and Rapunzel, and the baby who was promised to that greedy imp, Rumpelstiltskin, these children are born as the result of interactions that include all of nature, and their parents are swiftly punished for being unappreciative of their benefactors, even if they have no idea who some of them are. Such punishments always exploit parents' greatest fear, which is that the child that came to them from who knows where will be sent back there by one of the secret forces that brought her into existence in the first place.

If a child is murdered by a fairy, spirited away by Rumpelstiltskin, or imprisoned in a high tower by a witch, parents know that the world will become uninhabitable. It will be as though carbon or hydrogen has been subtracted from the atmosphere. All of nature will be lessened. This terror is heightened by the fact that gifts do not have a discernible origin, which is why they come as a surprise and why the king is unprepared for the feast that he had many months to plan. Even a king's pantry and a king's judgment are insufficient to the task of expressing gratitude for a child, because it is just as difficult to give thanks for a new life as it is to understand where new life comes from. And although the king is solely to blame for the wise woman's anger, everything under his dominion suffers the consequences, including plants, animals, and those neighboring princes who think they can cancel a curse with a sword and a can-do attitude.

More recently, E. B. White had a great deal of fun with the premise that gifts conceal their origins in *Charlotte's Web*, a novel in which a spider and a rat work together to save the life of a frightened spring pig who learns that he was born for slaughter. When Charlotte spins the words "Some Pig" into her web, followed in subsequent weeks by the words "Terrific," "Radiant" and "Humble," no one doubts that it is Wilbur who is terrific, radiant, and humble rather than the large grey spider in the rafters. She is counting on the fact that people will believe that her web is proof of divine revelation rather than proof of her own ingenuity and hard work. When "Some Pig" appears one misty morning, Mr. Zuckerman, the farmer, is dizzy with excitement. He tells his wife, "There can be no mistake about it. A miracle has happened and a sign has occurred here on earth, right on our farm, and we have no ordinary pig"! No mistake about it? "Well," says Mrs. Zuckerman, "it seems to me you're a little off. It seems to me we have no ordinary *spider*."[26] Everyone thinks this is a preposterous notion. It is immediately dismissed and never spoken of again. Instead, hundreds of people get dressed up to come to the pigsty to marvel at Wilbur, who is a winsome but otherwise ordinary beast. On Sunday, the local minister preaches a sermon on signs and wonders. No one preaches a sermon about Charlotte. She dies alone, but assured that her friend will never become a pork roast.

Gift thinking is usually more concerned with the spider than the pig, as it were. Mauss always emphasizes that cycles of exchange are obligatory, public, and reciprocal: those who get must give back, although they might be allowed to raise the political stakes by waiting a while or by giving more than they were given in the first place, as in sumptuary competitions such as potlatch. After Mauss, people tend to be interested in gifts that are spontaneous and difficult to source. These gifts do not move in a straight line between giver and recipient, but in a circle that orbits into darkness.[27] Whatever its form or situation, the gift is always sanctioned by life outside of life, although it need not dwell with the dead or the gods. In his book *The Gift,* Lewis Hyde is interested in material gifts mainly because of what he believes they can teach us about creative ones, and he is particularly attentive to the moments when a talent or an object "passes out of sight" or "goes around a corner before it comes back." During this "passage into mystery" people can't see the hands that reach for the gift and then pass it along, and this darkness is where the gift gathers the vitality that it moves through the world.[28] Hyde's wonderful interpretation of "The Shoemaker and the Elves" helps to illustrate how this process works. In this fairy tale, we meet a shoemaker who for some reason cannot figure out how to make a shoe that anyone wants to buy. As a result, he is starving and friendless.

When the story begins the cobbler is heading to bed, having cut out his last piece of leather, which in the morning he intends to sew into yet more footwear that no one will take any interest in. However, during the night he is visited by naked and barefoot elves, who turn this scrap into an exquisite pair of shoes. The shoemaker is "speechless with astonishment," which suggests that his transformation is off to a good start.[29] He sells the shoes immediately and uses the proceeds to buy enough leather to make two pairs of shoes, a pattern that repeats night after night. Curious about the source of their good luck, he and wife stay up one night to watch the little men at work. In thanks, they make the elves tiny suits and shoes. Once dressed, they disappear for good, leaving the shoemaker to fend for himself, although he feels no anxiety about their departure, because a subtle change has taken place that makes him capable of doing the elves' work for himself. Hyde is interested in this change, and reads the tale as a parable about awakening talent in a man who has lost his confidence, or perhaps never had any. The shoemaker works as hard as he can, and when he has done his miserable best and fallen asleep some magical creatures arrive to help him. Their real task is to make him aware of his own ability, which is why they vanish only when the shoemaker has demonstrated that he has finally mastered his craft. Now, having received proof of their pupil's excellence, they are free to wield needle and thread elsewhere.

For Hyde, the elves embody a capacity within the shoemaker's mind that was dormant or inaccessible. They come in their own good time, because creative labor "sets its own pace," which is one of the important ways in which it is different from work that can be measured by a fixed standard of productivity or paid an hourly wage, and why it is embarrassingly reliant on long stretches of seemingly fruitless endeavor, false starts, and idleness, including sleep. Work depends on "the will," Hyde writes.[30] Creativity requires disciplined commitment to a task, but it must also contain something that cannot be scheduled and often takes considerably more time than you thought you had. If not, the task might as well be undertaken by a high-order machine.

When I first began to think about gifts my children were very young, and I was still close to the origin of their lives. They came to me against expert medical forecasting and despite the lesions and scars that fill my pelvis, whose most common side effect, aside from chronic pain, is infertility. Bowel, rectum, fallopian tubes, ovaries, abdominal wall, ligaments, and tendons: all colonized by endometrial tissue, all damaged. Endometriosis is a disease in which a reproductive system commits suicide, leaving behind a mess that no one can clean up. To cure it you'd have to gut me like a fish, get rid of all that throbbing meat. No experience in my life so far has done more to make me feel the demands of gratitude, which is too often associated with sugary platitudes rather than with deep astonishment in which there is as much terror as joy. I've since learned that people who think deeply about gratitude do not pour syrup on it. They do not write advertising copy for brands of herbal tea, or inspirational slogans to be printed on yoga mats. Like agony and malfunction, having a child made me feel like a child, because I was out of control and constantly amazed. All my adult confidence was gone, but so was my compliance with rules I don't believe in. I once made strict writing schedules and stuck to them with iron discipline; now this feels like a waste of time, not a prudent use of it. Now it seems prudent to stare out the window and make a donation to the day. I try to anchor my labor as a scholar in this state of mind. I have never known anything truer or more free.

Like the shoemaker, most of us try to find a place for creative labor within our work, whether it involves the making and sale of commodities or writing about the humanities in universities that are almost as obsessed with taking inventory as a retail operation—how many publications, talks, grants, students, committees? I have often sat across a desk from someone who is using a fingertip or a pen to count the number of lines on my

CV in order to determine whether I have met this or that benchmark of productivity. Usually the answer is no. On these occasions I feel ashamed of my increasingly unproductive nature, but not sufficiently ashamed to become the kind of worker my superiors would like me to be. As a profession, we don't seem concerned by the possibility that our accounting systems might produce ideas that gather dust on a shelf, like all those boring shoes that no one wanted to buy. I cannot understand this, as either a scholar or a lover of shoes.

Paul Celan told the people of Bremen that in thanking one another they were also thinking with one another, a shocking claim to fraternity for a Holocaust survivor in the late 1950s. Hyde also emphasizes the role of gratitude in the giving and receiving of gifts. Again, this has nothing whatsoever to do with etiquette or good manners. "We cannot receive the gift until we can meet it as an equal," he writes, and therefore we must "submit ourselves to the labor of becoming like the gift."[31] A polite "please" and "thank you" is not what is being asked here, and is likely to get in the way. The other day I felt unaccountable rage when I walked past my neighbor's house and saw a bedazzled sign that read "There Is Always Something To Be Grateful For!" propped up beside an artful arrangement of pumpkins. I suppressed an insane desire to run up the front steps, smash the sign, and kick the pumpkins into oncoming traffic. We receive the gift only when we greet it with a corresponding part of ourselves, and that part is not covered in glitter. Not all that is given is good, and some of it is painful beyond measure.

We don't tend to feel much gratitude for things that we have paid for or earned on the clock, and Simonides feared that this would make it difficult for his customers to appreciate or even understand his poems. He was angry about money at the same time that he tried to bank as much of it as he could, on the grounds that it was the only form of attention he was likely to receive in an era when *charis* was on the wane. However, we might be grateful for our ability to earn money, and recognize that some of that ability—much more than we would like to admit—depends on things we cannot control or take credit for, including the families and social structures we are born into. Earlier I criticized Agamemnon for refusing to honor Achilles, but the *Iliad*'s greatest warrior is not blameless either. At the beginning of the epic he is disinclined to acknowledge that his mother is in league with the gods, and unwilling to concede that some of his success depends on nothing more than having the right talent for the time—killing, in this case. Like humility, the labor of gratitude is difficult, because it draws our attention toward those aspects of our lives for which we can neither be congratulated nor faulted. In this way, it allows us to meet the gift like an equal, and other people as well. For Hyde, this is why the elves will not leave the shoemaker until he has reciprocated their generosity. It is fair to ask why creatures with a dab hand at sewing can't fix their own wardrobe problems, and the answer is that the shoes are not the problem, and neither is reciprocity, if it is understood only as repayment for services rendered. When he gives thanks the cobbler proves that he has learned to express the gratuity within his own life. From now on, that elfin quality will be visible in the shoes he makes, and everyone will want to buy them in order to feel it in themselves.

Nothing is said in "The Shoemaker and the Elves" about the shoemaker's customers, although it is clear that they are able to tell at a glance that something special is coming out of the workshop. Who knows what good they will do with that feeling? We might even say that it "awakens part of the soul," which is how Hyde describes the effect of creativity on the maker as well as the recipient.[32] It alerts the innermost part of people, not just their intellects, but needs and abilities of which they may not have been aware. In this sense, the elves are no more outside of the shoemaker than Charlotte's web comes from outside the barnyard. On the contrary, it comes from inside her body and represents a surprising heightening of proficiencies that are already part of her nature and essential to basic activities like trapping and eating food. The fact that she is moved to help to prolong her friend's life even as she is living out the final days of her own, spinning a sac to contain her innumerable children at the same time that she is extolling Wilbur's radiance, has everything to do with the foreknowledge of mortality that she was born with. Her compassion for a pig who might not be allowed to live out his natural lifespan comes in part from her own instinctual desire to live until her children are born and safely housed. And if the elves seem faintly human, despite their magic natures and pointy ears, that is because they too are a surprising extension of the cobbler's own innate capacities, which were for some reason out of his reach. In order to access them he needed to be provoked by exhaustion and desperation, or perhaps by a good night's sleep, just as Charlotte was provoked to put her web to an unexpected use by Wilbur's fear of being butchered.

A two-handled solid gold cup, a poem, a child, a web, a pair of shoes. With varying degrees of strength, each pulls people into relationships with those who once ignored or tried to kill them. When we meet the gift like an equal we also meet other people like an equal, and perhaps all of nature, which is why gifts are always associated with the exposure and strengthening of hidden solidarities. It is also why thinking about the gift so often leads to theology of one kind or another. Sometimes the God of monotheism is called the Giver, the source of all gifts, although it is not possible for most of us to sense that we are intimate with the entirety of creation and obliged to act accordingly. If "the kingdom of God is within you," as the gospel of Luke avers, then we are each seeded with infinity, larger inside than out, like the magical interiors in children's stories.[33] And many, including Jesus, argue that we become aware of this gratuity through our most fundamental inclination toward ourselves, namely love. When asked by a teacher of rabbinical law to identify the most important of the commandments, Jesus identified two, and they are versions of one another: love God and love your neighbor as yourself.[34] These are not presented as separate enterprises nor as sequential ones. The rabbi agrees with Jesus's edit, which is not surprising, because these ideas are as central to the Torah as they later become to the gospels, the epistles, and the Koran. Worship, like charity and compassion, is a surprising extension of the innate impulse to care for your own life.

In meditating upon the commandments, many have observed that we can never love one another enough and will always feel guilty as a result.[35] I feel the truth of this, but I bear in mind Simone Weil's belief that the *quality* of the attention we bring to others is what matters, not the number of people we try to attend to. This was not a merely academic question for Weil, who shortened her life by choosing to share the pinched living and working conditions of French factory and farm workers throughout the 1930s and early 1940s, despite her advanced degree in philosophy and her poor health. Her early death was hastened by starvation and exhaustion. The French philosopher Emmanuel Levinas, who wrote at length about obligations among neighbors, believed that love for others requires "donation without reserve," and Weil is one of the best examples of this principle that I know of.[36] Nevertheless, she writes this: "The love of our neighbor in all its fullness simply means being able to say to him: 'What are you going through?'" This question offers "a recognition that the sufferer exists, not only as a unit in a collection, or a specimen from the social category labeled 'unfortunate,' but as a man, exactly like us."[37] Weil acknowledges that it is difficult to understand even one suffering person as anything but a specimen of misfortune, and I am not sure that it is any easier to see the concealed misery of a privileged person. Not all suffering is visible.

"Donation without reserve" suggests constant effort, more and more giving to more and more people. This is not how Weil thinks about the divine imperative to love. She believes that the refinement of attention that allows us to recognize someone as an individual rather than a type requires as much rest as exertion. Although she always praises hard work, intellectual as well as physical, and did a great deal of both, she also insists upon the importance of periods of quiet inactivity in which we wait, watch, and listen without striving for anything. In fact, she believes that the primary value of intellectual training is to make us understand the difference between clock-watching productivity and creative labor in which the mind at rest becomes able to solve the problems we have posed to it. In these moments the intellect opens to intuition. If we are very fortunate, the soul will also empty itself "of all its own contents in order to receive into itself the being it is looking at, just as he is."[38] How extraordinary.

Weil, who was Jewish by birth, did much of her writing in occupied France. Her thinking is shaped by the events of those years and by the rise of Fascism that she witnessed throughout Europe in the previous decade, crisis conditions in which it becomes clear that the injunction to care for others, particularly the stranger and the outcast, is not just a private spiritual or intellectual imperative, but a political one. Despite the interlocking climate and refugee crises of our own time, few people believe the gift to be a political principle or essential to the interpretation and enforcement of the laws of nations, even though this is exactly what the Italian political philosopher Giorgio Agamben has been arguing since the early 1990s. He writes that laws are always founded and sustained by grace, which he calls "the exception." In an early book, *Homo Sacer*, whose front cover features a photograph of the floorplan of Auschwitz, Agamben focuses on the violence of the exception, beginning with the oldest Roman laws, which were founded by sovereigns who established their right to rule through the designation of a sacred man, or *homo sacer*: an outcast criminal who could be murdered with impunity and had no status within the judicial order that his banishment helped to create. At its origin, Agamben argues, the Roman Empire formalized a tradition in which law is "made of nothing but what it manages to capture inside itself through the inclusive exclusion of the *exceptio*: it nourishes itself on this exception and is a dead letter without it."[39] Law creates a circle of inclusion on the basis of those it excludes from protection, judgment, and even humanity.

Agamben's arguments often turn to the totalitarian and genocidal political regimes of the twentieth century because they provide the most extreme contemporary examples of what can happen when leaders define their states through exceptions. The Executive Orders with which newly elected President Donald Trump sought to ban refugees and visitors from seven predominately Muslim countries raised international alarm in January 2017 not only because the Orders were plainly discriminatory, but because they revealed Trump to be the kind of leader who asserts his authority over the law by stripping large numbers of vulnerable people of their status within it. Auschwitz is often Agamben's limit example of this kind of "state of exception," in which a leader's power grows in proportion to the number of people who are made powerless. Chancellor Angela Merkel's decision to open Germany's borders to a million Syrian refugees at a time when most other nations in Europe and around the world were either closing their doors or enforcing quotas is a powerful attempt to reverse this history. This welcome shows the other side of the state of exception, which saves rather than kills or excludes.

Exceptions are as dangerous as they are necessary. They can take as well as give, and this irresolvable conflict is implicit in the terms gratuity and gratuitous. The former is generally understood to be a gift, the latter an offense. But why, when they mean the same thing? The only difference between them is that one is a noun, the other an adjective. This fact doesn't stop us from condemning behavior that falls outside the accepted standards of reason and good judgment by calling it gratuitous. No one who speaks of gratuitous spending or violence, for example, is issuing praise. Yet many people are comfortable with the idea that those who exceed accepted standards of conduct or achievement should receive special recognition, even when their achievement serves no straightforward purpose. I would not want to live in a world where people did not ride jet skis into open ocean in order to surf 100-foot-high waves, or concoct obscenely expensive meals out of foraged weeds, although I'm not sure where these activities fall on the spectrum between genius and decadent lunacy. It would be easy to assume that the difference between gift and offense rests on the distinction between excessive behavior that harms in the first case and helps in the second, but this distinction is not reliable. The ambivalence I am describing is embodied by the *homo sacer*, who could neither be protected nor judged by the laws that his sacredness established, and for this reason was more powerful, more helpless, and more dangerous than other people.

In his later writing, Agamben is primarily concerned with the generosity of the exception, not its abusiveness. He finds this generosity particularly well articulated by the canon laws of the Byzantine and Latin Churches of the sixth and seventh centuries, where exceptions do not lead to the building of concentration camps and gulags or to travel bans. They lead to "the occasional restriction or the suspension of the efficacy of the rigor of the laws and the introduction of extenuating circumstances" that acknowledge the "weakness" both of those who interpret the law and of those who are governed by it.[40] In other words, they lead to humility and mercy. An exception can offer clemency in circumstances that might otherwise warrant punishment or open a door that might justifiably be locked. Roman canon law valued these moments because they exposed human administration to the "mysterious divine praxis undertaken for the salvation of humankind."[41] In the modern democratic state, few politicians or lawyers believe that their work should be interrupted by divine praxis or that their jobs involve saving anyone's soul. This does not mean that we can do without exceptions, simply that we cannot pray for them.

In *Homo Sacer*, Agamben attempts to imagine secular sources of power that might be strong enough to challenge human fear and arrogance.[42] He does not seem to be satisfied by the results. In later books, including *The Kingdom and Glory* and *The Highest Poverty*, he looks for this power in the epistles and the early church, where he finds a lived commitment to the idea that life can never be fully brought under the control of any set of rules or system of measurement, no matter how rigorous and encompassing.[43] There is something within a life that cannot be contained even by the most virtuous regulations, including those of a monastery or place of devotion, and it is this irreducible fraction or essence that we recognize in ourselves and others when we are able to ask, "What are you going through?" It is also this irreducible fraction that is capable of placing pressure on the very rules that are designed to control it. This is why Agamben, like some other political philosophers in our time, is so interested in Paul. His letters, gathered in the New Testament, provide the richest and most influential meditations we have on the indivisibility of gift and law.

The theologian Stanislas Breton calls Paul "ever the exception."[44] This is true on several counts. More than any other evangelist of his time, Paul travelled constantly throughout the Mediterranean in order to prevent Jewish law from becoming a closed border, an exclusive patrimony, or a dead letter. For this reason, Breton beautifully calls him "the man of … transits, setting his foot upon the soil only in order to immediately leave it again."[45] A Greek-speaking and Hellenized Jew of the cosmopolitan diaspora who was also a Roman citizen, a Pharisee who became an apostle, a member of the Jewish élite who became a common laborer, Paul embodies contradiction and itinerary. Even tent-making, the trade by which he may have earned a living after his conversion, served people who made their home wherever they went and had to learn to deal with whomever they met there.[46] Often these meetings went very badly for Paul, who was flogged in synagogues, stoned in the streets, imprisoned by Roman authorities, and shipwrecked three times in the course of his travels. He managed to enrage Romans and Jews alike, and for the same reasons: his contempt for hierarchies and for laws that supported them, even those that were believed to come from God. It is not surprising that he was sometimes in conflict with imperial administrators, given that the Empire's taxes reduced many to penury and that the *Pax Romana* was enforced by an army that the historian Karen Armstrong describes as "the most efficient killing machine the world had yet seen; the slightest resistance met with wholesale slaughter."[47] Before he was killed by that machine, Paul's deepest conflicts were with the original apostles and with Jesus's early supporters in Jerusalem, mainly because of what they regarded as his scandalously openhanded interpretation of the Torah.

In his ministry, Paul was often lax about Jewish dietary and hygienic requirements, including circumcision, because he believed that Jesus had revealed the divinity of every individual no matter what or with whom they ate, how they performed ablutions, or how they marked their bodies. In his much-quoted letter to the Galatians, he claims, "There is neither Jew nor Greek, slave nor free, male nor female, for you are all one in Christ Jesus."[48] Paul's Jesus is not a king who will liberate the Jews from their Roman oppressors as King David liberated their ancestors from the Philistines. Nor is he the leader of a Jewish reform movement meant to correct the avarice and self-interest of Jerusalem's ruling class. He is Christ the universal messiah, Son of God, and he is no more or less interested in the Jewish struggle for self-governance than in the freedom of a Gentile slave or a pagan tradesman.[49]

None of this is an endorsement of anarchy. "Before the law was given, sin was in the world," Paul tells his Roman converts, and humans were condemned to spiritual death by Adam's original disobedience.[50] God calls

Moses to Mount Sinai and gives the Jews the life-saving commandments, although it turns out that he is unimpressed by those who merely do as they are told. Paul writes, "when a man works, his wages are not credited to him as a gift, but as an obligation," and neither charity nor worship should be understood as waged labor.[51] In his letters, Paul repeatedly comments on the grueling length of his work day, which sometimes began before dawn and extended into the night, and Armstrong speculates that he must often have preached the gospel in the workshop while hunched over his bench and stitching together the pieces of leather from which his tents were made. She also speculates that the reason his writing becomes so large over time is that his hands were too stiff from gripping his tools to form a delicate script.[52] Paul spoke to workers *as* a worker who understood the difference between a wage and a gift. Jesus often makes the same distinction. He tells his followers that God is more interested in what they do "in secret" than on the street, and cautions against the mistaken belief that public displays of piety will please him, including prayer, fasting, evangelism, and charity. A man who makes a display of his good deeds gets what he deserves, Jesus says, which is high self-esteem and the good opinion of other men. Those are his wages, paid in full. And anyone who approaches Jesus with a checklist demonstrating a lifetime of right conduct, like a bureaucrat in search of a promotion, will be told, in a tone that brooks no further discussion, "I never knew you."[53]

Mosaic Law must be honored—on this matter, Paul is clear. And yet it cries out to be broken, because the faithful are "not under law, but under grace."[54] "The law was added so that the trespass might increase," Paul teaches the Romans, "but where sin increased, grace increased all the more, so that, just as sin reigned in death, so also grace might reign through righteousness to bring eternal life through Jesus Christ our Lord."[55] Here and throughout the epistles, the remarkable purpose of the law is to provoke sin so that God's grace increases in turn, one form of excess creating space for the other. Notice that the moral distinction between gratuity and gratuitousness loses its clarity here. Those who give with abandon and those who take more than they have a right to are alike to the extent that they both open the law to the divine. "The gift is not like the trespass," Paul insists, yet often the trespasser brings the gift.[56]

In his reading of Romans, Alain Badiou argues that divine grace is "translegal," or "the opposite of law insofar as it is what comes without being due."[57] Grace is always undue, an event that can never be earned or willed. However, as Paul's interpreters from St. Augustine to the present day have observed, the Pauline conception of grace is nothing as straightforward as the opposite of law. Paul often emphasizes the violence he committed against Christians before his conversion, insisting, "I am the least of the apostles and do not even deserve to be called an apostle, because I persecuted the church of God." "But by the grace of God I am what I am," he continues, and we sense that the gravity of his sins is in fact commensurate with the visionary role that God granted him. Paul suggests as much in Timothy, where he writes that despite—or perhaps because of—his history as a "blasphemer and a persecutor and a violent man," the "grace of our Lord was poured out on me abundantly."[58]

Grace enters when human will steps out of the way, or is shoved. Thus Paul repeatedly presents himself as a paragon of sin. Here he tells his Roman converts that their forefather, Abraham, was a paragon of faith:

> It was not through law that Abraham and his offspring received the promise that he would be heir of the world, but through the righteousness that comes by faith. For if those who live by law are heirs, faith has no value and the promise is worthless, because law brings wrath. And where there is no law, there is no transgression.[59]

Long before Moses climbed Mount Sinai, Abraham leads his son Isaac to the top of Mount Moriah to perform the sacrifice that God has demanded. The enormity of his belief summons the angel who at the last possible moment spares the life of the child and proclaims Abraham father of nations and of the chosen people. This covenant precedes the Laws of Moses, and it comes from trust so profound and absolute that a man holds a knife to his only son's throat. In Paul's view, the law that is later given to the Jews is meant to provoke moments like this. Law marks the porous border across which humans and God bestow gifts on one another; it is the threshold where trust must begin, not where it happily comes to rest in the fulfillment of a set of requirements. And when angels come to earth, it is always because people have given freely, as Abraham does, or because they have taken so much from one another that God intervenes to set things to rights. These are the exceptions that Paul places at the heart of Christianity, and for which he gave his life.

In Paul's mind, the faithful and the sinner are both closer to the gift than a respectable person will ever get. This is difficult to bear, because most of us are respectable people, and we like the warm glow of virtue that we feel. We also recognize that law-abiding decency is of genuine benefit to others. I pay very high taxes to support public health care and education, and I am convinced that these systems strengthen my society, ragged though they are in some regions of Canada. I am furious with anyone who compromises this infrastructure for personal gain. Yet Paul believes that exceptional states of mind and soul do a better job of creating deep gratitude because they strip away comfort and self-satisfaction until all that is left is the uncontrollable gratuity that comes from God. Considering his concern for the poor and persecuted of the Empire, Paul would certainly have supported public services that diminish social disparity. However, he would not have believed that they were capable of erasing the differences among Greek and Jew, slave and free, man and woman. Only his God can do that.

If Paul's ideas are easy for you, then you will not need to turn to a children's story, as I do. I find it helpful to consider that in *Charlotte's Web*, Wilbur's life is saved by the combined efforts of a spider and a rat: not a lamb and a kitten, but animals that are disliked and feared. When Wilbur first meets Charlotte, he thinks she is cruel because she talks about how much she enjoys drinking the blood of her prey. And Templeton the rat—my favorite character as a child—is gluttonous, lazy, and does nothing for anyone without being paid for it in food. Together, they persuade everyone, including Wilbur himself, that he is a miraculous creature whose life is an exception to the rule that governs other pigs. Here I see a mild version of Paul's thinking. The key players in E. B. White's story are the spider who gives everything and the rat who gives as little as possible; the obedient old sheep who believes that a pig is born for the butcher as surely as autumn follows summer, and that this is how it has always been and ought to be, achieves nothing except as the bearer of bad news. Actually, that's not nothing. The sheep explains the rule, which is the first step to bending it. Signs and wonders, swerves and transformations: these come from the unpopular animals who keep to the shadows and see a life worth saving where others see a fact of nature or a tasty meal.

I do not believe in God. I hope this does not mean that I am a thoughtless person who lives by coins and law alone. Increasingly, I wonder whether faith is a form of vulnerability that I barricade myself against, and whether my mind has faculties that I could only know about if I had chosen to train it differently. On the plus side, I have no difficulty feeling what Stanislas Breton describes as the "incessant givenness" and "anonymous generosity" of life, and I am relieved to discover that I am in honorable company.[60] Many people whose ideas about the origins of responsibility and power are not rooted in faith nevertheless feel that the universe is home to an abundance that occasionally breaks in upon our senses, or rises to the surface of our emotions, producing feelings that range from quiet joy to teeth-rattling awe. In an essay called "Givenness," Marilynne Robinson writes, only "when we are presented with an astonishment of some sort, a threat or an insight, are we inclined to realize that a moment is potentially capacious and transformative."[61] Robinson may be the most celebrated Christian writer of our time, but she never assumes that faith is the only way to experience givenness or to understand the ways in which it challenges our laws. Even when the gift is not expressed or created by worship, the edges of comprehension are where hope appears.

* * *

Is there anyone who more fully communicates the craving for astonishment than Annie Dillard? "We don't know what's going on here," she writes delightedly at the beginning of *Pilgrim at Tinker Creek*, a book in which she follows not just Ralph W. Emerson, Henry D. Thoreau and John Muir, but all of those naturalist-philosophers, past and present, who believe that the best way to understand what is gratuitous in yourself and in the world is to get down on your hands and knees and study the contents of a pond.[62] Or to get on your feet and walk through a garden or an orchard, better still a forest, as Dillard is doing one afternoon when she sees something she's been looking for a long time. She sees a tree and all the grass that surrounds it on fire, "each cell buzzing with flame." She writes that this vision "was less like seeing than like being for the first time seen, knocked breathless by a powerful glance. The flood of fire abated, but I'm still spending the power."[63] Still spending the power.

"What is going on here?" Dillard asks again, much later in the course of her pilgrimages to and around Tinker Creek.[64] It is her constant question. This time she is wondering why nature's profusion is often cruel, as illustrated by the 10 percent of all insects who contribute to their ecosystems by kidnapping and slowly devouring their fellows, a process that Dillard finds difficult to square with the luminous regard of a cedar tree. We may not understand why the earth is host to so many hunters and parasites, or why the bitterest suffering is inherent within fertility, but it is always clear that what is going on in Dillard's writing is the recruitment and spending of creative power that comes from passionate attention to the entire terrain of physical life. Most of the time that terrain is not transfigured as it is at the beginning of *Tinker Creek*, nor does it need to be, because Dillard is exhilarated by sights that make most people yawn. She spends three years hoping to track a muskrat, schooling herself in the lore of river rodents, and when she finally sees one floating down the creek she writes, "my life changed." "I felt a rush of such pure energy I thought I would not need to breathe for days."[65] The unexpected appearance of this muskrat does considerably more than give Dillard the oxygen she needs to write a dozen or so pages about muskrats. It makes her a new creature. She notices that this replenishment is brought about by the "self-forgetfulness" that is required for the close observation of animals who do not thrive on our attention, and wonders "if we do not waste most of our energy just by spending every waking minute saying hello to ourselves."[66] Like many people, she goes to the woods (or the river, the quarry, the mountains) to suspend the process of greeting herself and instead be greeted by something that takes little interest in our kind and yet can shoot us a look of fire.

It is not easy to forget about yourself. For Dillard, solitude and dehydration are prerequisites, but for me a flock of birds will do. I remember last autumn when every day at twilight the bare trees in my backyard filled with starlings. All of a sudden, as though in response to an urgent summons, hundreds of birds flew through the air in great whirling clouds and then alighted, singing in loud alarm or jubilation. They arrayed themselves in neat rows on the branches as though with the help of a bird valet. I stopped whatever I was doing and rushed outside to hear their evensong, which ended after a few minutes, when they flew away as abruptly as they arrived, again as though in response to an authoritative signal. I felt blessed by the lavishness of their visitation. They vanished when winter came and now, in midsummer, in a fourth month of unstoppable pain, I dream of their return.

Particularly when I feel vulnerable in body and mind, I crave what the political philosopher Jane Bennett calls "not-quite-human capaciousness," which she sees in all the chemicals, proteins, and particles from which the physical world is made, including starlings. This vitalism cannot "dissolve completely into the milieu of human knowledge," she writes. Despite the fact that "non-living" and living things share a common substrate—bones, for example, contain minerals found in the earth's crust—and that we are acted upon by things and processes that we think of as inanimate, like the earth's capacity to create hard mineral structures within soft tissue, to which we apparently owe the existence of our skeletons, people tend to resist the idea that we are always, even in small ways, not ourselves. "I've learned," writes the falconer-poet Helen MacDonald, "how you feel more human once you have known, even in your imagination, what it is like to be not."[67] That feeling comes from placing yourself "entirely at the world's mercy."[68] Jane Bennett argues that some of our resistance to this surrender can be attributed to the vanity of the type of humanism that places our own intelligence at the center of nature. I think some of it can also be attributed to the difference between what we can articulate as knowledge and what we experience as emotion and intuition. The rest comes from the inherent elusiveness of life outside of life, which Bennett fittingly calls the "*out-side.*" She compares it to the conception of God as the Absolute, a word she traces to the Latin roots *ab* (off) and *solver* (to loosen). Thus the "absolute is that which is *loosened off* and on the loose."[69]

It is not always a simple matter to tell the difference between capital and lower case forms of the absolute, or especially useful to try. When Annie Dillard describes her vision of a tree on fire she knows that for many readers it is impossible not to think of Exodus and of Moses, trembling before the angel who appears as a herald of the Lord in the flames of a burning bush. This is Moses's first direct encounter with God, and he is not sure what is happening. "I will go over and see this strange sight," he says, "why the bush does not burn up."[70] At this early stage of his career he is a full-time shepherd, a man who knows how nature works. The fact that his curiosity pulls him closer to a bush in order to investigate its perplexing qualities is not irrelevant to what happens next, which is that God speaks to him and endows him with the eloquence and magic by which he will lead his people out of bondage in Egypt. God gives Moses power and tells him how to spend it. *Pilgrim at Tinker Creek* often invokes the Abrahamic faiths, not just by frequent quotation of the Bible, the Talmud, and the Koran, but by the implicit suggestion that awe at matters such as the hourly growth rate of bamboo or fire that does not consume what it burns is a way of allowing oneself to be addressed and shaken by a form of life that is not identical with ours. In none of her writing does Dillard feel the need to decide exactly what form of life this is or assume that she has the ability to do so.

Thoreau, who was a pilgrim at Walden pond more than a century before Dillard went to Tinker Creek, is confident that the "tonic of wildness" awakens "the most original part" of a person.[71] "We need to witness our own limits transgressed," he writes, "and some life pasturing freely where we never wander."[72] That wild life is in us too, he believes, and can never be fully domesticated, because it is divine. Having witnessed it in the woods and ponds around Concord and felt it within himself, Thoreau begins to spend it on various forms of civil disobedience. He doesn't only want to make himself a new creature, but his fellow citizens as well, and particularly the taxpayers of Massachusetts. The essay "Slavery in Massachusetts" is his scorching condemnation of the support given by the Federal government, the state Governor, the press, and the citizenry to the Fugitive Slave laws of 1850, which required Northern States to assist slave owners in their attempts to recover their runaway property. Toward the end of the essay, Thoreau asks, "what signifies the beauty of nature when men are base?"[73] And then he answers the question in the same way that he does at the end of *Walden*: the experience of wildness reveals laws that are more generous and just than those of a slave-holding country, and perhaps of any human administration. In the first water lily of spring he sees those laws that have "prevailed longest and widest, and still prevail," even among men who are driven by racial hatred, moral complacency, and greed.[74]

Wildness is not always beautiful or perfumed. In a chapter of *Walden* called "Higher Laws," Thoreau sees a woodchuck in the woods and feels tempted to "seize and devour him raw," not because he is particularly hungry—he has an ample bean harvest, remember, and a string of fish on the line—but because he loves "the wild not less than the good" and is cautious about his ability to distinguish between them.[75] He relishes a fried rat for dinner from time to time, and is not discomfited by the scent of a dead horse decomposing in the heat a short distance from his cabin.[76] Unlike Dillard, Thoreau welcomes the sight and smell of death, writing, in his incomparable prose, "I love to see that Nature is so rife with life that myriads can be afforded to be sacrificed and suffered to prey on one another; that tender organizations can be so serenely squashed out of existence like pulp." Like *pulp*? He is delighted that "sometimes it has rained flesh and blood!"[77]

Here I recall that Marilynne Robinson describes astonishment as "a threat or an insight."[78] Its most literal form is petrification: shock so acute that it turns flesh into stone, as Medusa did. Astonishment is brought about by monsters as well as gods, terror as well as joy. Sometimes it is strangely difficult to tell these states of mind apart. For this reason, Thoreau shows no sign of preferring the beauty of a lily to the stench of a decaying animal, and is enthusiastic about plagues of frogs and blood, which strikes me as a little unwise, or maybe as proof of unusual courage. Even Moses was terrified by the burning bush, and offered God many reasons why he was the wrong man to lead the Jews out of captivity. Thoreau knows what can happen to people who feel that they have been directly addressed by God. His essay "A Plea for Captain John Brown" is about the militant Abolitionist and devout Christian who believed that God had called him to lead an armed slave revolt. As is well known, the rebellion of 1859 was quelled, and Brown was charged with treason and hanged.[79]

This should not be understood as failure. It is testament to the sacrifices required to challenge the most unjust laws, including the Fugitive Slave laws. I like to read Thoreau's essay beside Toni Morrison's *Beloved*, which gives a full account of those sacrifices, and is also the most Pauline novel I know, featuring an epigraph from the letter to the Romans, and not one but three men named Paul. Baby Suggs, the old woman bought out of slavery by her son, tells her community of escaped and freed slaves that "the only grace they could have was the grace they could imagine," and she preaches this message within a golden bower of trees deep in the forests of Ohio.[80] But no one imagines that a fugitive slave will cut her child's throat to save her from capture or that the dead child will one day return to life as a young woman, just as no one imagines that her return will at first be a miracle and gradually become unendurable. In the end, Beloved takes almost everything from her mother Sethe, and the women of the neighborhood have to exorcize her before she takes everything from them too. Even after she disappears, she is not gone. Sometimes people catch sight of her in the woods or feel her in the wind. Paul D thinks, "He can't put his finger on it, but it seems, for a moment, that just beyond his knowing is the glare of an outside thing that embraces while it accuses."[81] Beloved is the outside thing; she is not the kind of "loneliness that can be rocked" to sleep but the kind that "roams" and is "alive, on its own."[82]

Unlike Thoreau, Morrison does not believe that nature reveals laws higher than the human. Beloved is the name given not to one murdered child but to all who were taken in slavery, and she becomes a permanent part of the woods, the air, the soil, and the waterways of this world. Nature is not a retreat from human administration; it is filled with presence that was once human, including that of the fugitive and lost, and so is the wildness it offers us. This capaciousness is frightening and uncategorizable, beyond anyone's knowing or control, loosened off and on the loose in a fearsome way. Beloved is certainly not the kind of grace you can imagine. Then again, grace is never what you can imagine. Her murder in infancy becomes a plank in the Abolitionist platform precisely because it shows the unimaginable lengths to which a slave woman will go to protect her child's freedom.

More than fifteen years after the publication of *Beloved*, Morrison wrote a foreword in which she describes how she felt when she quit her job in publishing and began to consider writing a novel based on the historical figure of Margaret Garner. Morrison recalls that she felt *free*, but that this heart-pounding sensation was so close to panic and fear that at first she did not know what it was. Then she realized that it was the feeling of possibility, and that she would use it to write about women and men who were not allowed to feel it or decide what to do with it if they did.[83] Not immediately knowing how to classify a state of mind is central to freedom, as Morrison describes it here and in the figure of Beloved, who forgives and accuses, gives and takes, blesses and curses, reminds and obliterates, and can never be localized or brought under control any more than the wind can be. Perhaps this is why people tend to describe astonishment as both essential and useless; they do not always know what to do with it but they know that they cannot do without it. Even when it does not lead to the writing of a Pulitzer Prize-winning novel or to the overturning of inhuman laws, it makes people feel less reduced by their circumstances, however fleetingly.

As a young woman, the writer and activist Barbara Ehrenreich saw a forest fluoresce, much as Annie Dillard did. She insists that the experience did not place pressure on a law or moral precept or ask her to change her life. She did not wish to discuss it with a lawyer any more than she wished to discuss it with a priest. In fact, she insists that her vision of incandescence "had nothing to do with right or wrong, good or evil, kindness or cruelty, or any other abstractions arising from the human tribal life." "Whatever I had seen *was what it was*," she writes, "with no moral valence or reference to human concerns."[84] It made her fear that she was mentally ill, but also persuaded her that her experience of "overflow," in which the "heavens had opened and poured into me, and I into them," addressed her central question about life: "What is actually going on here?"[85] As an adult, Ehrenreich sought to answer the question as a research biologist and then as an advocate for American women and the working poor, but she later concludes that a life cannot be understood only within the physical or cultural dynamics of the species—human tribal life. Nor does she believe in God. She believes that her formative ecstatic experiences reveal the presence of "runaway processes driven by positive feedback loops, emergent patterns, violent attractions, quantum leaps, and always, as far ahead as we can see, more surprises" that are inherent within matter and within our own perceptual processes.[86]

Glimpses of runaway life, even those that call one's sanity into question, are both a provocation and a source of renewal that is hard to live without. Ehrenreich describes the depression that overtook her in late middle age when her visions ended. One of the great world literary projects of the new century, Karl Ove Knausgaard's autobiographical novel cycle, *My Struggle,* spends several thousand pages describing his efforts to express the outside of his life in order to stave off suicidal despair. Knausgaard is so deeply drawn to the sacred that he wrote a novel about the Old Testament called *A Time for Everything* and then joined a group of writers who were translating the Hebrew scriptures into Norwegian. However, he speaks for many when he writes that he can never embrace institutional Christianity or any other religion, and that God is "a wild notion" he "could never entertain as a belief."[87] He also speaks for many when he writes, "constantly, continually, a storm blew through our world," and admits that this storm of energy, which he believes to be the true subject of the Bible, fills him with as much terror as joy, and makes him fear that he will drink himself to death, as his father did, or find some quicker way to end his life.[88] Knausgaard's frank exploration of the varieties of exhaustion that drive people to despair, including public forms such as genocide and terrorism, has made *My Struggle* an international phenomenon.

In the second novel in the series, *A Man in Love*, Knausgaard describes falling in love with the Swedish writer Linda Boström, and the birth of their first child. He writes, "the world lay at my feet, open, packed with meaning."[89] If for some reason I was asked to choose one word that best described the entirety of *My Struggle* it would be this: *open*. This is the feeling of freedom and immanence that Knausgaard craves. But over time what is open always begins to close, the clock ticks again, circadian rhythms emerge, passion cools, and everyone becomes absorbed in the daily round of activities that life requires. After the birth of his first child, Knausgaard experiences this return of the ordinary as a great loss, but he also discovers that he now has the momentum that he needs to finish writing the novel that he has been working on with little success for over five years. It is as though he is able to harness some of the roving availability that came with new love and pull it into a novel about the history of angels, from the book of Genesis to the present day.

As Knausgaard finishes this novel, *A Time for Everything*, he feels that "a kind of light burned within me, not hot and consuming but cold and clear and shining." This light releases so much energy that it replaces the need for food and sleep and creates what he calls "the best moments in my life."[90] *A Time for Everything* is about the sources of this energy, and about the "struggle the Bible speaks of," which is not the creative struggle of an individual to write novels, but the much larger struggle of our species to resist "the darkness that descends again and again on person after person, generation after generation, century after century, until the despair is unendurable."[91] Knausgaard imagines that for the inhabitants of the ancient societies described in the Hebrew scriptures, angels illuminated this existential darkness, and their presence as ambassadors of God was enough to imbue life with meaning. But he speculates that beginning with Christianity, which shifts the meridian between divine and human by incarnating God as a mortal man, angels are gradually put out of a job; their services as *angelos*, or messengers, are no longer required because the message is already on earth, it is here, in the body and in mortal experience, rather than in the distant heavens and a transcendent order of being. And so over time angels gradually lose their power to bring gifts and curses, until they are fully unwilded. Slowly, and particularly throughout the Renaissance, they became carnal beings with earthly appetites, and then cherubic little *putti*, no longer terrifying emissaries of the divine.

Part the breast feathers of any seagull, and you will see it: "a tiny little arm … thin as a piece of wire," last remnant of the fiery beings who once guarded the tree of life.[92] Knausgaard imagines that over the millennia, angels gradually devolved into scavenger birds, their wings shrinking, their noses hardening, their chain mail feathering, their hands sharpening into claws. Now they live on scraps on the outskirts of human settlements, bring no gospel, and have nothing to offer other than a proclivity for eating our garbage. The angels are gone, but the despair is not.

Like the fictional sixteenth-century theologian Antinous Bellori in *A Time for Everything*, who describes the dying cherubim he saw as a child in the woods of Northern Italy and hopes that his writing will restore them to power, Knausgaard is always reaching into the forest. It is not an angel that he hopes to find there, sword in hand, or any sign of the cross. *My Struggle* is driven by Knausgaard's search for the sacred, but that search does not lead him back to faith or to nature. It leads him to that part of his own mind that is not controlled by what he calls the "constables of the consciousness."[93] This is the wilderness of intuition, and Knausgaard's central aim in writing *My Struggle* at breakneck speed—almost 4000 pages in three years—was to knock the constables off their feet in order to access the only aspect of his identity that he believes to be more than a collection of cultural and familial influences. He feels that only this gratuitous fraction of his mind can help him to resist the existential terror that beginning in adolescence led him to blackout drinking, drug use, and self-mutilation.[94]

It has to be said that this work comes at a very high price for Linda Boström, and for Knausgaard himself. Despite her history of manic depression, including a suicide attempt and a period as an inpatient in a psychiatric ward, Knausgaard leaves her to care for their infant for six weeks after he moves into his office to finish *A Time for Everything*. Boström calls him, distraught, several times a day, and threatens to leave him and take their daughter with her. He tells her to leave if she must, but that he cannot stop writing until the novel is done, no matter the consequences. In *The End*, the final volume of *My Struggle*, we learn that when the first books in the series are published in Scandinavia, Boström has another breakdown and has to be hospitalized again. It is hazardous to chase the clear and shining light—many saints and mystics have attested to these hazards, including the fictitious Antinous Bellori—but it is more harrowing for Knausgaard to live without it. In the end, it creates feelings of betrayal within his family that may never be healed. Yet he feels driven, as a matter of survival, to describe experiences of abundance that by definition elude description and at the same time seem to come with a built-in demand to be shared, much as a visit from an angel is never a private matter, but always changes the fate of an entire people. Every vision of largesse carries an imperative, which is that the recipient has to find a way to express what she has felt and thus to make space for the extra life that is now indispensable. *My Struggle* is the form that Knausgaard found. Many readers, including me, feel that these books are not just about moments of radiance, but radiant in themselves.

I will never move into my office to write for weeks at a stretch, perhaps because I have never felt self-loathing so deep that I cut my face open with shards of glass, as Knausgaard did. It is true that I usually prefer solitude to company, and books to life, and that my children often chastise me for being so absent that I am not even aware that I am muttering under my breath. "Who are you talking to?" they ask suspiciously, "Why are your lips moving?" "Where *are* you?" I tell them that I'm thinking, and then I do my best to pull my attention out of whatever internal labyrinth I'm wandering in and toward the math homework that needs doing and the story of what happened on the schoolyard at lunch hour. I am grateful to Knausgaard for charting these internal labyrinths, but I am equally grateful to those who know how to be where they are. I need to get better at this. As so often, I turn to Marilynne Robinson, whose body of work is deeply attuned to what she calls "the resurrection of the ordinary." Those words come from her iconic novel, *Housekeeping*, and they refer to the life of Sylvia Foster, the widowed mother of three young girls, who is as "constant" and as "unremarked as daylight."[95]

This is the best description of motherhood I have ever read. The work of housekeeping is to conceal the work so that children never sense fragility or weakness, at least not enough to make them doubt for an instant that the stable domestic patterns created by love are part of nature, that they are just how things are, and could not stop any more than the sun could decide to stop burning. This is the danger that we work to conceal from children, even though we know that in the end they will see that their parents are not like the reliable ball of flaming gas in the sky, but vulnerable in every way, and prone to unconscious muttering. When this realization takes place, the hope is that somehow the steady and unquestioned light of childhood will be enough to illuminate a lifetime. It isn't loving that is hard but the incessant labor that it requires: feeding, clothing, cleaning, teaching, and, above all, absorbing the primordial emotions that children are born with and that they are not afraid to express. These emotions are as powerful and active within them as the volcanic heat at the center of the earth or the nuclear storms that are said to give birth to galaxies. Responding to this emotion with patience and intelligence is the hardest part of mothering.

All of Robinson's novels are filled with suicides and transients—people who for any number of reasons cannot be constant, will not create daylight. One of Sylvia Foster's daughters deliberately drives her car into the lake, orphaning her children; another burns down the family home to live as a vagrant. "A house should have a compass and a keel," Robinson writes, like Noah's ark, and she is faithful to those who stretch conventional perceptions of what goodness or community or family should be.[96] But she is also interested in people like Sylvia Foster, a woman who is content to stay at home all her life, cooking and cleaning, planting and harvesting, and never dreaming of the outside. One evening as Sylvia digs new potatoes in her kitchen garden she is astonished by the summer wind: "What have I seen, what have I seen. The earth and the sky and the garden, not as they always are. And she saw her daughters' faces not as they always were, or as other people's were, and she was quiet and aloof and watchful, not to startle the strangeness away."[97] The moment of strangeness that Sylvia experiences here gives her an intimation of absolute life, and unlike her husband and daughters, she is the kind of person who can find a place for it inside the house. Her constancy, her ability to tend and foster, is precisely what reveals something hidden within the earth, sky and human face. She doesn't know why on this particular evening the wind has startled her like this, but she knows that she needs to hold on to the difference it has made even though it is not clear what the difference is.

Moments like these are not just a matter of looking but of being looked at differently. "It is as if the interstellar spaces, and all the random atoms into which we will one day vanish, turned a kind of incomprehensible but utterly comprehending attention toward us," writes Christian Wiman, echoing Annie Dillard.[98] In "From a Window," he gives an example of what this feels like to him:

Incurable and unbelieving
in any truth but the truth of grieving,

I saw a tree inside a tree
rise kaleidoscopically

as if the leaves had livelier ghosts.
I pressed my face as close

to the pane as I could get
to watch that fitful, fluent spirit

that seemed a single being undefined
or countless beings of one mind

haul its strange cohesion
beyond the limits of my vision

over the house heavenwards.
Of course I knew those leaves were birds.

Of course that old tree stood
exactly as it had and would

(but why should it seem fuller now?)
and though a man's mind might endow

even a tree with some excess
of life to which a man seems witness,

that life is not the life of men.
And that is where the joy came in.[99]

Like all of Wiman's later works, this poem was written in the shadow of his diagnosis in his late thirties with a rare and aggressive form of cancer. It suggests that what he sees from a window, namely the doubling of a tree's foliage by a rising flock of birds, changes what he sees in a more general sense, just as Sylvia Foster is startled first by the wind and then by the inexplicable foreignness of her daughters' faces. This change is produced by "some excess / of life" that is both endowed by Wiman's mind ("Of course I knew those leaves were birds") and independent of it. The result is a transition from grief—"Incurable and unbelieving"—to joy. That joy comes from what the man sees from his window, but also from the feeling of being seen by something that for a moment relieves him of his solitude.

For many people, this solitude is unbearable even when it is not filled with physical or emotional agony. Surely this is why Sylvia Foster cherishes strangeness, just as I cherish the autumn evenings when the local trees fill with birds. This excess, which Wiman calls "saving otherness," is often revealed by suffering, although it is also to be found in pleasure.[100] Even Simone Weil, who went to great lengths to make her physical life as punishing as possible, believed that God is present in the "beauty of the world," including erotic love. St. Augustine felt that divine grace made God his lover, and there is a long tradition of Christian devotional writing that likens faith to eroticism, but this is not what Weil is thinking of. In fact, she observes that the history of Christian thought has been inattentive to sensuality in its own right—a "terrible gap," she calls it.[101] In the late 1980s, the theologian Rowan Williams gave a talk called "The Body's Grace" to the members of the Lesbian and Gay Christian Movement in London, in which he argues that eroticism between flesh-and-blood human beings—including gay human beings–creates contact with God as surely as faith can. This was a novel idea at the time. He writes that sexual desire creates an "entry into some different kind of identity" in which "I am no longer in charge of what I am" because my body is "recreated by another person's perception."[102] Sexuality is not an analogy for the experience of God's love, or some debased version that we poor mortals must make do with, Williams says. It is the direct experience of the Absolute. A lover is someone who holds up a mirror from an unexpected angle and says, "Look at who you really are, or could be." Desire allows us to ask of one another what Paul asked of his God: Here, make something new of me.

Pre-monetary *charis* recognized that people renew each other all the time by doing things like driving their spears into the earth in the middle of a war zone, or offering a double-handled solid gold cup rather than homicide to a well-armed stranger, and that the beautiful things that people make are surprising too, whether they are crafted with words, leather, or precious metal. These forms can be so startling that it is as though they were made by creatures that hail from some other precinct of existence and arrive here still breathing hard and giving off heat. Even the most modest acts of invention reveal that gifts are not just at work in the lives of people we think of as being exceptionally creative, like novelists and poets, but in every aspect of living.

If the organizational psychologist Adam Grant is to be believed, gifts even exist in corporate America—not in splashy displays of philanthropy or tax-exempt donations to registered charities, which are more about brand-building than anything else, but in the daily and often unremarked operations of any profitable business. This is not the kind of donation for which a CEO receives a standing ovation or her name on the wing of a building. Grant argues that although in the workplace most people are "matchers," meaning that their treatment of others is governed by expectations of reciprocity, it is demonstrably clear that only "givers" create wealth. Matchers are motivated by a sense of responsibility and fair play, and they help people who have helped them in the past or may help them in the future, but *quid pro quo* does no more than keep the cycle of industry moving efficiently. Givers, who donate time and attention to others without calculating the consequences or expecting a return, are the people who drive profit, including the most important forms: happiness, respect, motivation, and compassion. Givers don't act according to the law of reciprocity; they know that their generosity will have to go around a corner or two before it comes back.[103]

Grant is a social scientist who teaches future entrepreneurs and executives at Wharton, people who disrupt industries and found multimillion dollar companies with the help of business plans I could not understand even if I studied them for a decade. I cannot imagine that he would consider a fairy tale to be a respectable source of evidence for anything, much less a study in entrepreneurship. However, Grant also works as a consultant to companies looking to increase their productivity, and so I present him with the story of the shoemaker, who was, after all, a failing businessman who needed to figure out how to turn his brick-and-mortar store around. Confronted by this case study, Grant is likely to argue that the elves emerge from a deep reservoir of goodwill that the shoemaker created through acts of kindness that he has forgotten about, because he is a giver who doesn't keep a running tab of who owes him. Unlike takers and even matchers, who want to get paid now, before the money and the favors dry up, his actions are governed by faith in the future. Let's assume that a man who cuts out the last piece of leather and goes to bed thinking that his situation will look different in the morning has always been optimistic about what's coming next. And it turns out that he is right to be optimistic, because some of the people he helped in the past have not forgotten, and they have been quietly consulting one another about how to reach out to their former benefactor without taking credit. "Hang on," says one. "I just got a LinkedIn request from some faery folk." Grant believes that gifts emerge from social networks, but it seems to me that givers feed an energy overload that is created by the sum of all enterprises taking place within nature, not just human ones. Giving to other people feeds this overload, but so does giving to a task, even one as humble as making shoes. If this is true, then the shoemaker isn't rescued by the hidden actions of an individual or even a group, but by the impersonal abundance that travels through all the circuits of life and occasionally sheds into the human domain. This overload takes on agency and is able to act without our intervention, which is why it sends the shoemaker help in a nonhuman form.

Versions of this idea are to be found in many accounts of creativity. Artists in all genres describe the process of invention as both an act and an event—donation to a task and trust in an uncertain future. Heidegger called it an "overflow, an endowing, a bestowal" that comes from beyond the visible resources of any individual or culture.[104] More than half a century later, Derek Attridge calls it "otherness," which he defines as "that which is, at a given moment, outside the horizon provided by the culture for thinking, understanding, imagining, feeling, perceiving."[105] All agree that without something that comes from beyond the horizon, invention doesn't happen. To open the senses or receive an endowment of any kind one must travel to the edge of the law and then lean on it until the surprise comes, but in the secular realm this journey is undertaken without divine instruction and its effects are never calculable or imbued with moral authority. A surprise is an access of energy. What happens next is anyone's guess. This is why Attridge cautions that there "is no necessary correlation" between being a good artist and a good person, and that the only stable connection between creativity and ethics is imaginative openness.[106] Heidegger's thinking remains enormously influential, and yet he actively supported the Nazi regime and after the war never apologized even to his Jewish admirers, including Paul Celan.

There is danger in openness, and it can't be avoided, because without danger there is no grace. Certainly grace was hazardous for the Greeks, in whom a *charis*-event created a state of vulnerability so acute that it either turned a stranger into a brother or into someone whose throat you pierced with a spear, depending on his answer to your gesture of goodwill. And Adam Grant argues that givers are to be found at the bottom as well as the top of the American workplace hierarchy because generous people are always in danger of burning out or being taken advantage of. Yet there is never any question that the gift is worth every risk. If the body's grace requires that "I am no longer in charge of what I am," so do all other forms of creativity. Rowan Williams's belief that sexuality is one of the primary ways in which we transform one another shows how deeply the need for grace is rooted in our emotional and physical being, and how much we are willing to wager in order to experience it. Unsurprisingly, gifts that seem to come directly from God require endangerment of the most extreme sort, as is clear in the story of Abraham's near-sacrifice of Isaac and in the letters that Paul wrote to his embattled groups of Christian converts in the years before his execution for sedition.

I have insisted from the beginning that grace is always astonishing, but it is also true that people put themselves in the path of grace even if they do not always know it. Gifts do not respond to summons, but this does not mean that summons are futile. This delicate contradiction is at the heart of Chapter 22 of Genesis, in which all of Abraham's preparations for the sacrifice of his son are described in detail. He cuts firewood, loads the donkey, travels to the mountain top, builds the pyre, binds the child, raises the knife, and not for one moment does he imagine that God will intervene. Not once does he scan the heavens for a pair of wings or scout the bushes for the ram that will take Isaac's place. But what is Abraham doing on Mount Moriah, if not patiently preparing the ground for the coming of an angel? And what is Paul doing, if not the equally impossible work of teaching people how to obey a law that demands to be broken?

This demand turns Abraham into the father of nations and Paul into an apostle, just as it calls the elves to the cobbler's workshop. To the very last, the cobbler is obedient to the rituals of his trade, cutting out the final scrap of shoe leather even though it can't possibly save him from penury. The elves don't come until he has done everything that routine requires of him; only then, when his will is all but destroyed and his cupboard is bare, do the faeries arrive, twinkling with life. In this regard the shoemaker is like the prince in "Sleeping Beauty," who ignores the old man who warns him about the wall of thorns that has already killed many kings' sons. "I do not fear to try," he says earnestly. At the very moment when he approaches, sword held high, the curse relents and the thorns bloom. I get the feeling that the prince has more than lucky timing on his side. His willingness to place himself at risk helps to turn the thorns into flowers, just as his kiss is necessary to awaken Rosamond from sleep. It is not enough to wait out the curse, even though he cannot abbreviate it by even an hour. Nevertheless, he has to push against it, as others pushed before him. In their way, these fairy-tale characters share the rigor of the biblical men who abide by the rules so fully that they unknowingly conjure their own rescue.

***

Emmanuel Levinas writes that no one can ethically "be approached with empty hands and closed home."[107] His thinking took shape in post-Holocaust France, and was steeped in both continental philosophy and Judeo-Christian theology, but it would not have been unfamiliar to Homer or the Brothers Grimm. To be faithful to the world, and not just responsible to the rule of reciprocity, you must keep wealth in motion and you must open doors, which are two ways of saying the same thing. It's not easy. If it were, we wouldn't have all the countervailing stories of locks and greed. In a day filled with the relentless clamor of other people's needs, I sometimes think of life behind the hedge of thorns with longing; my mind darts into the sleeping kingdom, and I imagine a delicious somnolence, like the melting feeling of a summer afternoon. Then I think, don't be a fool, it's not summer in there, it's absolute winter. It's not sanctuary, it's exile. This is where your hands cup dust and you die of loneliness in a very tidy house.

2

Charity

Pity and charity may be at root an attempt to propitiate the dark
powers that have not touched us yet.
MARILYNNE ROBINSON[1]

For some, charity is made out of spun sugar, the preferred food of saints. For others, it evokes an ongoing history of violence that includes the "white savior industrial complex," as Teju Cole calls it.[2] For others still, charity is like one of the dormant seeds found in the unsealed tombs of pharaohs that, once planted, turns out to contain ancient and essential nutrition that cannot be found in our modern granaries. The word comes from Greek *charis,* with tasting notes of *agape* and Latin *caritas*. I propose that *eros* has a role to play too, although it is less canonical. All are forms of love. All depend on the intuition of something incalculable in the human presence, the quality that some people call givenness, which includes the dark powers that swirl within and around us. Even so, Mary Douglas is right to observe, "though we laud charity as a Christian virtue we know that it wounds."[3] If you grew up buying most of your possessions at charity shops, as I did, the word feels like a punch in the stomach. Early Christians felt it too, which is why the authors of the Gospels issued the much-quoted but frequently misconstrued instruction to give to the needy without letting your left hand know what your right hand is doing. In our time, this phrase is usually cited in contexts of malfeasance or idiocy. Neither is germane to Chapter 6 of the Gospel of Matthew where the instruction originates. Here Jesus advises that giving should take place in secret, not just to avoid public displays of piety and the self-congratulation that accompanies them, but because it must be a mystery even to the giver.[4]

When the early modern scholar and Protestant reformer William Tyndale undertook the first translation of the New Testament into English, working directly from the original Greek, he chose to use the word love rather than charity to describe these movements of gift. It is well known that Thomas More found the decision heretical, in part because he thought that the word love was too ordinary to express either God's relationship to humanity or the divine imperative to care for others, particularly the deprived and outcast.[5] Yet presumably Tyndale chose the word precisely because people knew what it meant. They knew what it felt like to love and be loved, and they could use that knowledge to restore emotional depth to the act of giving and to complicate the idea of need. Not everyone needs help buying food or finding shelter, but is there anyone who does not need love? Seen this way, it becomes easier to understand giving as a fundamental response to what is most astonishing in oneself and in others. If not, it is no gift, but a calculation. Not love, but a tactic or therapy. As cold as charity, people say, and with reason.

Mary Douglas's reasons are not so different than Tyndale's. In her foreword to Mauss's *The Gift*, called "No Free Gifts," she connects charity with pre- or non-monetary traditions in which the purpose of giving is never just to take care of a person's body, but to confirm that she is fully alive as both a social and an absolute being. Douglas's argument is not that we should stop giving to those in need or that gifts are necessarily a form of arrogance, but that "refusing requital puts the act of giving outside any mutual ties."[6] Her argument is that in order to shorten the distance between giver and recipient we need to give *more*.

At the beginning of a novel called *Some Hope*, Edward St. Aubyn writes that the novel's protagonist, Patrick Melrose, "moved in a world in which the word 'charity', like a beautiful woman shadowed by her jealous husband, was invariably qualified by the words 'lunch', 'committee', or 'ball.'"[7] Like St. Aubyn himself, Melrose is the son of an English aristocrat and an American heiress, yet he is very much in need of charity. Despite having been disinherited by his mother, who was always more interested in caring for opportunistic strangers than for her son, more money is not what Melrose is after. St. Aubyn's autobiographical novel cycle is about Melrose's attempt to recover from being repeatedly raped by his father and abandoned by his mother, experiences that led him to several decades of drug addiction, and frequent visits to Emergency Rooms, rehabilitation centers, and psychiatric wards on both sides of the Atlantic.

Melrose feels that only an act of mercy can release him from this suicidal storm. At the end of *At Last*, the fifth and final novel in the series, he experiences such a moment in the garden of the psychiatric hospital where he is a long-term patient. Suddenly and without explanation, something "unseen and unprovoked ... invaded his depressive gaze, and spread like a gold rush through the ruins of his tired brain. He had no control over the source of his reprieve." He calls it "gratuitous beauty." It is not brought about by his physical surroundings, which are wintry and bleak. It is not brought about by love for another person or for God, in whom he has no faith, nor by the conscious granting of forgiveness. Perhaps it is just a rogue surge of dopamine. Melrose doesn't know where the feeling came from or whether it will ever happen again, only that under its influence his depression "simply yielded to another way of being."[8] He has no idea what he has done to earn this temporary release, only that he can't live without it. The reader doesn't know either, although having followed him through five novels and forty years of his life we can see that he has softened the defensive irony that he learned from his father, which turns out to be far more addictive than heroin and almost as deadly. The hope that begins in *Some Hope* is connected to Melrose's new willingness to be gentler with himself and others, which over the years leads him to understand that if he is to survive he will need to find a way to remember his parents without rage, grief, and terror. If he thinks about the discrepancy between what he needed and what they gave him he will not survive. He needs to discover a form of generosity toward their memory.

A performance of *Measure for Measure* is what prompts Patrick Melrose to imagine this generosity. In Shakespeare's play the words mercy, charity, and grace are spoken in almost every scene. His Royal Grace Vincentio, Duke of Vienna has the unenviable job of enforcing the law while granting exceptions, knowing that his authority as Sovereign depends upon getting the measure right. If law is too brittle or grace too easy, then both fail, and Vienna with them. By his own estimation the Duke has been getting the measure wrong for quite some time. Over the years he has made it his practice to ignore the city's "strict statutes and most biting laws," with the result that his subjects have come to mock rather than respect them.[9] His remedy is to disguise himself as a friar and appoint an unyielding Deputy in his stead, decisions that underscore the extent to which charity concerns the spirit as well as the state. At first the Duke's stratagem seems cruel and cowardly, made worse by the fact that while dressed in the habit of a holy man he gives lectures on divine grace to all the people whom his Deputy abuses. But gradually it begins to seem that the monk's robes are not just a convenient fraud, but a lesson in humility that the Duke is teaching himself so that he can then teach it to his subjects. In the end he comes out of hiding and rains mercy on those who have lost hope, including an unrepentant prisoner deemed too drunk to go to his own execution.

As the Duke pardons this man, Barnardine, he distinguishes spiritual from "earthly faults." He tells the prisoner that he has a "stubborn soul / That apprehends no further than this world." "Thou'rt condemned," the Duke says, and there's nothing I can do about it other than to pray that you take the pardon I offer you and use it "to provide / For better times to come."[10] If Barnardine needs to apprehend further than this world to save his soul, so does the Duke, although he has the additional burden of worrying about Vienna. His alias as a monk persuades him that his power to forgive does not come from his title or political office, or even from within his own humanity, but from the very region that he counsels Barnardine to believe in and to orient his life toward: the spirit, the divine. At the beginning of the play, the Duke says that he cannot bear to unleash the fury of the law on his people after so many years of being kind, which is why he needs to protect his reputation by hiding behind a proxy; but as he pardons Barnardine he seems to acknowledge that although he is addressed by his subjects as your Grace, he is not the true source of charity. If it is important for the Duke to distinguish spiritual from earthly faults, and to recognize that his jurisdiction extends only to the latter kind of infraction, then it is equally important for him to recognize that when he grants clemency he is not himself. The mistaken belief that the law is nothing more than an extension of his own prestige is a form of stubbornness every bit as serious as Barnardine's.

Stubbornness. Aristotle counseled against it. The word compares the stuck mind to a dead tree stub too deeply rooted in the earth to be moved, and long past usefulness. By the fourth century BCE, the Greek cities no longer operated primarily as gift economies, and unlike the poet Simonides of Keos, who had to muddle through the transition to coinage, Aristotle feels no nostalgia for the old days. Nevertheless, in *The Ethics* he praises the civic practice of erecting a Temple of the Charities (or Graces) in a public place, and believes that charity is fundamental to human happiness and to the functioning of the kind of state that promotes it. Although Aristotle admires money and democracy, which emphasize the material equivalence of commodities and the political equality of citizens, he fears that they might obscure the ethical importance of attending to those attributes of people and things that elude standard measures. He argues that even when laws are perfectly just they cannot be equitable because they are universal, and therefore unresponsive to the contours of the individual case. True justice, he writes, arises not from the evenhanded application of the law, but from "a *correction*" of it.[11] He goes on to write that the law must be as pliant as the soft leaden rulers used by masons on Lesbos to measure the stones of irregular shape and size for which the island seems to have been known. In our century, the island of Lesbos is known as an entry point to Western Europe for refugees, not as a source of building materials. Aristotle is unlikely to have foreseen this, yet his analogy holds. Like a skilled stonemason, the equitable state or man "is not overly just," and he and his neighbors are much happier for it.[12]

Aristotle and the Duke of Vienna do not agree about the source of charity, although they do agree that it is essential to individual and collective wellbeing. They also agree that it relies on the willingness to apprehend further than this world—not as far as the divine, perhaps, but certainly as far as the hidden qualities of mind, experience, and circumstance that make it dangerous to measure everyone by the same laws without bending or in some cases suspending them altogether. The alternatives are injustice and misery.

The Patrick Melrose novels offer a scathing critique of the Anglo-American aristocracy, but St. Aubyn does not tackle the problem of how an entire social class might become less stubborn. It is miracle enough that Melrose occasionally catches a glimpse of some other way of being; everyone else will have to shift for themselves. For more than four decades, the question of how they might do so has been of primary importance to the South African Nobel Laureate, J. M. Coetzee. His work considers the social force of charity as well as the range of forms it is capable of taking, some of which are very strange. The transition from apartheid to non-racial democracy does not lessen his interest in these questions, but it does change the way he answers them. Over the years, those answers cover far more ground than I have just done in reaching from *charis* to *caritas*, although these are key points of reference for Coetzee's thinking about the transformation of the state as well as the individual. Taken as a whole, his life's work suggests that only acts and experiences of charity can deeply alter the way people value themselves and others; but it also suggests that despairing people don't always have the capacity to bring about this alteration no matter how hard they try, especially if they live in a state governed by iron rather than leaden rules. As a result, the gifts that proliferate in Coetzee's later work don't come from people. They come from further afield, as gifts so often do.

* * *

The merciless spirit of Franz Kafka hovers here and requires a moment of obeisance. This will just take a minute. I exaggerate only slightly when I say that all of J. M. Coetzee's apartheid novels reimagine the fate of Gregor Samsa, the loneliest insect of the twentieth century. It is crucial to Kafka's parable that Gregor locks his bedroom door at night even when at home, and that he spends the first quarter of the story trying to unlock that door with his brand-new insect jaws, because he knows that if can't get to the train on time he will lose his job and forfeit on his father's debts. Eventually he succeeds in turning the door handle, at the cost of a painful injury, but before he does so his mother sends for a doctor and his father sends for a locksmith. Kafka writes that the promise of their arrival heartens Gregor a great deal, and that he "felt himself drawn once more into the human circle and hoped for great and remarkable results from both the doctor and the locksmith, without really distinguishing precisely between them."[13] Naturally, neither the locksmith nor the doctor ever arrives, and Gregor never reenters the human circle. In the end, his sister Grete chases him back into his bedroom and turns the key in the lock again, but by this point incarceration is a formality. Incarceration within utilitarian relationships *is* Gregor's disease—its primary cause, symptom, and consequence—so it's no surprise that he confuses locksmiths with physicians, just as it's no surprise that neither of these healers ever shows up.

Gregor Samsa scurries through a world of numbers—clocks, train timetables, accounts receivable, salary, debts—not of charity. Missing a single train is enough to bring down the full wrath of his employer and the heavy weight of an insect carapace. The loneliness that sends Gregor out of his natural body sends Coetzee's early characters out of their minds. I do not know of another writer, living or dead, whose characters spend so much of their time in a swoon. Their ability to pilot their own minds is so weak that whenever they try to think about others (often, but not always, across racial lines) they either fail to leave the enclosure of their own skulls or are thrown into states of delirium, sometimes in the middle of a conversation. All of Coetzee's early work is devoted to understanding this problem and how to overcome it, and so is a large body of scholarship about how the sympathetic imagination functions or fails in his writing.[14]

For years, Coetzee tested the proposition that imagining others is key to resisting a political system that tried to keep people apart, even as his nonfiction writing argued that apartheid destroyed the capacity to imagine others. When in 1987 he accepted the Jerusalem Prize, awarded to writers who explore the freedom of the individual within society, he claimed that apartheid "stunted" the mind and placed South African literature "in bondage."[15] A later essay, "Apartheid Thinking," developed the infinitely more startling thesis that the Afrikaners who created the apartheid state in the mid-twentieth century, under the guidance of political philosopher Geoffrey Cronjé, were "possessed by demons."[16] This might sound like a metaphor or a joke, but Coetzee is not a jokester, and he asks us to take his outrageous thesis seriously. He then proposes that if we are to understand these men, we must "inhabit with part of ourselves Cronjé's position as writing subject. In reading him we must make an effort of projection, entering his language, listening closely to what he says, and even more closely to what he does not say."[17] In this case, we are being asked to think with demons.

Brace yourself, there is further trouble ahead. As Coetzee points out in several essays of the 1980s, the diseases of the imagination that infect the state also infect all of its citizens, including its critics, dissidents and revolutionaries. As a result, when he writes about manifestations of state paranoia he never exempts himself from scrutiny. He knows that the "paranoia of the state is … reproduced in the psyche of the subject" and invades "the very style of the self," and he acknowledges the dizzying possibility that even his own self-scrutiny is a symptom of the self-loathing produced in writers subject to censorship.[18] When he polices his own language of analysis and diagnoses himself with the same pathologies that he is studying, I sometimes wonder whether to applaud his self-awareness or mourn his self-doubt. One of the qualities that Coetzee professes to admire in Tolstoy's later work is the value it places on an orientation to the truth rather than unattainably "perfect self-knowledge," but the impulse that guided Tolstoy is not sufficient for Coetzee, at least not in the work he wrote under apartheid. In his essays of this period, he often comes closer to what he calls "the bad infinity" found in secular confessional writing, in which the desire to tell the whole truth about oneself regresses into corrosive uncertainty.[19]

Bad infinity is of a piece with the hermeneutics of suspicion that dominated scholarship in the humanities throughout the 1980s and 1990s, and to some extent still does, but it is also a symptom of apartheid thinking. Coetzee recommends that we project our minds into that of Geoffrey Cronjé, even though he has often argued that apartheid made this projection nearly impossible. He is not alone. In *Country of My Skull*, her now canonical memoir of the Truth and Reconciliation Commission hearings, Afrikaner poet and journalist Antjie Krog speculates that one of the lasting disorders produced by apartheid is the inability to "think [one] self into other positions."[20] Pumla Gobodo-Madikizela, who worked as a clinical psychologist with the TRC's Human Rights Violations Committee, makes a similar claim in *A Human Being Died That Night*, where she describes the process by which torturers are psychologically disabled in the course of carrying out their dehumanizing work.[21] Writing not about the torture chamber but about daily life in the United States and the UK, Paul Gilroy argues that race thinking deforms the "intimate consciousness" by which people come to know themselves, at the same time that it "obstructs empathy" and makes it "impossible even to imagine what it is like to be somebody else."[22] When in 2015 a white nationalist shot and killed nine African Americans in a Charleston church, the poet Claudia Rankine reflected on her country's ongoing history of racial hatred and took white empathy off the table for good: "there really is no mode of empathy that can replicate the daily strain of knowing that as a black person you can be killed for simply being black," she wrote in *The New York Times Magazine*.[23]

This is a central wager of Coetzee's body of writing. But here is another, pursued with equal conviction: people crave each other like food, like oxygen, especially when they are in pain. If we cannot dream ourselves into one another's lives then we must find another way, and there will be no rest until we do so. Some survivors of the Charleston massacre publically forgave the shooter, and many who testified before South Africa's TRC forgave atrocious crimes, including torture, rape, and murder. Reflecting on such gratuitous acts of forgiveness, Jacques Derrida emphasized that they cannot be fully understood. "This zone of experience remains inaccessible," he wrote, "and I must respect its secret."[24] There is no mode of empathy or effort of projection that brings such acts within our comprehension.

For me, Coetzee's most moving novel of the 1980s is *Life & Times of Michael K,* which is about a starving Colored man who spends much of his time in inaccessible zones of experience. As an infant K's hare lip makes it impossible for him to nurse, and requires his mother to feed him with a teaspoon; as an adult, he plans to return to infancy, believing that he can live on water drawn from a well with the help of a teaspoon suspended from a long piece of string. After his mother dies in the middle of a civil war, K begins fasting, first because he has no money and then because he loses his taste for food that he does not grow himself, in stealth, on land abandoned by white farmers who have gone into hiding. "Who are you?" is a question that many people ask K as he wanders the South African countryside alone, trying to evade military checkpoints and forced labor camps. He cannot respond. He has almost no capacity to see through the eyes of others, no matter their race, and no intimate awareness of himself. "What does he see?" wonders K when the foreman of the work gang into which he has been conscripted looks at him. "What am I to him?" Toward the end of the novel K is incarcerated in a prison camp hospital where he is treated for malnutrition. "What am I to this man?" he asks of the white doctor who takes a great interest in him. The medical officer returns the query: "I might ask the same question of you ... the same question you asked: What am I to this man?" None of these questions are answered. All these men can do for one another is pose or hear the question, state or witness the need.[25]

The doctor tells himself that if he cannot understand why his patient would rather die than accept his help, then he should lock himself in a toilet stall and shoot himself in the head. Coetzee has often written about white people who feel this way.[26] In his early novel *In the Heart of the Country*, a farmer's daughter named Magda feels that she will only be able to inhabit her consciousness with some consistency if she can convince her Colored servants Hendrik and Anna to call her by her proper name, rather than the customary Miss or *Baas*. Alas, Hendrik and Anna have serious problems of their own, and are no more interested in helping Magda with her metaphysical project than in working on her farm for free when her money runs out. In *Waiting for the Barbarians*, the unnamed Magistrate of a frontier settlement becomes convinced that his moral survival depends on imagining the inner lives of people who hate and fear him. He rescues a barbarian girl who has been maimed and partially blinded by the Empire's interrogators, and begins to try to inhabit her experience in the torture chamber. It's not the physical details that preoccupy him—the way heated metal is brought close to an eye in order to burn the cornea, or tiny knives inserted and twisted under skin, or pressure applied to ankles so that some of the fragile bones that compose the joint splinter– but the possibility that the mind of a prisoner permanently closes to other human beings: a father closed to a daughter, a daughter orphaned even while her father still fights his torturers in front of her. "What does she see?" is the question with which he concludes his meditation.[27] We know better than to expect an answer.

Unlike Magda, the Magistrate and the medical officer, the homeless Colored man who tries to befriend K at the end of *Life & Times* is not trying to assuage his own guilt. He is an unrepentant pimp and thief, perhaps worse, and it is not clear what he wants from K in exchange for a few hours of companionship and a couple of roasted sausages other than the opportunity to offer hospitality to a man in even worse shape than himself—a dying man with no control over his bowels or bladder, dressed in filthy rags, destitute and semi-conscious. "It is difficult to be kind ... to a person who wants nothing," the man says to K with genuine puzzlement.[28] "I have become an object of charity," K thinks when one of the pimp's women tries to perform oral sex on him for free.[29] This is not a helpful gesture under the circumstances, and not one that K enjoys, but the desire to give seems to be more important than whether or not K appreciates what he is given. He cannot digest the wine or the sausages either, vomiting them up, but the pimp still insists that he join their picnic.

In a novel that centers on a starving man named K it would be foolish not to think of Kafka's hunger artist.[30] Some readers see K as a hero of the resistance who manages to escape everyone who wants to feed him in order to feed themselves, and there is profit in this view.[31] But when I think about the pimp and his women, whose situation is almost as dire as K's own, I consider the cost of not wanting anything or anyone. In Kafka's parable, the hunger artist's audience does not understand why he fasts; they see him as an amusing curiosity when instead they should see that when he refuses food he also refuses *them*. The irony is exquisite: those who are entertained by the artist are unknowingly taking pleasure in the experience of being hated. In the end, when the artist fulfills his dream of starving to death and his forgotten corpse is pulled from its cage, replaced with a sleek young panther, the passersby see only the contrast between the two tenants of the cage, but we know that they are similar. The panther will eat you alive; the artist refused to eat. Both are a threat. Kafka's artist is one of Michael K's literary great-grandfathers, but K lives in a far more demanding world than the one Kafka invents. There is no one who grasps the bars of the hunger artist's cage, peers in, and says, "What am I to you? I need to know, or I will starve too." There is no one who says to the artist, in tones of real distress, "It is difficult to be kind to a person who wants nothing." "You must not be afraid to say what you want, then you will get it," says K's strange benefactor in the final pages of the novel, but K is not afraid to say what he wants.[32] He has no idea what he wants, other than to be left alone with his secret garden and his teaspoon.

In the late 1980s, Coetzee invented a man who both resembles Michael K and is his opposite. South Africa had recently emerged from a prolonged State of Emergency, during which police and paramilitary forces unsuccessfully attempted to crush the overwhelming resistance to apartheid, escalating violence throughout the country to unprecedented levels. During this time, both of Coetzee's parents died; more shockingly, so did his son, although his death was not directly caused by the country's turmoil. *Age of Iron*, the novel that emerges from this desperate period, is about a retired classics scholar named Mrs. Curren, who is dying of cancer, and about a vagrant Colored man named Vercueil, who is not afraid to say what he wants or to become an object of charity. When Mrs. Curren returns from her final visit with her doctor, having been told that she has weeks to live and given a prescription for narcotic painkillers, she finds that Vercueil has set up camp in her spacious back garden, where he drinks and sleeps his days away. She tolerates his presence but is shocked by his idleness and ingratitude. When she hires him to do some work in her garden, he performs his tasks derisively and without effort. Outraged, she says, "I am not giving you money for nothing." We "can't proceed on a basis of charity," she insists, as Vercueil drinks the coffee she has brought him and then pockets his unearned wages. "Why?" he asks, spitting a large globule of coffee-colored phlegm at her feet. "Because you don't deserve it," she tells him. "Who deserves anything?" he asks.[33]

To show the absurdity of the idea that there is no relationship between labor and wages, and to shame him for his indolence, Mrs. Curren gives Vercueil her wallet and challenges him to empty it. He does. He is not even a little bit ashamed. In the time it takes him to get to the liquor store and back, she comes up with a better answer to his question about charity. She says, "the spirit of charity has perished in this country. Because those who accept charity despise it, while those who give give with a despairing heart. What is the point of charity when it does not go from heart to heart?" It is easy to see that in trying to turn Vercueil into her employee Mrs. Curren is replaying an old story: white *Baas*, Colored servant. But we know that she doesn't want or need another employee. For one thing, she already has Florence, maid-of-all-work. What she wants is to be cared for by someone who has no obligation to care and every reason not to. "Care," she thinks: "the true root of charity. I look for him to care, and he does not. Because he is beyond caring. Beyond caring and beyond care."[34] Mrs. Curren is wrong to believe that she can use money to make Vercueil love her, which is why he says that it makes no difference how much she pays him or whether he works for his wages, because although he is happy to take her money and her hospitality, he doesn't want anything from her and will not give anything in return. Who deserves anything?

Over the course of the novel, Mrs. Curren opens her home to Vercueil and to the young black revolutionaries who use her servants' quarters as their base before they are both murdered by the police. Hosting strangers who would happily see her dead is not enough to revive the spirit of charity in the age of iron, not even close. Mrs. Curren is a former professor, and just as she believes that Vercueil could use a refresher course on the labor theory of value—despite his maimed hand, the result of manual labor—she also believes that Bheki and John, the teenage revolutionaries, will benefit from her lectures on Thucydides and the dangers of the Spartan warrior code.

Coetzee would not have borrowed Hesiod's phrase "Age of Iron" if he did not believe that the fall of the Greek Empire had something to say to late-twentieth century South Africa, but the historical merit of the comparison does not matter. He wants to bring Mrs. Curren to the realization that there is nothing in her library that will make it possible to think her way into Bheki or John's experience; instead, she must stop thinking, stop lecturing, because her belief in the usefulness of her knowledge only widens the distance between them. If they are ever to learn to care for one another, from heart to heart, it will have to begin with her willingness to put her authority down.

When it comes to teaching intellectuals to get out of their heads, Coetzee is ruthless. To read him as a scholar is to be constantly afraid of how you might need to change your life. In the final pages of *Age of Iron*, after Bheki has been shot in the township and John shot in her house, Mrs. Curren finds herself lying under a bridge in a pool of her own urine. She refuses to return to her home, feeling that it has been defiled by the brutality of the police; disoriented and in agony, she falls asleep, and awakens only because some feral children who think that she is dead are poking a sharp stick into her mouth in hopes of harvesting any gold teeth they can pull out of her jaw. The roof of her mouth is raw and bleeding, but the children will not stop until Vercueil comes to rescue her, reeking of urine himself. He carries her in his arms to the side of the road, where the two lie together on a piece of cardboard, scarcely speaking. He is not beyond caring, although for the first time in her life Mrs. Curren has a physical sense of what it is like to be beyond care, valued only for the wealth that can be extracted from her body. Earlier in the novel she imagined Vercueil as an insect, a dog, even a husband. Now she sees him as an angel of mercy. Or is he an angel of vengeance? When the two return home, Vercueil lies in bed beside her as her pain becomes unbearable, and she reflects that as a white person in South Africa she has lived a doll's life, hollow and heartless, disconnected from all other people and living things. Vercueil enfolds her in his arms, smothering her to death. "From that embrace there was no warmth to be had," Coetzee writes in the novel's appalling final line.[35] This is a mercy killing, but it is not exactly an act of love.

* * *

No one would wish for less empathy in the world. If the curriculum at my daughters' public schools and those of their American cousins is any indication, we are more concerned with teaching our children to imagine others than ever before. This was certainly not part of any lesson plan I can recall from my own childhood. When my daughter was in first grade, her school piloted a program called "The Roots of Empathy," in which a woman brought her baby into the classroom once a month so that the children could study his development and learn to read his needs. My daughter adored these visits and discussed them enthusiastically, although they made no discernible improvement to her treatment of her own younger sibling. "Remember baby Myles," I would call out, half-facetiously, in the midst of some screaming altercation, and my daughter would glower at me as though I had crossed the last frontier of decency. "That's different," she'd mutter.

"No, it's not," I would tell her. "The only difference is that it is easy to take care of someone else's child for a few moments, and very difficult to take care of your own sister." This line of analysis achieved nothing, other than to intensify my daughter's scowl. Reading Michel de Montaigne's "On Repentance," a late-sixteenth century essay about the difficulties of knowing one's own mind, much less anyone else's, I was startled by this passage: "In what we have to deal with, there are hidden elements, at which we cannot guess, particularly in human nature: silent states that make no show and are sometimes unknown to their very possessors."[36] Over the last fifty years or so, we have developed rich vocabularies to describe human differences—those of race and gender, class and sexuality, nationality and religion, among many others—and instead of "silent states" we now refer to the unconscious. I prefer Montaigne's older language, because to my twenty-first-century ears it preserves the strangeness of human being. In addition to the differences we know how to name, there are hidden reservoirs of venom and nectar within any individual, and we guard those reservoirs, even when we are not aware that they exist.

Whether we are newly interested in empathy because we feel that it is under threat or because we now recognize its importance to increasingly fractured forms of civic life, I cannot say. I can say that in the new century, there has already been a great deal of scholarly interest in the subject, all of it dependent on our desire and capacity to enter the minds of other people, either face-to-face or with the help of works of art.[37] These arguments are complicated by the fact that we also know imagination to be a highly partisan faculty, credited with aiding the rise of modern nationalism and imperialism, and prone to many catastrophic forms of systemic error, including unconscious bias. Some who study the social effects of empathy insist that it too is morally neutral, and that there is no guarantee that the ability to imagine others makes us willing to care for them.[38] A stint on a school playground should lend some empirical support to this hypothesis, although it is just as likely to challenge it, given that you will probably see a wide variety of behaviors on display, from shunning, taunting, and hitting to moments of surprising kindness. In his landmark study, *The Conquest of America*, Tzvetan Todorov argued that our imaginations are both too unruly and too obedient to dominant beliefs to be swayed by any moral precept. He also argued that the Spanish conquistadors of the fifteenth and sixteenth centuries did an excellent job of understanding the imaginative lives of Meso-Americans, especially their cosmology and social organization, and then used that knowledge to murder them by the millions. He calls this "understanding-that-kills."[39]

Of course, the conquistadors travelled to the Americas with the explicit intention of harvesting the region's wealth by any means, including slavery and genocide, and it is hard to conceive of anything that could have dissuaded them from this purpose or changed their belief in the lesser humanity of the people they encountered—an inferiority that the Spaniards had long been conditioned to perceive by countless stories and images in circulation in early modern Europe.[40] Works of art can open our minds to others, but they have just as often deformed the imagination so that we cannot see who is in front of us. Nevertheless, the danger of misunderstanding should not prevent us from teaching children to imagine how their classmates think and feel. No one wishes for less empathy in the world. But we do know that it breaks down with alarming regularity, both within communities and at their edges, and that people are overly confident in their understanding of others, often with devastating results.

In the early 1990s, when empathy was not yet a keyword either in the zeitgeist or in academia, Martha Nussbaum argued for its capacity to stretch narrow forms of allegiance, including racism and nationalism.[41] Some two decades later, she changed her mind, as is a philosopher's right. In *Political Emotions,* she writes, "empathy … can be deployed by sadists."[42] In more ordinary terms, it can also be deployed by marketers, social-media influencers, news organizations, and other reality-shaping agents. This is understanding-that-sells ideas, beliefs, and commodities. In her later work, Nussbaum argues that love is the most effective way to counter narcissism, as well as the contempt and disgust that fuel the desire to persecute others: "all of the core emotions that sustain a decent society have their roots in, or are forms of, love—by which I mean intense attachments to things outside the control of our will." And, as Nussbaum also argues, love always entails vulnerability, which is why it is inextricably linked with other aspects of life that elude our control, including the "anxious confrontation with … mortality and finitude."[43]

We teach children this, too. Every time we read a fairy tale we enter a world in which someone who feels unloved runs out of problem-solving strategies and then has to wait to be welcomed back into the circuitry of life by routes that cannot be anticipated. A fairy tale never spends much time describing the years of futile effort in which a person makes shoes that no one wants to buy, prays for a child, or struggles against poverty, abuse, or unfair animal enchantment. These lonely years are given a terse summary, and then the tale begins with the miraculous return of abundance: an elf, a child, a fairy godmother, a kiss. As we know from "Sleeping Beauty," a gift must be met with gratitude or it will provoke a new failure of love—in this case, a missing invitation to the feast and a forest of thorns. In "Sleeping Beauty," unlike in life, this punishment comes with an expiry date, and a surprise. The curse stipulates that the kingdom will revive after a hundred years, and as far as I can tell there is no codicil that requires a stranger to enter the realm in order to complete the process. But we sense that without the prince the awakening would be incomplete, for the very reason that he is an interloper who eludes the predictive wisdom of the thirteen women and the terms of the curse itself. His kiss is enlivening because it is uncalled for.

Outside of myths it is hard to say where this "gush of life" will come from or when.[44] I borrow this lovely definition of grace from the Israeli novelist, David Grossman. He uses it to describe the experience of reading the short stories of the Jewish-Polish modernist Bruno Schulz, which help him to overcome the paralysis he feels in the wake of the Shoah, because the wild liberty of Schulz's imagination somehow slips the noose of the Fascist 1930s and surges off the page. If Schulz's remarkable stories have this effect on Grossman, it may be because many of them are *about* the gush of life. "How can one not succumb and allow one's courage to fail when everything is shut tight, when all meaningful things are walled up, and when you constantly knock against bricks, as against the walls of a prison?" Schulz asks. Then what he calls "the age of genius" erupts, and every form is revealed in its hidden and fluid essence.[45] In Schulz's work, this energy always comes from a sacred recess outside of ordinary time—the thirteenth month, the twenty-fifth hour. New life arrives in the night, or on the winds of an otherworldly storm.

There are no otherworldly storms in Coetzee's writing, but there is sustained attention to the forms of abundance that revive the spirit as well as the social contract.[46] In the 1980s, he more than once called apartheid a "failure of love."[47] Beginning in the 1990s, he abandons the idea that we can love only those we are able to imagine and invents a group of people who are more interested in what they can learn from their hearts than from their minds. One of them is Fyodor Dostoevsky. This was strange subject matter for a South African writer in the early 1990s, when the country was celebrating Nelson Mandela's release from prison and looking ahead to the first fully democratic elections after almost 350 years of colonial rule. It is not surprising that *The Master of Petersburg* has attracted so much less scholarly attention than Coetzee's other novels. Set during the winter of 1869, the novel is about a period of political and personal crisis in Dostoevsky's life. His stepson Pavel has fallen from a high tower to his death, or jumped, or been pushed by the police or by his fellow revolutionaries, and Dostoevsky returns to Petersburg from exile in Germany in order to visit his son's grave and try to reconstruct his last days. He never learns whether Pavel's death was an accident, suicide, or politically motivated murder, and his anguish is deepened by a failed love affair with his son's former landlady, Anna Sergeyevna. In the novel's chilling final scene, Dostoevsky sits down at a desk in Pavel's rented room to begin drafting *The Possessed* in the pages of his son's diary, perverting details of the boy's life to craft a novel of sexual voyeurism and pedophilia that looks as though it were a confession written in Pavel's own hand. In a state of near-derangement, and terrified by the ruthlessness of the revolutionaries his son was working with, he forges his son's words as a provocation to God. God remains silent, as we knew he would.

There is much that is deliberately menacing in Coetzee's depiction of the creative forces that act upon Dostoevsky as he begins to invent one of his most disturbing novels, whose title is variously translated into English as *The Devils*, *The Demons*, and *The Possessed*. Above all, these forces are indifferent to the person who has called them. Cold, faceless, and primordial, they do "not belong in his world" and have no concern for it.[48] When Dostoevsky yields to them and begins to write, as though possessed, he believes that he "has passed through the gates of death and returned; nothing can touch him any more. He is not a god but he is no longer human either. He is, in some sense, beyond the human, beyond man."[49] In Dostoevsky's mind, there are irresolvable conflicts between Christian faith and secular creativity, the constraints of morality and the pliant freedom of novelistic imagination, divine law and the demands of a nascent revolution, and these conflicts help to explain why he is often shamed by the things he is able to think, and why he distrusts his capacity for invention as much as he cultivates and lives by it. As a Christian, Dostoevsky knows that Christ will return when least expected, and although he is certain that the alien presence in the room is not Christ, he also knows that it is leading him back to life. It's not the resurrection he watched for and not the one he wanted, but it is a rebirth nonetheless, although it returns him to a life that he believes accursed. Coetzee's Dostoevsky feels sure that to pass beyond the human is to be damned. Coetzee is not so sure.

From a secular standpoint, it is hard to know what it means to say that someone is possessed by a demon or visited by a god. Yet in all of Coetzee's later work, this is just what is said. The most important acts are those that take place when people are not in command of themselves, when they feel powerfully moved by forces that they cannot name or understand. "What can one make of episodes like this," asks Elizabeth Costello in the novel that bears her name, episodes that are "unforeseen, unplanned, out of character"?[50] She poses herself this question after recalling an incident that she has never told anyone about in which she bent topless over the body of a dying man to lick and suck his penis. Aiden Phillips did not request this act as he lay incapable of speech or movement. Costello performs it because months earlier she removed her shirt and posed for Aiden, and as he painted her face and breasts she felt that a goddess shone through her and united her with all the divine women whose bodies have been adored by the painters and sculptors who depicted them—Artemis, Athena, Hera, and above all, Mary, mother of Jesus. "I was not myself, or not just myself," she thinks.[51] As she labors over Aiden's inert body, Costello knows that her behavior is inexcusable, possibly criminal. She cannot explain the impulse that grips her any more than she can explain the feeling of having been blessed as an elderly man of very modest artistic talent painted her naked torso. But she feels certain that when she takes Aiden's penis in her mouth her intention is to love him, and that what she hopes to create is not *eros*, or the access of divinity that the Greeks called *agape*, but *caritas*: the loving care bestowed by on one person by another.[52]

What can one make of episodes like this? "Are they just holes, holes in the heart, into which one steps and falls and then goes on falling?"[53] Dostoevsky thinks so, and there are moments when Elizabeth Costello thinks so too. However, Coetzee places more faith in the impulses that enter through these openings than in the conscious workings of the mind, including the techniques by which people make reasoned arguments or endeavor to empathize with other living things. Costello spends a lot of time listening to and making formal arguments, often about what and whom it is morally desirable for a human being to imagine or represent. Is it ethical to compare American factory farming with the Holocaust? What is the difference between an animal as a metaphor and an animal as blood, bone, and sinew? Should a novelist recreate historical scenes of torture and murder in order to conjure the specifics of depravity, or does this kind of writing simply release more evil into the world? Is it true that the academic humanities lost their way during the Renaissance, when the study of human enterprise parted from the study of God?

In each of the lessons given in *Elizabeth Costello: Eight Lessons*, she is standing behind a podium at a university, a writer's conference, a tribunal or, in one instance, on a cruise ship where she has been hired to edify the guests with a talk on the future of the novel, a subject that has long ceased to interest her. When she is not lecturing, she is often sitting in an audience listening to someone else address one of the questions that I just listed. By the end of the novel, she is dead and in some sort of purgatory; in any case, she is a long way from the academic circuit where she made and listened to intelligent and well-researched arguments about what tasks the imagination should take on, and to what end. There are at least two kinds of lessons unfolding in this book: those delivered from behind a lectern, and those that take place after hours, when Costello meditates on the inadequacy of everything she has said or heard. Increasing physical infirmity makes her more and more skeptical of the lectern. It's not thought that guides her actions and beliefs any more, but emotion—passionate, indefensible, and often imprudent emotion.

Costello's skepticism about the limits of argument is deepened in the afterlife, where she is told she must remain until she completes a written statement of belief to the satisfaction of the demanding and humorless members of a committee that will decide whether she is ready to take on whatever tasks await the dead, or needs to spend a little longer in the transit zone while she learns to articulate the convictions that guided her in life. Producing a credo proves very difficult for Costello, because the moments in her life that mattered most to her were the ones in which she had no idea what she believed and felt so unlike herself that she could only describe her experience in the language of deities and devils, visitations and falls. Therefore, after much mandatory revision of her writing assignment, she testifies that she cannot outline the beliefs that she lived by, for two reasons. First, because there "are matters about which it is appropriate to keep one's peace, …, even before the ultimate tribunal"; and second, because "beliefs are not the only ethical supports we have. We can rely on our hearts as well."[54]

Here she anticipates another aging and infirm Australian novelist who loses confidence in credos: J. C., the writer at the center of Coetzee's later novel, *Diary of a Bad Year*. This loss of belief is a problem, because J. C. has agreed to contribute to a book of essays called *Strong Opinions*.[55] Alas, in old age his main opinion is that opinions don't count for much, especially strong ones. Neither does the sense of authority that allows writers to produce them, unless that authority is shot through with a vatic availability that reveals that the author is not himself, or not only himself, but speaking with the assistance of some "higher force."[56] J. C. is not concerned with assigning this force a source or a name, and neither is his doppelganger, J. M. Coetzee. What matters to him is that it is not reducible to human will or intellect. "Behind every paragraph the reader ought to be able to hear the music of present joy and future grief," he thinks; in short, the writer's "existential condition," which is by definition as precarious as the reader's own.[57]

Instead of fulfilling his commitment to the editor of *Strong Opinions*, J. C. finds himself rereading Dostoevsky's last novel, *The Brothers Karamazov*, which makes him feel "more and more vulnerable," and moves him to helpless tears, no matter that he has read the novel countless times.[58] "It is the voice of Ivan," thinks J. C., "as realized by Dostoevsky, not his reasoning, that sweeps me along."[59] The emotion contained in that voice resonates with J. C.'s own anguish and makes him a confederate of Elizabeth Costello, and, more surprisingly, of her sister, the Catholic nun and missionary Sister Bridget, who is invited to speak at a university convocation in Johannesburg and uses the occasion to declare, rather tactlessly, that the academic humanities are dying because they do not address people's deepest needs and have no tools with which to offer succor to people seeking "guidance in perplexity."[60] Only the word of God can offer this comfort, she argues, which is why the humanities do not deserve to rise from their deathbed.

Sister Bridget's faith leads her to devote her life to caring for those in extremity, primarily orphaned African children with AIDS. It also leads her to a frankly hostile assessment of the value of secular creativity. She cannot imagine a richer or fuller career for an artist than one spent carving an icon of Jesus on the cross, year after year, until the sculptor's hands become arthritic.

She thinks that physical beauty is a delusion, a fleeting distraction, and that the Hellenism that underpinned the emergence of humanism throughout the European Renaissance is fundamentally untrue to the brutality of life, particularly the lives of the impoverished and afflicted in Southern Africa. Missionaries did not impose Christianity on the Zulus, she argues; the Zulus chose to follow Christ because the agony and abandonment of the crucifixion reflect the reality of human suffering. (Here Sister Bridget overlooks the fact that a good deal of that suffering was inflicted by the missionaries themselves and by the colonial governments they served—she is no historical materialist). Elizabeth Costello is keenly attuned to misery, but she is not persuaded by her sister's arguments, although she does share her belief that the alleviation of grief and perplexity, including loneliness, requires openness to a higher force. When she gets back to Australia from Johannesburg she writes to Bridget about the time she removed her blouse and posed for Aidan Phillips, and the point of the letter is to defend "acts of humanity" that come from "the overflow, the outflow of our human hearts."[61] Costello argues that the attempt to understand these moments of overflow without attributing them to a deity is the true vocation of the humanities.

Costello counters her sister's attack on secular art by defending physical beauty as a blessing, and painting as a kind of worship. "That is what the Greeks teach us," she concludes, "the right Greeks."[62] Not the authors of the Greek Bible, in other words. In her letter, Costello imagines the Italian painter Correggio in his early-sixteenth century atelier, painting a model who lifts her naked breast like the Virgin offering her nipple to her child, and she tells Bridget that all the men in the room, the painter's assistants and the visitors to the studio, would have felt the electricity of that scene and known that they were witnessing a moment of immanence in which the sacred shone through the carnal. Costello has to admit that the sight of the half-naked woman would have aroused those men in such a way that adoration and desire were intermingled, and she hurries to emphasize that the woman's beauty nevertheless revealed the presence of an angel. But the truth is that there is a moral wildness here that makes lust and reverence equally available, and the wrong Greeks knew it as surely as Costello does.

Costello omits her final meeting with Phillips from her letter, and she is probably right to think that Bridget is too stubborn a thinker to be told such a story. The same may be true of the members of the tribunal who want to know what she believed in when she was alive. Even so, her omission lends support to Bridget's claim that the academic humanities are in crisis not only for all the familiar economic and political reasons, beginning with the transformation of universities into corporations, but because scholars rarely set out to produce arguments that help people to respond to the uncontrollable emotions that shake them hard, often past endurance. This chapter of *Elizabeth Costello* is called "The Humanities in Africa," but it is clearly a lesson about the humanities more generally. If there are limits to Bridget's understanding of creativity that is not explicitly devotional then there are also limits to Costello's ability to find a place in her defense of that creativity for the experiences that have moved her most deeply throughout her life, and haunt her thoughts and memories. If her defense of art cannot accommodate and voice her own perplexity, including the unpredictable ways in which her heart overflows, then it fails in every way that matters. What companionship can she offer someone who is gripped by similar confusion? These questions come sharply into focus in places such as South Africa, where there is widespread poverty and trauma, but they do not disappear in places where there is relative plenty.

In fact, these questions came most sharply into focus for Coetzee after he emigrated to Australia in the early 2000s. After decades of teaching literature at the University of Cape Town, and in the midst of a career as a global intellectual of rare versatility and erudition, he became the patron of "The J. M. Coetzee Centre for Creative Practice" at the University of Adelaide, which "investigates how creativity can be shaped by collaborative processes and examines the impact of emotional states, such as inspiration or melancholy, on creativity."[63] In this same spirit, Costello testifies before the ultimate tribunal that beliefs are not our only ethical supports. We can rely on our hearts as well, she claims. This is true, although it has to be said that the heart offers ethical support of a rather complicated kind. It does not always ratify existing conventions about how a person should think or behave any more than the outflow of love can always be counted upon to advance the interests of a "decent society" rather than the interests of zealots and fanatics, who always profess passionate affection for their nations, but whose definitions of decency do not correspond with Martha Nussbaum's, or with mine. Love cannot always be marshaled toward the good any more than the imagination can be, which is one of the reasons why love makes us so vulnerable. If we cannot fully control the emotion, we cannot fully control its effects either. J. C.'s heart drives him to a tawdry passion for his beautiful amanuensis, who is young enough to be his daughter. In a novel published just a few years before *Diary of a Bad Year*, *Slow Man*, Paul Rayment's heart drives him to an unrequited love for his "frail care" nurse, and to seek to become godfather to her three children.[64] And Costello's heart prompts her to do risky things that she cannot explain and was too embarrassed to write about when she was alive, even in a private letter. She believed that in performing fellatio on a dying man she was trying to call down a god, and that when a dockworker tried to rape her and then incinerated her clothes, he was possessed by a devil that entered her body and is still waiting for a chance to get out and stretch its leathery wings. These ideas don't come from trying to step into other people's minds, and they don't offer ethical support for what already exists. Instead, they create the crisis in consciousness that demands some fundamentally new way of reckoning.

Costello refuses to write about these experiences in her novels or lectures, although she would be a better writer if she did. Her refusal helps to explain why her creativity has stalled and why she is best known for a novel she wrote in her youth. Unlike the Dostoevsky of *The Master of Petersburg*, she is unable to find a form in which to express intuitions that do not seem appropriate for the world. In her view, they do not belong to the domain of reasoned belief, and she will not attempt to pull them into it; she cherishes them precisely because they open onto a realm that she cannot account for. Unsurprisingly, her career as a dead person deepens her commitment to this realm. It can be dangerous to step into holes in the heart, which is why Coetzee blamed demon possession for the invention of apartheid, but it is also dangerous to try to seal them up. They admit the forces that go by many names and create surprises of all sorts, including the prince who walks through flowers to kiss the beautiful girl at the center of a still-drowsy dominion.

Perhaps we can understand Elizabeth Costello's kiss in precisely these terms, even though she bypasses the mouth and goes directly to the groin in a way that would be impossible in a story written for children. Nonetheless, when she leans over Aiden Phillips's body she is trying to make him feel blessed, as she once felt under his eyes. It is impossible to know whether she succeeds. Like the endings of *Life & Times of Michael K* and *Age of Iron*, the scene hovers ambiguously between *caritas* and cruelty. These novels are not fairy tales, yet it is clear that what Costello hopes to give is charity of the kind that can only take place when she is a stranger even to herself, vulnerable to the silent states within and around her.

* * *

No contemporary writer has thought more richly about Christian forms of charity than Marilynne Robinson. This is why all of her novels are about housekeeping, which has very little to do with laundry and sweeping the floors, and a lot to do with the way people love each other. Often, Robinson's families are cobbled together on the road or in the neighborhood, not defined by bloodlines. It is loving care that creates a family, which is why in *Gilead* she meditates at some length upon the Fifth Commandment. She observes that it creates a threshold within the Laws of Moses because it links the first four Commandments, which taught the Israelites how to treat their God, with the final five Commandments, which taught them how to treat one another. In the voice of Reverend John Ames, the novel's narrator, she proposes that the injunction to honor one's mother and father is therefore the hinge between the metaphysical and the social, the eternal and the temporal, the divine and the human. That's a lot of pressure on one law. The Fifth Commandment has to bear the weight from above of the four laws of "right worship" and the weight from below of the five laws of "right conduct," which are at least as demanding.[65] In the minds of the faithful, those laws against murder, adultery, theft, lies, and covetousness press up toward God as demonstrations of righteousness, just as acts of worship are prerequisite to the workings of a sanctified society. In the middle, somehow communicating between both domains, there is the love between parent and child.

This relationship is the occasion for *Gilead* itself, which takes the form of a letter that is a sermon as well as a family history written by a dying father to the very young son who will have to grow up without him. "You have been God's grace to me," Ames tells his son in this letter, "a miracle, something more than a miracle."[66] *More* than a miracle. That is quite something for a minister to write about an ordinary child. At the end of his life, Ames sees divine grace in evidence everywhere, but especially in the bond between parents and children. In some instances, that bond is violated, as it is by Ames's namesake and godson, Jack (John) Ames Boughton, who fathered a daughter in his adolescence and never acknowledged her, even after she died of poverty and neglect in early childhood. He could have saved her life if he had been willing to claim her as his own. This failure is especially painful for Reverend Ames, whose own firstborn child, also a daughter, died along with his first wife in childbirth. Ames thinks that if a child is an act of grace, then it will take another to rescue Jack Boughton from the lifetime of misery that his refusal to be a father brought him.

Not that this refusal ever weakened Jack's parents' love for him. If anything, his inadequacy strengthened it, for reasons that Ames intuits from the reverence that he feels for his own son, which is not contingent on what the boy does or does not do in his lifetime but rooted in the wondrous fact of his existence. If his son's actions ever call down shame and grief, as Jack Boughton's have done, then Ames's love would need to increase proportionately in order to prevent his child from ever losing sight of his inalienable value. Ames will not be around to love his son this way, which is a large part of what worries him about dying.

This is the core of the Fifth Commandment, in the Reverend's view: it demands the "right perception" of other people, beginning with the people with whom one has the greatest intimacy, and places that perception at the horizon between the heavens and the earth.[67] If that horizon links the child to God, it also links her to society, which is why the Fifth Commandment opens onto five laws about how best to conduct oneself in a community in the interests of peace and collective prosperity. In *Gilead,* as in the Old Testament, the law of right perception demands that one honor "the *being* of someone," her "mysterious life," not her appearance, actions or circumstances.[68] This law drives John Ames's father to spend a month walking through Kansas in a middle of a drought, parched and half-starved, in order to find and pray at his own father's grave, even though the two men were bitterly opposed in life, and then to spend another week tending the neglected and overgrown graves of strangers. Over the course of three generations, it also drives members of the Ames family to become Abolitionists, to fight against the Confederates, to preach in support of American involvement in the Second World War, and, in the case of Jack Boughton, to fall in love and have a son with a Black woman at a time when almost every state in the union declared their relationship a crime.

For most people, it is easier to see the mysterious being of a child than that of an adult. A child's social identity is weak, not yet hardened by choices and demands. In this sense, a child is an unobstructed mystery. I learned this when my own children were infants. When I looked at them I could see that they had never existed before, but also that they are elemental, like wind or fire or carbon. Even now, when they are long past infancy, I look at them and see rushing water or a tornado or one of the great molecular upheavals by which planets are born. This intuition is not unique to me. Because of it, harm done to children, especially if it is clearly traceable to political actions or omissions, enrages and moves people in ways that the suffering of adults cannot. It is as though life itself were being assaulted and declared worthless. Hence the power of child activism against climate crisis, and the global outcry provoked by the photographs of the drowned Syrian boy, Aylan Kurdi, whose body washed up on a Turkish beach in September 2015 after his family capsized while attempting to make the illegal crossing into Greece. Like the photographs of migrant children held in metal cages at the US border with Mexico, these images shake the soul. They arouse utmost despair and rage, but they also remind people that when the laws of states will not yield to exceptions they become murderous, both for those they protect and for those they exclude. It is one thing for adults to make this argument, with articulate appeals to human rights or some other formal mechanism of inclusion, but quite another to embody it as a child does. A child calls for the exception because he is almost universally visible as an exception in a way that no adult can be. Simply by existing he reveals the life outside of life that is elsewhere hidden.

There is a scene that occurs in various forms in many of Coetzee's apartheid novels, although it is never important to the plot or dwelled upon at any length: a poor woman, a minor and usually nameless character, clutches her dead infant to her chest.[69] This scene takes place on the novels' peripheral vision, but it is part of a larger pattern in which relationships between parents and children are destroyed by the state, and it is central to Coetzee's decades-long investigation of the spirit of charity. Whatever specific form those abuses take, whether they occur in feudal Russia or in a prison camp for barbarians, they share in common a tendency to enforce parsimonious forms of self-interest that destroy the generosity essential to the sustenance of new life. These mini-pietàs illustrate that the law is dead. And they quietly echo the task that is taking place at the center of the novels in which they appear, which is always the same: a person is struggling to love a parent or a child. In either case, the person senses that caring for the inalienable "*being* of someone," rather than for whatever social identity she has been assigned, is a way of resisting political systems designed to obscure that being so fully that it becomes invisible, covered over by accidents of birth or circumstance.

This is why the Magistrate sets out to be the barbarian girl's father, not just her lover or benefactor. It is why Dostoevsky begins to write *The Possessed* in the hopes that it will resurrect his stepson. Michael K. is thankful that he has "no desire to father," but then he turns the earth into his surrogate mother and his harvest into his children.[70] When he thinks of his mother Anna's death, he imagines that in her last moments she was looking through him to the memory of her own mother, reaching toward her as a child craves comfort in distress. "To me she was a woman," he thinks, "but to herself she was still a child calling to her mother to hold her hand and help her."[71] So is the dying Mrs. Curren, who looks past the daughter to whom she is writing her story and cries out to her own mother, saying, "look down on me, stretch forth your hand!"[72] "I come from a line of children without end," thinks K, and of course this is true of everyone, although it is more clearly true of the people who live in the Age of Iron.[73]

Under these conditions, only a child—or the parent who is visible in the child—can be appealed to for mercy. The appeal is made, but the bond cannot bear the pressure that is placed upon it. The Magistrate is no more capable of being a father than Michael K. is, and we know that Mrs. Curren's daughter will never receive her mother's letters. In turn, Mrs. Curren imagines that her own mother will refuse to hold her hand no matter how she begs, and will instead choose to soar unencumbered into the heavens. For Hesiod, this failure is what defines the Age of Iron, when even parents and children become unable to respond to one another's absolute life. The revival of this response becomes a central concern of Coetzee's later writing, particularly in *Disgrace* and the *Jesus* novels, which examine charity as a political force as well as an aesthetic and emotional one. For this very reason, namely their interest in the way the "overflow, the outflow of our human hearts" restores life to law as no legislator can, these novels push hard on the relationship between parent and child.[74] The bond holds.

The equitable man is not overly just, says Aristotle. Nor necessarily a man, adds Coetzee. In *Disgrace*, she is a woman who boards dogs and runs a market garden with the help of her entrepreneurial black neighbor, Petrus, until she is raped by three black men and decides to keep the pregnancy that results. To her father David's bewilderment, Lucy refuses to report her rape to the police or protect herself from further attacks by leaving her isolated homestead in the Eastern Cape. To his greater bewilderment, she says that in South Africa in the late 1990s, when the nation's constitution was being rewritten and the terms of human engagement revised at every level of daily life, what happened to her is a "purely private matter" rather than a crime that should be handled by the legal system.[75] The novel makes it clear that the country's courts are so overburdened that there is no point in expecting legal redress, or even basic forms of police competence, but also that these procedural problems are not what drive Lucy's refusal. She blocks her father's every attempt to understand why she is willing to surrender everything, including her life, to men who see her only as a body to be abused or an economic opportunity to be exploited, but she offers few explanations of her own and we have little access to her reasoning, which remains inscrutable to the end.

Disgrace, published in 1999, remains Coetzee's most controversial novel. It has attracted more attention than any of his other works, by a wide margin, and lost none of its capacity to disturb. Last year, a particularly attentive student approached me after a lecture, brandishing his copy of the book. "I am astounded by this novel," he said, throwing the book down on the desk in front of us. "Astounded!" There was wonder in his voice, but also frustration and anger. I told him that although I have been reading and teaching Disgrace since it was first published, I too am astounded by Lucy's behavior, and so are many readers. I am the oldest of four sisters, I am the mother of daughters, and I am a member of a family repeatedly battered by the rape and murder of girls and women. Disgrace has grown more difficult for me over the years, not less. It would be unprofessional of me to tell my student any of this, because our job is to tell one another what we know, not who we are. And I don't mean that it is difficult for me to talk about the novel as an intellectual in the controlled environment of a classroom or conference hall. Wake me up at 3:00 am on any night of the year, hand me a cup of coffee, and within minutes I could give a coherent lecture on this novel, or on any number of related topics. (Let us agree never to put this preposterous claim to the test.) I mean that it is difficult for me to live with the ideas contained in this novel, as it is always difficult to think outside the forms of justice codified by law. At this point in my life, I know better than to hurry past this discomfort, because a state of astonishment is exactly where Coetzee's novels ask us to be.

In the vast critical archive on Disgrace, it is axiomatic to remark upon David's racism and sexism. He is stubborn, and knows it. "I am not receptive to being counselled," he tells the members of the tribunal convened to review the charge of sexual harassment brought against him by a Coloured student at the university where he teaches literature.[76] He is, on the other hand, highly receptive to eros. The god of love possessed me, he tells the tribunal by way of explanation, "I was not myself."[77] As in much of Coetzee's work, one form of love blurs into another, to disturbing effect. David has a standing appointment with a prostitute until she realizes that he has come to consider himself a father to her sons; he seduces and later rapes his student Melanie Isaacs and then wonders whether to call her daughter; he feels the deepest love for Lucy but fears that she finds it incestuous. After the loss of his job, he moves in with her and becomes a volunteer at the local Animal Welfare League, a charity that has had to shut down for lack of funds. He gives charity to the charity, in effect, and then to Bev Shaw, the woman who keeps the place going and whose tenderness toward the animals she treats moves him so much that he becomes her lover even though he finds her completely physically unattractive. She reminds him of sanctimonious Christians, he claims. So cheery and benevolent that they raise the devil in him.

After the attack, Lucy tells David that he is no longer her father. She says that he cannot help her because she is "a dead person," not the daughter he knew.[78] His grief is so deep that he feels as though he is dying, too. He has already tried to imagine the scene of her rape, but this exercise in empathy has done nothing to help him understand why she refuses to defend herself or to confront Petrus when it turns out that one of her attackers is living under his protection and is now her neighbor. He is the youngest of the three, a disturbed and possibly mentally handicapped teenager named Pollux. When David catches him peeping through a hole in the wall at Lucy as she bathes, he kicks and sets the dog on him, seized by the old rage of a white master who is entitled to teach his servant a lesson. Another instance of stubbornness. Lucy rushes outside to cradle the boy where he lies, arm bleeding, and as she does so her bathrobe slips open to reveal her breasts, already swollen in pregnancy. David and Pollux stare, transfixed. "A stillness falls."[79] The pièta is broken when Pollux scrambles to his feet and runs off, yelling death threats. Here is another of those disquieting moments in which erotic, paternal, aesthetic, and divine forms of love cross unpredictably into one another, all made equally available by the body of a woman, who in this case tends to the injuries of a man who is also a child and simultaneously one of the fathers of her child to come.

David finds Lucy's solicitude incomprehensible. When he pushes her, yet again, to explain herself, she speaks so quietly that he can't hear her words. Perhaps she cannot hear them either. Enraged, he calls Pollux a "jackal."[80] Echoing the *Iliad*, the *Aeneid* briefly relates the story of Pollux and his twin brother Castor, who shared death between them, each spending one day in the underworld while the other lived on the earth.[81] The name is one of many allusions by which Coetzee widens his story, reaching from the fall of Lucifer to the epics of Homer, Virgil, and Dante, and from the New Testament to Romantic negative capability. More importantly, the name is a reminder that Pollux is a mystery, not fully accessible even to himself. The same may be true of Lucy, who cannot account for the care she gives him. It is one thing to protect the boy from prosecution in the interests of peace, and to withhold judgment in light of the systemic brutality that he suffered under apartheid, but quite another to allow him to watch her bathe and then to kneel beside him, breasts exposed, gently nursing his wounds like a mother, or perhaps a wife.

"When you give to the needy," writes the author of the Gospel of Matthew, "do not let your left hand know what your right hand is doing, so that your giving may be in secret."[82] It is a waste of time for David to try to understand Lucy's behavior by imagining her rape. If it turned her into a dead person, it also dissolved her ability to articulate the principles that guide her actions. She is like Elizabeth Costello in purgatory, who refuses to explain the beliefs that she lived by and instead points to her heart. This is not recalcitrance, but a fact of life outside of life, which is that beliefs and the arguments that shape them have no place there. They are the work of the right hand. The left hand serves the secret, which is where charity comes from.

David knows what it is like to act on an unjustifiable impulse. "I was not myself," he told the tribunal. Throughout his life, this is a condition that has often led him to take what he wants from women. If he intends to continue to be a father and soon a grandfather– and if he intends to help rather than hinder the social transformation of his country– he has to turn it into a condition in which he gives with equal recklessness.

"He does not understand what is happening to him," David thinks as he weeps uncontrollably while escorting the bodies of the dogs he euthanizes to an incinerator.[83] The words apply broadly. Like his daughter, David finds himself increasingly gripped by love for causes that seem unworthy of it. He goes in search of Mr. Isaacs to confess what is "on his heart"—not on his mind.[84] He says that his crime was not that he acted on his desire for Melanie but that he did not act fully enough; he took but did not give, he was not willing to be burned up by the fire that she ignited in him. He was still himself even when he wasn't. This is not the frank confession of guilt that either the reader or Mr. Isaacs might have hoped for, but he invites David to join the family for dinner anyway, a generous act if not a disinterested one. David's suspicion that his host is involved in the church in some capacity is borne out by the general abstemiousness of his household, in which there are many prayers but no corkscrew with which to open the bottle of wine that David brings to the table. Although there is the hospitality of a shared meal, and hands joined during grace, there is no Eucharist or gratuity here. Dinner is followed by more invitations to prayer and by an impromptu sermon about how God might want David to seek forgiveness for his sins. And then, several hours after he has retreated to his hotel, there is a phone call from Mr. Isaacs, a final admonition: he will not ask the university to reinstate David or to grant him clemency of any kind. God has chosen his punishment and he must accept it. David assures his host that clemency never crossed his mind.

If this is charity, it isn't worth much. It bears no resemblance to the scene that plays out between the sermon and the final phone call, when David stumbles into a bedroom in search of Mrs. Isaacs and Desiree, Melanie's younger sister, to apologize for the harm he has done to their family. This is Mr. Isaacs's idea, a task undertaken at his instruction, but he would not approve of what happens in that room. David gets to his knees, then bows his forehead to the ground as though in prayer. He is not sure that this is the right thing to do or that it is sufficient to the occasion at hand. The women stare. They have no idea what the occasion at hand is. A stillness falls. When David raises his eyes to look at Desiree, "the current leaps, the current of desire."[85] This uncontrolled desire is closer to love than anything Mr. Isaacs has to offer. It reminds David that his lust for beautiful young girls has not lessened, and it makes him ridiculous, even grotesque. It reminds him, yet again, that he does not understand what is happening to him.

It is not difficult to see how this encounter anticipates the debate between Elizabeth Costello and Sister Bridget in "The Humanities in Africa." In *Disgrace*, Coetzee is less concerned with the value of the academic humanities in a poor country than with the inefficacy of an institutional Christianity that has replaced the secret paths of charity with conventional rituals of atonement and forgiveness in which leaps of desire, which are not always distinguishable from leaps of faith, have no role to play. As embodied by Mr. Isaacs, the church has no more to contribute to the process of social repair than the police.

That repair begins with indefensible love. The fact that this love can never be asked for or encoded in law is precisely what allows it to be given. No reader of *Disgrace* that I know of has ever argued that Lucy is morally required to act as she does, and there is no guarantee that any good will come of her actions. Other than Petrus, who has never known the protection of the law and who stands to gain from Lucy's renunciation of it, the only person within the novel who is not appalled by her behavior is Bev Shaw, who runs the defunded Animal Welfare charity. If as readers we struggle to understand Lucy's conviction that the creation of a more equitable society demands that she love men who despise her, perhaps it is because we have not yet lost our senses, as David does when he is doused with kerosene and set on fire during the attack. One eye swells shut, the flange of an ear catches alight; he plunges a hand into the toilet to douse the flames on his skin, and then realizes that none of the European languages that he speaks are intelligible to his African attackers. Sight, hearing, touch, and speech are all partially disabled. From this moment on, David's sensorium is under reconstruction. Nothing less than this reconstruction, Coetzee implies, will make it possible to see the value of people in whom it was previously hidden from view.

This drastic proposal does not originate with Coetzee. He is drawing on the Gospels, which are closely attentive to the relationship between revolution and phenomenology. As Jean-Luc Nancy argues in a beautiful little book called *Noli Me Tangere*, it is a central premise of the Gospels that all the senses and faculties of self-expression need to be revised if people are to learn to understand themselves, one another, and the earth in a new way.[86]

This is why the miracles often involve curing problems with sentience—the blind, the deaf, the dumb, the lepers, the mad– and why Jesus continually tells his disciples, often in a thoroughly impatient tone of voice, that they are not to take the parables literally. Or perhaps even the miracles. "How is it you don't understand that I was not talking to you about *bread*?" Jesus asks in the book of Matthew, after he has fed first the 5000 and then the 4000 with an impossibly skimpy supply of loaves and fishes, and delivered a parable in which he compares the Pharisees and Sadducees, keepers of the law, to bad yeast.[87] Understandably, his disciples believe that these events are all connected by the common theme of bread, and that they are being reprimanded for forgetting to pack any. "Are you still so dull?" Jesus asks in exasperation.[88] I suppose the answer has to be yes.

If it were no, the disciples might resemble David Lurie at the end of *Disgrace*. He sits in the yard behind the Animal Welfare clinic with his bandaged eye and ear. Out of love for his daughter, he works to see the invisible and hear the inaudible. No one will thank him for caring for the souls of dead dogs or writing an amateur opera about Lord Byron in the underworld. On the contrary, these absurd enterprises render him a laughingstock. But they are not about dogs or song any more than the miracles of divine provision are about yeast and flour. The purpose of those interventions in materiality is to provoke states of astonishment that allow Jesus to shift attention from the needs and afflictions of the individual body to the abundance of spirit, as he is always trying to do. He fills empty casks with wine and baskets with food, and then says, what matters is not that I can multiply or transfigure what already exists, or even that I can restore life to the dead, but that "I have food to eat that you know nothing about."[89] This claim is so much stranger than the ability to tinker with quantities that to understand it requires new eyes, ears, hands, and mouths.

Unlike Marilynne Robinson or the authors of the Gospels, when Coetzee sets out to cure stubbornness by looking further than this world he does not see God; or rather, he does not give the name God to what he sees. Nor will he divide the generous desire to give from the abusive impulse to take, but instead unites them in much the way that Giorgio Agamben does when he refers to both mercy and tyranny as states of exception. If this is the state in which we leave David Lurie at the end of *Disgrace*, it is also where we meet him again, fifteen years later and halfway around the world, in *The Childhood of Jesus* and its sequels, *The Schooldays of Jesus* and *The Death of Jesus*. This time he is an unobstructed mystery several times over. He is a young child, a refugee who has arrived in a new land without a name or any recollection of his former self. He might be dead or in transit between one kind of life and another, as Elizabeth Costello is at the end of the book that bears her name. As in the Blessed

Groves of the *Aeneid*, where spirits prepare to be reborn by shedding their memories, the boy has forgotten where he comes from and who he once was; all particulars of identity have been washed away during the ocean voyage that carried him to the Spanish-speaking New World, along with the stranger who decides to become his father. This New World is so coolly reasonable that it could be run by Houyhnhnms. When David disembarks in a town called Novilla with his adoptive father, Simón, they pass through a "charity station," and immediately realize that they have arrived in a place where charity does not exist.[90] Their new home is benevolent but stingy, kind but passionless, fond of cold showers and picnics that consist of unsalted bean paste on crackers. In this frictionless place there is no injustice or inequality to be redressed, no corrupt power to be overthrown, no God to worship or obey, little sorrow or striving, no history or future. Nevertheless, David embodies charity and demands it of everyone he meets. It is as though with this character Coetzee reaches back through all of his writing, detaches charity from history, and places it at the very center of human being.

"All great gifts come out of nowhere. You should know that," says Simón to Inés, the woman he plucks off a tennis court and invites to become the boy's mother.[91] Why should she know that? She seems to, because she is willing to accept a stranger's conviction that a child she has never seen before is her son, much as Simón is willing to accept the boy's belief that the universe is filled with empty spaces where life pools and hides. The boy claims that numbers do not proceed in an orderly fashion from zero to infinity; they float in haphazard configurations, and to move from one to another requires stepping across a crevasse into which one can fall, and then keep on falling.[92] These dark spaces between numbers and words are like holes in the heart, and David's insistence that they matter more than the rules that people have invented to stitch up the mind is what marks him as the "escape artist" and the "lifesaver" that he aspires to be.[93] He wants to pull people out of the nowhere places that they tumble into—the flooded holds of ships, the ocean, and above all the gaps between numbers and words that he will teach people to see when he grows up and becomes a magician.

Like messiahs, magicians always require two teachers: a lawyer and a criminal. In each of the three *Jesus* novels, Coetzee provides David with both, beginning with the schoolteacher, Señor León, whose name echoes his cardinal principle– respect for *la ley*. Like every other state employee, he believes that "the law is enough," and insists that David be sent to a boarding school because he is an unteachable child who will not apply his exceptional intelligence to mastering ordinary methods of reading, writing, and counting.[94] David will not submit to the lessons of the classroom any more than he will submit to existing beliefs about the way the physical world is organized, and the only people who really understand this refusal are Emilio Daga, a thief who gives David a cloak of invisibility; and Dmitri, a rapist and killer.

It has taken me several years to understand why I find the *Jesus* novels so unsatisfying. At first, I thought the problem was allegory, which runs the risk of becoming either weightless or heavy, but Coetzee has written allegorical novels before, including *Waiting for the Barbarians*, which shakes me no matter how many times I read it. No, the problem is not allegory. Then I thought that the problem was repetition. True, Coetzee has never before written about what Jesus might have been like as a displaced kindergartener who borrows from both Harry Houdini and Harry Potter, but the deeper imaginative structures of the *Jesus* novels are familiar. The same can be said of the relationship between *Life & Times of Michael K* and *Age of Iron*, yet I am amazed by both. No, the problem is not repetition. It is that all his life Coetzee has written about people who struggle to become exceptions but are instead confronted by the iron power of the rule. In the figure of David, Coetzee for the first time imagines somebody whom those laws cannot touch. He is a natural-born "pillar of grace," from start to finish.[95] Even the disease that kills him at the age of ten is idiopathic. His adoptive parents have to work hard to protect him from rule enforcers like the censor and the school board, but David is largely unaware of their labors, and by the final book in the series, almost everyone he encounters acknowledges that he is extraordinary. The problem for me is that grace is too easy here, and law too brittle. Everything in these novels feels unreal.

Every few years, I teach an Honors seminar on the writing of J. M. Coetzee. At the beginning of the term I look ahead to thirteen weeks to be spent in relentless confrontation with extremity, and I flinch. Occasionally I think, "Never again." I teach other, more joyous seminars, and my colleagues would not complain if I retired this particular course from my rotation. I created it, and it is mine to teach or abandon as I wish. But I suspect that I will never abandon it, because Coetzee's ability to tell the story of extremity, of people who are overtaken by the forces that reduce all the weak tools to ash, is almost unparalleled. So too is his ability to imagine the resources of mind and spirit that sometimes appear to those people when all else is gone. Those resources go by old and unfashionable names, but I have found, again and again, that my students recognize them. "What is *caritas*?" they ask. "What *is* charity as a moral or political category?" Shift the vocabulary and they know what loving kindness is, they understand care, and they are no strangers to holes in the heart. Our conversations are charged with urgency, as though we too were living through a State of Emergency, or a transition from white supremacy to true democracy, or the collapse of what we thought we knew—and we are, that is exactly what we are living through. The *Jesus* books are about a beloved child who embodies this transformation and brings it to all he meets, but I don't feel the mystery, and I don't feel the dark powers either. I don't believe that any student will come to me, eyes wide, and say, "I am astounded by this book." Who knows, I might be proven wrong, and I might change my mind. This is not a particularly scholarly observation, but it was J. M. Coetzee who taught me to trust it. No one can spend decades reading his work, as I have done, and emerge with any faith in the value of intellect alone. We can rely on our hearts as well, if we are willing to risk being ridiculous, to become as improper as a child, perhaps to stumble and fall without dignity.

3

Secrets

Before watching Wim Wenders's film, *Wings of Desire*, I had no idea that in their eternal study of human beings angels find it necessary to take so many notes. The immortals invented by Wenders and Peter Handke remember our every thought and gesture, but when Damiel and his old friend Cassiel reconnoiter to review history and discuss the day's research they each pull out a little notebook and read their jottings aloud, more like scrappy beat reporters of the 1950s than timeless creatures of air. Above all, they are excited by inexplicable and spontaneous behavior. "Today I heard a subway conductor shout 'Tierra del Fuego!' instead of announcing the station name," reads Cassiel. "Nice," says Damiel, nodding enthusiastically. "Today I saw a woman fold up her umbrella in a rainstorm and let herself get drenched."[2] Cassiel beams. Amazing! This conversation takes place in the front seat of a convertible parked inside a luxury car dealership, but at this point in the film we already know that the Berlin Public Library is the best place to study the contents of a mind. All the angels of Berlin congregate there. After hours, they stand around and watch the custodial staff vacuum.

When Cassiel arrives in this temple of books he takes a moment to savor the readers' internal voices, his eyes closed and face lifted to the ceiling, but what seems to fascinate the angels more than anything are the *acts* of reading and writing.

These perplexities have to be watched carefully and at close quarters. How does a book or a pen make a mind sing out in quite this way? Trying to answer this question, the angels eavesdrop on the library's patrons, peering over their shoulders and settling down beside them at desks and in carrels. Whenever I imagine angelic compassion, or even divine intercession, I see

FIGURE 3.1 *The angel Cassiel, played by Otto Sander, listens to readers' internal voices. Source: Wim Wenders.* Wings of Desire. *Performed by Bruno Ganz and Otto Sander. 1987; The Criterion Collection, 2009*

the beautifully attentive face of the actor Bruno Ganz in this scene, as he nestles beside a reader, running an invisible finger over lines of print and then picking up a pencil to play with it. "It's wonderful to live as spirit and testify for all eternity to only what is spiritual in people's minds," he will soon say to Cassiel. "But sometimes I get fed up with this spiritual existence. I don't want to always hover above. I'd rather feel a weight within, casting off this boundless freedom and tying me to the earth."

Toward the end of the film, Damiel does cast off his freedom and fall to earth, mainly because he is in love with a circus acrobat, but his decision is foretold by this early scene in the library. When he strokes a page of text and twirls a pencil through his fingers we can see that for Damiel these actions allow the spirit to shine through the flesh. In this film, as in life, people do all sorts of things with their bodies in order to feel but also be free of them for a moment: they fly on trapezes, dance, drink, make love, or, in desperation, leap from buildings to their death. But in the eyes of the angels who watch them, people are most ecstatic and yet most at home in themselves when they read and write. *Wings of Desire* begins and ends with a hand filling a page with script, and eventually we realize that the hand belongs to the ex-angel, who records his autobiography just as he promised Cassiel that he would. For Damiel, to be mortal is to be able to say, "I have a story," and then pick up a pen and write it down. Now he is as weightless as paper, but also fully embodied. Now he can testify to spirit, but as a sensual and social being.

As far as I know, Wim Wenders is alone in his belief that angels visit libraries to worship people just as people visit holy places to worship the divine. He is by no means alone in the conviction that writing moves the mind in two directions at once: deep into the self, and out into the social life that governs the self but can also be transformed by it. One of the loudest complaints made in the avalanche of books about our digital era is that virtuality thins self-awareness and degrades social interaction precisely because it does not bring the mind into contact with itself, with the result that people have less and less of themselves to share with one another even as they spend more and more time sharing.[3] At their best, these arguments express the old fear that we will lose our ability to access and express interiority, and that without it we will have little to offer each other, no matter how often we broadcast our thoughts and activities.

For as long as I can remember, the same image has flashed into my mind in the seconds before I fall asleep at night: an enormous grappling hook tethered somewhere in the sky, or perhaps it is a plow, digs deeply into the earth and slows the planet's rotation. In other versions, I am using my own fingernails, strangely strengthened and enlarged, to stop the world. I don't feel like one of the angry fairies or snubbed wise women who bring life to a halt because of an unanswered claim on gratitude. I make no such claim on anyone. What I feel in these dreams is that for a moment I have entered the time of the angels, where it is possible to get a clear view of everything. I am hungry for this view, perhaps because I was raised by parents who spent most of their days sitting nearly motionless in front of easels or drawing boards, trying to reveal invisible things.

My parents grew up in very violent households, and they live with the consequences, which are sometimes unbearable. I now understand that their ability to see hidden life is central to their survival every day, which is why it was so important to them to teach us to see that life even where others did not, and always to feel it in ourselves, no matter the circumstances. It is true that some of their techniques were startling, and unlikely to be endorsed by parenting or financial experts. In the late 1970s, my father moved our family to a neighborhood whose residents were so despised that the city changed its zoning laws in order to expropriate everyone's homes and turn the area into parkland. City Hall granted him a special dispensation to buy and renovate a condemned cottage on the condition that within twenty years it would be purchased by the city for a pittance and then bulldozed like all the other houses on the strip, and in exchange, my father agreed to invest his borrowed money and more than a year of his full-time labor in a dwelling that would steadily lose value until it was turned into a picnic spot.

He felt that he was the winner in this transaction, and in the end he was, although throughout my childhood our neighborhood was synonymous with poverty and criminality. The city declined to connect it to the municipal sewage system, turned the local school into a residential training center for prison guards, and left the motorcycle gang to its own devices. Between the student prison guards and the gangsters, who had many shared interests, the neighborhood bar achieved a wide radius of notoriety, as did the motel across the street. And then, for no discernible reason, the mood began to change. Well before the twenty-year expiry date, but long after many people's houses had fallen down or been razed, the city relented. It became legal to buy, sell and renovate property for the first time in decades, and developers smelled opportunity. Now my parents' house is worth many times what my father invested in it, and so is the lakefront land that it sits on.

My father does not pretend to have seen any of this coming. His decision was not the result of a long-range analysis of the real estate market or of anything else. He and my mother moved to the neighborhood because it was cheap, and unlike most people who have any choice about where to live, they were only mildly concerned by the Hell's Angels's clubhouse beside the playground. They looked at the place in the same way that they looked at whatever they were painting: with patience, curiosity, and minimal judgment. They looked at their daughters this way too. I spent many hours of my childhood sitting or standing in my father's studio while he painted me, and it took me years to realize how rare it is to be looked at by someone who is not trying to figure out which of their needs you might serve or how best to appraise your utility to whatever system they are in charge of. I don't need one hand to count the number of times this has happened to me since. It is far more shocking than most forms of erotic attention. What my father gave me as a child was the knowledge of what it is like to be regarded in a spirit of steady and open inquiry, and the understanding that it is important to get the results of that inquiry down on paper in case you have seen something that other people might need tomorrow or next year.

Whether these transfers of grace happen, and to what end, has nothing at all to do with the medium in which thinking takes place. It has to do with the thanking in the thinking, and this mystery has been at issue since the first cuneiform wedge touched damp clay. Unsurprisingly, historians are divided on the question of how and why the Sumerians invented phonetic writing in the fourth millennium BCE, but the archeological record clearly shows that the new technology was first used to answer questions like, "How much wheat is in the storehouse today?" "How many people live in your household, and what are their occupations?" not questions like, "What are the unique dimensions of your consciousness?" "What do you think and feel when you walk around this world?" The great majority of the surviving tablets reveal that the Sumerians developed cuneiform to serve the needs of accountants, archivists, and bureaucrats, not poets or philosophers.[4] In a pragmatic sense, writing was invented to regulate the public sphere, yet from its opening line, the Sumerian *Epic of Gilgamesh* turns inward: the oldest extant poem, recorded at the beginning of the second millennium BCE, explores the relationship between kingship and the "secret things" of human existence.[5]

The *Epic* is about a monarch's desire to be known everywhere and eternally. "I will proclaim to the world the deeds of Gilgamesh," promises the speaker of the prologue.[6] The King of Uruk left behind two monuments to those deeds: a city and a story, both made of stone. This was a man who wanted to be remembered. The *Epic* is about his desire to rule in his people's imagination forever, but more than anything it is about his need to solve the mystery of our relationship to the gods, nature, and death. When Gilgamesh realizes that his worldly authority cannot prevent his dearest friend Enkidu from dying, he takes off his royal garments, puts on the skin of a lion, and goes to ask the gods why death is the penalty for human life. When posed this question, immortal Utnapishtim does not have much to say to Gilgamesh by way of comfort, other than "There is no permanence," but he does give the King two gifts.[7] The first is the tale of how human beings became so numerous and noisy that the immortals found it impossible to get any sleep, so they decided to flood the earth and drown everyone, and the second is an underwater plant that restores youth. Gilgamesh loses the plant, but he takes the story of the flooding and repopulation of the earth, a "secret of the gods," back to the people of Uruk, and engraves it on a stone for everyone to see.[8]

The first poem ever written down is about a king who carries news from the gods into a walled city, strengthening his own position as a leader and at the same time revealing the vulnerability of all people. The secret is a stone inside the city's fortifications, but it is also a door onto a revelation about the divine wrath that sent six days and nights of torrential rain, and the divine mercy that saved one family and two of every living thing. In other words, the secret is not a stone like any other; it pulls the imagination beyond Uruk's ramparts and challenges the power of the king who was strong enough to bring the story that revealed his own weakness. The scribes who recorded versions of Gilgamesh's story over thousands of years seem to have been thinking carefully about how building a wall and telling a divine secret needed to be shown as conflicting expressions of the drive to rule a people, which is perhaps why these actions begin and end the text of the *Epic*. They are also constantly paired throughout *Wings of Desire*, and above all in Wim Wenders's decision to headquarter his humanist angels at the Berlin Public Library at a time when that city was still divided by one of the most infamous walls of the last century.

In the ancient worlds, libraries reflected the military power of generals and emperors. The Medes and Babylonians who conquered Nineveh in 612 BCE deliberately buried the library where the *Epic of Gilgamesh* was housed; as a result, cuneiform became obsolete, and the Mesopotamian cities disappeared from the archaeological record until the mid-nineteenth century, which is exactly the kind of outcome that the Medes and Babylonians were hoping for.[9] Beginning in the mid-eighteenth century, and particularly after the French Revolution and the seizure of the clerical book collections, the public libraries of Europe were founded in support of a new idea: the modern secular nation.[10] Wenders's seraphim want to understand human interiority, but they also want to understand the lasting trauma of twentieth-century German nationalism, and they intuit that these two projects converge in the stacks and carrels of a public book collection. Many scenes in *Wings of Desire* are set in crowded places, including subways, nightclubs, busy streets, and the circus, but the library is where internal voices emerge from their murmuring solitude to chorus together in the way that makes Cassiel throw back his head in rapture. Only in a reading room can an immortal study the relationship between the fingerprint and the flag.

The most famous audio sculpture made by the artist Janet Cardiff and her partner, George Bures Miller, is called "The Forty Part Motet," which premiered in New York City one month after the attacks of September 11, 2001.[11] The curators at PS1 MOMA decided to make the piece available to visitors twenty-four hours a day, and it became a place of gathering and vigil. Now "The Forty Part Motet" is part of the permanent collection of the National Gallery of Canada, and tours almost continually.[12] Visually the piece is simple, even austere: in an otherwise empty room, forty black pedestal speakers are arranged in a large circle, each broadcasting the voice of one member of the forty-part choir that is singing "*Spem in Alium*," "Hope in Any Other," a devotional song by the sixteenth-century English composer Thomas Tallis. When Cardiff was recording the choir, she spontaneously decided to leave each person's microphone on during a break, capturing their chit chat and coughs, their laughter and breathing, their whispers and yawns. If you stand in the center of the circle you will hear these private sounds merge together, just as you will later hear the choristers' voices combine in harmony, but by moving from speaker to speaker you can also eavesdrop in a way that is impossible in real life. It is as though you are standing half an inch away from a stranger, leaning your face into theirs. A few minutes later this person stops clearing her throat or chuckling and begins to sing a soaring vocal line from a piece of music that is almost 500 years old. Every time I have seen this piece I have been shocked by how moving the transition is.

When I am walking around a gallery of contemporary art I dutifully read the artists' and curators' statements, which all sound alike, and I approach each piece feeling in command. When I step into the circle of "The Forty Part Motet" I stop thinking, because I am shaken by emotions so strong that I cannot understand where they came from. Where were they just a few moments ago when I was reading art theory and feeling bored? Now it is as though a key has turned in a lock that I didn't know existed, something vast has been let loose in the room, and I can't imagine where it was hiding. I sometimes feel that I can tell the difference between the ideas that I form in my mind, using the knowledge that I have gathered over the years, and the ideas that seem to form outside of me and then appear, like visitors. One feels like the deliberate working out of a project I have set in motion, the other like a presence that pushes gently and then with increasing force, as a child pushes when it works to be born. This is the kind of presence that "The Forty Part Motet" reveals.

It also seems to be the kind of presence we crave in a crisis. The writer Patricia Hampl beautifully conjectures that in difficult times people want to hear "the sane singular voice, alone with its thoughts, maybe to assure ourselves that sanity does exist somewhere, and the self, the littleness of personhood is somewhere alive, taking its notes."[13] She traces this insight to the first essayist, Michel de Montaigne, the aristocrat who retreated to his library from the vicious civil wars of sixteenth-century France, and instead of writing an historical analysis of the religious sectarianism of his time, invented a new literary form devoted to the private idiosyncrasies of the individual mind: his own. To those who lament, "I have done nothing today," Montaigne replies, "What! Have you not lived? That is not only the fundamental, but the most noble of your occupations."[14] This anxiety about productivity feels so contemporary that it is hard to believe these words were written over 400 years ago. Everywhere I look these days I come across books that encourage me to reclaim my wastrel self—the part that wants to sit and daydream, to go in search of lost time rather than clock it, to reflect rather than move fast and break things.[15] Dreamland is the only habitat for which evolution prepared me, and I've always thought it was a small and unstable niche. Now we are all being invited to enter it, and to follow the path of Montaigne, in the conviction that the singular voice is inherently emancipatory, not just for the person in retreat, but for everyone who is able to listen in.

When she won the Nobel Prize for literature in 2007, Doris Lessing gave an acceptance speech called "On Not Winning the Nobel Prize," in which she says that writing comes from an "empty space" within the mind.[16] It is not on the blueprint, but it is how blueprints are made. It is the origin of sovereignty as well as solidarity, and home to that small fraction of the self that stands a little outside of circumstances and for that reason has the potential to stretch them. Lessing talks about the desperation for stories that she has seen in some of the world's poorest people, even when every day is dominated by the search for calories and water, and describes a pregnant woman standing in line for drinking water during a drought in Zimbabwe, where Lessing grew up and where she returned many times as an adult to stock vacant libraries and schools with books. While the woman waits, her two young children clutching her legs, she is reading a few chapters of *Anna*

Karenina that have been ripped away from the binding and somehow made
their way into her hands. After she has received her ration of water, she has
to return her piece of the novel to the shopkeeper and walk several miles
home. At first I thought this anecdote was sentimental and untrustworthy,
but I have read enough of Lessing's work to know that sentimentality was
not one of her weaknesses. Her point is that the empty space is not just
where writing comes from, but where living comes from. She imagines that
this space is in each of us, and that it was formed by the original fire and
wind of the great explosion by which matter was first created. If she is
right that the very poor sometimes have a keener sense of this gratuity than
the affluent, it is because resistance to brutality demands it in a way that
comfort does not. I recall Winston Smith, who in the desolate opening pages
of *1984* realizes that he owns nothing except "the few cubic centimeters"
inside his own head, and must learn to reclaim them if he is to resist the
Republic of Oceania's lies.[17]

Beginning with Gilgamesh, writers have often felt that their words
come from someplace very far from humanity—from gods or angels or the
wilderness within the mind. Annie Dillard has a wonderful short essay in *The
Writing Life* where she describes a dream in which her old Smith-Corona
typewriter erupts, spraying ash all over her study and setting her desk on
fire.[18] Volcanoes flood the earth's surface with fertile liquid from its core,
enriching the land that everyone walks on, and good thinking in any genre
turns the author's mind inside out, just as a volcano reverses the earth. For
Maurice Blanchot, this is the very definition of the literary: what is "farthest
removed from existence as already revealed now reveals itself within shared
existence."[19] Derek Attridge expressed the same idea more than half a
century later when he claimed that writing "speaks to my inmost, perhaps
secret, being" and "utters thoughts I have long nurtured but never had the
power to express."[20] Many people are surprised to discover that what feels
private in their work, almost incommunicable, is what readers around the
globe respond to, not because they have seen it before but because it exposes
some censored aspect of their own inner lives.

I find that the writers who move me most deeply release some kind of
energy that compels me to do this work for myself. It is the strangest thing.
I often have to put the book down and stare into space because my mind
has begun to pay attention to the other words that are taking shape. I can
feel them getting stronger, but they are not on the page and have nothing to
do with what I'm reading. These words don't offer an analysis or critique of
the book in my hands; I couldn't use them to write a review or an argument
about it. Instead, they join up with whatever piece of writing I'm working
on at the time, adding a dimension I could feel but couldn't find, or perhaps
moving in an entirely new direction, one I'm not even sure I want to go in.
Sometimes they leap back to prose that I thought was put to rest months
ago, and they land at a precise point in the manuscript and break it open so

that I have to try to assemble it differently. Suddenly sentences that I thought were finished are a demolition site, covered in rubble and dust, but I can't say no to these new words. They are called up by the writer I'm reading, and even when I put the book down they don't go away, although they might fade a little, or get disorganized so that I have to fill in the gaps. I used to think that Blanchot, for all his verbal contortions, made this process sound too passive and too easy. Nothing reveals *itself*; it is deliberately revealed by someone, often by dint of great struggle. I still believe that, but at the same time I can see that Blanchot is right, because the deep self is just waiting for an opportunity to be seen and heard, and under the right conditions it really does feel like an eruption or revelation that changes everything.

* * *

In the *Homeric Hymn to Hermes*, the infant Hermes sets out to get Apollo's attention by stealing some of his cattle and then lying about it. It doesn't take Apollo long to figure out that Hermes is to blame, but he can't understand how his half-brother managed the theft. Apollo easily finds the footprints left by his cows, but the marks are unreadable:

> Well, well! This is remarkable, what I'm seeing. Clearly these are long-horn-cattle tracks, but they all point backward, toward the fields of daffodils! And these others, they are not the tracks of a man or a woman, nor of a gray wolf or a bear or lion. And I don't think the shaggy-maned centaur leaves such prints. What swift feet took these long strides? The tracks on this side of the path are weird, but those on the other side are weirder still![21]

The reader knows that to achieve this weirdness Hermes made the cows walk backward so that they would appear to be coming rather than going, and invented for himself a pair of sandals made of twigs and leaves, which he threw into a pool of water after he was finished with them so that they would not be discovered. Apollo thinks he's looking at footprints made by "little oak trees."[22] This doesn't make any sense, which is the point. The other point is that Hermes's trickery is intended to open up the hierarchy of the gods so that he will not spend the rest of his life living in a cave.[23] Apollo is so impressed by the godling's cleverness that he trades gifts with him and declares him a guide and messenger, although of the most equivocal sort. Sometimes his prophecies will be lies, and sometimes he will deceive the people who seek his counsel rather than tell them the truth.

Plato writes that Hermes embodies discourse, which is thus necessarily "twofold, true and false."[24] Hermes gains power by manipulating signs, and he teaches that representations depend on the multiplicity of meanings that give rise to hermeneutics, the interpretive practices that bear his name. To challenge a social structure—in his case, a pantheon—Hermes does strange and inventive things to the most basic mark that the body makes, namely a footprint. He makes cows walk backwards, and lo! it is as though they came from a field of flowers rather than Apollo's corral, and he weaves fantastic shoes that turn him into a walking tree. In 1641, the Reverend John Wilkins, one of the founders of the Royal Society, wrote a treatise on cryptography called *Mercury: Or the Secret and Swift Messenger*, which gave a general theory and many practical examples of how to circulate messages without being detected, and claimed the Greco-Roman god as patron of this art.[25] Hermes reveals the cryptographic potential within all tracks and prints, and shows that by baffling ordinary writing it is possible to disappear for a while and then, upon return, to be seen anew.

In the *Hymn*, Hermes is a poet-provocateur who is trying to upgrade his situation by astonishing the gods. The French magician and aerialist, Philippe Petit, followed Hermes's lead when he apprenticed himself to a Parisian printing house as a typesetter and invented his own font at the age of thirteen. Petit writes that there is a deep affinity between the graphic and the magical arts, which both depend upon conjuring presence.[26] But at least from the time of Herodotus, there has also been a deep affinity between the graphic and the martial arts. In *The Histories*, Herodotus claims that Demaratus of Ariston warned the Greeks of King Xerxes's planned invasion by sending a hidden message on a folding writing tablet. Demaratus, who had long lived in exile among the Persians but still felt affection for his former countrymen, scraped the wax from the surface of the writing tablet, carved his warning onto the wood, and then covered it up with melted wax so that the tablet would appear to be blank. The tablet reached Greece without attracting suspicion, and eventually the puzzled recipients decided to remove the wax in the hope that they would find something helpful underneath. When they found Demaratus's message, they shared it with the other Greek city-states. "Anyway, that is what is supposed to have happened," concludes Herodotus airily.[27] Herodotus also tells of a man named Histiaeus of Miletus, who shaved the head of a trusted slave, tattooed a message on his scalp, and then waited for the hair to grow back before sending him through enemy territory. When the slave reached his destination, he shaved his head again and showed the tattoo to its addressee, Aristagoras, who then organized a rebellion against the occupying Persian forces.[28] Whether or not we can trust the details of Herodotus's history, it is useful to know that as early as the fifth century BCE people were inventing ways to conceal and transmit words in order to more effectively wage war on one another.

Wax and hair sufficed to hide Greek intelligence from their enemies, but in later years these rudimentary tricks no longer served. Throughout his monumental study of the history of European cryptography, *The Codebreakers*, David Kahn argues that every major technological innovation in public communications produces parallel and nearly simultaneous innovations in the art of secrecy. The development of these arts is as central to European modernity as the printing press, which inspired the fifteenth-century poet, architect, painter, and composer Leon Battista Alberti to build the first device for generating polyalphabetic codes. His machine borrowed the central technological innovation of Gutenberg's press, which is that pieces of type are capable of infinite recombination, and anticipated one of its most important cultural consequences, which is that ideas became portable to a new degree. With each rotation of its interior wheel, Alberti's cipher disk reorganized the upper and lower case letters of the alphabet to produce codes more complex and secure than ever before.[29] In this moment, the double life of print began.

Print palmed the globe, but this does not mean that handwriting offered privacy. On the contrary, Jonathan Goldberg famously argues that throughout the sixteenth century the act of putting a quill to paper became inseparable from statecraft, thanks to the printing and wide distribution of penmanship guides that standardized written scripts and taught people how to turn themselves into "hands of the state."[30] In the pages of these guides, even the physical tools of writing—the penknife used to turn a goose feather into a quill with a sharp tip, for example—were represented as weapons to be wielded by people interested in improving their social fortunes, civilizing the native inhabitants of England's new overseas colonies, or upholding the commonwealth of nations with imperial England at its center.[31] In the same spirit, the statute that founded England's Post Office in 1657 was swiftly followed by the creation of a Secret Office, a center for cryptographic training and innovation, whose employees opened and read all the mail.[32] Like the Black Chambers that operated in major European cities from the seventeenth to the mid-nineteenth centuries, whose purpose was to open, decipher, and reseal all official diplomatic correspondence, the Post Office was created in part to keep an eye on the people who used it.[33] We are right to be outraged by the use of Facebook and other social media platforms for covert corporate data harvesting, government surveillance, and election rigging, but these strategies are not new.

I first became interested in cryptography when I heard Leo Marks, head of British Intelligence's S.O.E. (Special Operations Executive) during the Second World War, interviewed by Terry Gross on "Fresh Air." I was in graduate school in Philadelphia at the time, and riveted to learn that under some circumstances hermeneutics is literally a question of life or death. Popular culture has often depicted the men and women at Bletchley Park, who during the Second World War worked to break the codes generated by the German Enigma machine, thus preparing the ground for the invention of the computer and helping to win the war. Less attention has been paid to the people under Marks's supervision, most of them women, who read and eventually wrote poems for spies. At the beginning of the war, the Allies instructed their agents to embed their messages within a few lines of a well-known poem —the "source-text," it was called.[34] The most famous works of Shakespeare, Keats, Tennyson, Molière, Racine, Verlaine, and Rabelais became favorites because they were easy to remember and to verify. If a spy who habitually concealed her traffic, or enciphered messages, in the first stanza of Keats's "Ode to a Nightingale" made a coding error, the home decoder could consult a poetry anthology, a copy of Keats's collected works, or her own memory, and if she could ascertain that the agent had misspelled "numbness" or "Lethe," the hidden message might suddenly be revealed. I know that a woman poring over a poem is less cinematic than a scene in which a young Alan Turing stands in front of an enormous code-cracking computer, rattling with the effort of its calculations, but to me it is no less fascinating.

For the decoders, a great deal depended on the ability to decipher not only what was being said in a message, but by whom. Even penmanship bears the imprint of national style, as the Elizabethans knew very well. In 1941, "a rather *Germanic cast to the handwriting* in a Spanish-language letter from Havana to Lisbon" caught a mail censor's eye.[35] Sure enough, it turned out that the author was German and that the letter was written in code. Similarly, the Allies recorded audio "fingerprints" of the Morse transmitters whose radio messages they intercepted, which made it possible to recognize individual transmission rhythms or "fists," identify and compensate for habitual errors and "Morse mutilation," and track transmitters as they moved across Europe.[36] Even with Morse fingerprinting it was not impossible to forge someone else's hand, as Leo Marks discovered. In 1943, he began to uncover the most significant Allied intelligence crisis of the war when he noticed that of all the agents in Europe, the Dutch were the only ones who never made coding mistakes. Marks guessed that they must therefore be writing with the kind of leisure to be found nowhere but a jail cell. He was right. A German officer named Hermann Giskes was in the midst of perpetrating the longest fraud of the war, destroying the Dutch resistance over a period of twenty months through a *funkspiel* (radio play) in which one agent either ventriloquizes another or forces him to send misinformation in his own hand.

Leo Marks was a second-generation bibliophile, the son of Benjamin Marks, who was co-owner of one of the most famous antiquarian bookshops in England, "Marks & Co." In his diabolically witty memoir, *Between Silk and Cyanide*, he sets the scene for his epiphany about Herr Giskes: he was at his father's bookstore, sitting in Sigmund Freud's favorite chair and paging through a reproduction of the 1455 Gutenberg Bible, when he conceived the test code that would confirm his suspicion that the head of German intelligence in Holland was controlling the Dutch traffic. To Freud, Marks owed his intuition that a writer whose transmissions were always free of parapraxes, or slips in spelling and coding, was almost certainly not who he pretended to be; to Gutenberg, he owed the alphabetic mobility that came to define and to police the public sphere.[37] For this very reason, Marks eventually decided that he had to forget most of what he had learned from incunabula. In the final years of the war, and with the help of the young women who worked in the deciphering room, and went by the unfortunate name of F.A.N.Y.s (First Aid Nursing Yeomanry), he began to write original poems for each agent sent into Europe. This way, a German decoder with a fondness for Keats or Verlaine would not recognize the source-text when he intercepted it. Then Marks realized that turning the S.O.E. into a creative writing workshop only solved one of the weaknesses of book-codes: it made poems untraceable within the print archive, but even if "numbness" is not part of a quote from Keats, it is still instantly recognizable as a word to anyone fluent in English, and can therefore be used to crack open the mathematical logic of a coding system.

In the end, Marks decided that no matter how many weird things a person did to her fingerprints, she could not hide inside a word. Too many Allied agents were caught and executed, or sent to concentration camps. To protect them and their countries, he developed something he called a "one-time pad." It was printed on silk, and contained keys for enciphering messages not within words but within randomized letter patterns that were used once, cut away from the pad, and then burned. The most secure codes, Marks concluded, were those that owed no debts to print because they were designed to transmit their secret only once before they went up in smoke.

* * *

I have always felt that cryptography presents a radical version of a problem faced by all writers, which is how to express what is furthest removed from existence in a medium that has long served to regulate the most public aspects of who we are. Before Hermes was patron of cryptographers, he guided poets and the dead, and therefore embodied the belief that writing comes from the need to reveal life outside of life. He acted with this idea in mind when he wove sandals out of foliage and made footprints that scrambled Apollo's senses. "What swift feet took these long strides?" Apollo wonders. Not a man, woman, wolf, bear, lion, or centaur. Then what? Some kind of creature that Apollo has never heard of. One minute, he is looking at strange marks on the earth and wondering where his cows are. The next, he is confronted by the upstart maker of those marks, who wants to be his equal, or at least a place at the table. Here it is important to notice that Hermes's bid for recognition is oblique, more a matter of style than content. He doesn't approach Apollo with a placard reading "Full Rights for Half-Caste Divinities" or with any other direct appeal to fairness. The how of Hermes's message is what confounds the senses, not the what.

In order to bring about this change in a reader, the writer first has to bring it about in herself. Outside of myths, tree-shoes are not an option.

In the fifth book of the *My Struggle* series, *Some Rain Must Fall*, Karl Ove Knausgaard describes a scene in which he is looking out of a bus window at the spruce forests of his native Norway, and imagining whales in the depths of the sea. "Mist, heart, blood, trees," he writes. "What was it that enticed me with such power?" "Oh, if only I could write about *them*, no, not write *about* them but make my writing *be* them, then I would be happy."[38] The better part of Knausgaard's multivolume struggle consists of trying to figure out how to write a novel that does not feel made up, but as given as a tree or his own blood. This kind of writing always seems to come from what is felt rather than mastered in its entirety. Unlike Knausgaard, Marilynne Robinson believes that purely imaginary people and events are quite capable of "drawing the essence of what we know out of the shadows," although she too credits intuition with the ability to reach into that shadowland, which for her is also the home of the sacred.[39]

Over many years now, my experience of reading Robinson is that of going swimming in a backyard pool and then discovering, mid-stroke, that I am no longer floating in six to eight feet of chlorinated water but in the middle of an ocean. The shore is invisible, and something stirs in the fathoms beneath me. This feeling is not pleasurable; often it is unendurably painful. I learned long ago not to read Robinson's writing in a public place like a café or a park, because I might begin to sob. In her prose I can hear that I am being addressed as a holy being, and this experience is so rare and demanding that I have no skills with which to meet it. My knowledge means nothing here; it is like a broken toy, and I sense that the scale on which I understand my life is wrong. I can't say what the right scale is, exactly, only that it is closer to an ocean than a swimming pool, and that it is already available to me if I could grasp it, but it is no easier to grasp this new measure than it is to make a sentence out of mist. In an essay called "Freedom of Thought," Robinson describes this hint of hidden capacity and the way it helps her to escape the "tight and awkward carapace of definition," the "dead shell," into which we are all crammed by conventions of thought that are both imposed and internalized. What she hopes to create instead, both for herself and the reader, is a living presence made out of words, "something a little like a spirit, a little like a human presence in its mystery and distinctiveness."[40]

This is patient work. In conversation with President Barack Obama in September of 2015, Robinson says that the opening sentence of *Gilead*, which is spoken by the Reverend John Ames, came to her in a clear voice one day when she was sitting in a hotel room, waiting for her sons to arrive.[41] Thanks to the Reverend, she was able to write the novel in a matter of months, but at this point it had been more than two decades since the publication of *Housekeeping*, and I sometimes wonder about those years of preparation and waiting, if that is what they were. The epiphany comes quickly—a distinctive voice, speaking in perfect sentences—but perhaps after years of listening.

It is hard to imagine that a writer would deliberately extend those years by throwing obstacles in her own path. Yet this is just what Jhumpa Lahiri did when she decided that despite being the daughter of Bengali-speaking immigrants to the United States, and despite having won a Pulitzer Prize and been shortlisted for the Man Booker, among many other accolades, she would stop reading and writing in English in order to read and write exclusively in Italian instead. I can think of other people who have chosen to write in an adopted language, from Joseph Conrad and Vladimir Nabokov in the earlier twentieth century to Aleksandar Hemon, Yiyun Li, and Marjane Satrapi in the twenty-first, but they were all immigrants or refugees, not mid-career writers who had no need to leave home. In addition to renouncing English, Lahiri moved her family to Rome. In a collection of essays and stories called *In Other Words*, written in Italian, she tries to account for her decision to incapacitate herself so that she has to write "like a child, like a semiliterate."[42] At the beginning of the book, she describes her first days in Rome, where she arrives at the height of summer, her two children in tow, to find that she cannot unlock the door to the apartment she has rented. The key worked earlier but now suddenly it doesn't. After much panic, a locksmith arrives, and Lahiri is able to get inside, feed her children dinner, and begin to write—by hand, in a diary, in Italian. During the day, she confronts all the confusions of life in a new city. In the evening, she confronts them again on paper. She feels that she has entered "a state of complete bewilderment."[43]

It is also a state of metamorphosis. Every time she picks up a pencil, Lahiri feels as though she is writing with her left hand, "my weak hand, the one I'm not supposed to write with."[44] Her Italian is labored and filled with errors, but over time it gives her what she is looking for, which is a new direction for her writing, a new voice. One day, an entire story in Italian flashes into her mind, every sentence of it. This never happened when she wrote in English. The story is called "The Exchange," and it is about a translator who "wanted to be another person," not because she is unhappy with her life, which is filled with good fortune, but because she feels a need to know what other possibilities she might contain and whether they are improvements on the version she is familiar with.[45] She loves being alive and has no desire to kill herself, but she does want to "eliminate the signs of her existence," including her husband and her wardrobe, and so she moves alone to a foreign city with no possessions other than a few simple things to wear.[46] Here she lives quietly, with joy.

One day the translator follows a group of women into the apartment of a fashion designer, where a private trunk show is taking place. She enters, although admission is usually by invitation only and the door to the salon is hidden as well as unmarked. The women undress and begin to try on the clothes, which are all black and made to be interchangeable. At the end of the afternoon, the translator decides not to buy anything, although the clothes are beautiful and comfortable. She becomes distressed because she cannot find the sweater she came in. The designer locates *a* black sweater, hidden under a pile of other cast-off garments, but the translator is sure that it is not hers. It is ugly, scratchy, the wrong size. But what can she do? She puts it on and goes home. When she wakes up the next morning she sees the sweater and immediately knows that it was hers all along. Nevertheless, it has been subtly altered—by being lost and found? By being tangled up in the clothes of other women? By the hours that she spent standing in front of a three-way mirror examining herself from every angle? Whatever the reason, the translator decides that she likes this new version of her sweater better than the old one, and takes pleasure in the change.

I don't find it surprising that Lahiri names Ovid's *Metamorphoses* as her favorite book, or that she compares her decision to write in Italian to Daphne's transformation into a laurel tree. In Ovid's poem bodies change only under conditions of acute pressure, usually brought about by trespasses against social or natural law. Recall that Daphne runs not for the pleasure of it, but to avoid being raped by a god. Under similar duress, Io runs from Jove, Actaeon from Diana, Procne and Philomel from King Tereus, and on it goes. People and gods move out of bounds, whether by choice or by accident, and when they collide it becomes possible to exteriorize a form of life that was previously concealed by comfort. "The Exchange" is a gentle variation on these ancient stories of transfiguration, but even here it is clear that the translator is running for her life, just as Lahiri is. Like the black sweater, Italian reveals an "invisible, inaccessible" part of her.[47] Without it, she can neither write nor live.

In 2015, Lahiri sat down with the translator Ann Goldstein at the Center for Fiction in New York City for a public conversation about the Italian novelist Elena Ferrante.[48] Goldstein has translated all of Ferrante's novels into English, as well as *In Other Words*. In the course of their discussion, Lahiri reveals that although she has studied Italian for most of her adult life and dreamed of living in Rome since childhood, it was the experience of reading Ferrante's *The Days of Abandonment* that convinced her to give up English and make the move to Italy. Ferrante's name is never mentioned in *In Other Words*, but her influence is everywhere, beginning with Lahiri's account of the lock that will not open. Very similar scenes, including two children crying in the August heat, take place in *The Days of Abandonment*, which is about a novelist named Olga whose life collapses when her husband leaves her for his teenaged lover. Her hands malfunction—she drops things, breaks things, forgets how to manage keys, telephones, make-up, clothes, her body. She gets locked out of her apartment; another time she gets locked in with a sick child, a dying dog, an infestation of ants, and a recurring hallucination. She sees an abandoned woman from her childhood in Naples, the *poverella*, long dead by suicide, who now follows Olga around, dispensing advice and reminders about household tasks that need to be done.

Gradually, the *poverella* takes on a more interesting project. She sits down at Olga's desk and begins to write in her notebooks, in Olga's own handwriting. Since the births of her children, Olga has been unable to write. Now she begins again, not by summoning her resilience or determination, but by surrendering to the poorest and most despairing part of her mind: the *poverella*. She gets up in the middle of the night and writes page after page, always using the left hand. Only this disobedient hand can "fight fear" and "hold off humiliation," she thinks.[49] The verbs here are misleading. This is not a fight in the ordinary sense of strength against strength. Olga gives in to fear and humiliation just as she gives in to "obscenity" in the opening pages of the novel, deleting her middle-class gentility so thoroughly that she gets down on all fours and says to her neighbor, a near-stranger, "put it in my ass!" and then defecates in the park like a dog.[50]

The left hand knows nothing of decorum or law. The Gospel of Matthew promises that on the Day of Judgment God will tell sinners to take the first left to hell, and even in my parents' generation school children were often prohibited from writing with the sinister hand and forcibly restrained if they did so. My father-in-law, who went to British schools in South Africa, can attest to this. Unfortunately for educators of the 1950s and 1960s, the Gospel of Matthew also suggests that the left hand is the true source of gifts, including love, which also knows nothing of decorum or law. Any gift worthy of the name has to come from the left hand, says Jesus, because it comes from the most secret part of the self.

One might expect this to be a lonely place, but it turns out to be quite crowded. Lahiri's translator meets many women there, and exchanges some aspect of herself with them. Olga meets the *poverella*, and later her neighbor, Carrano, with whom she has traded only insults, accusations, and misguided sexual overtures. And then, quite by coincidence, she attends a concert and discovers that he is a renowned cellist, and that when he plays he is no longer a shambling middle-aged man, but luminous and commanding. She simply does not recognize him on stage, where he radiates vivacity that is felt by everyone in the room. This movement of gift is literalized in the final pages of the novel, where Carrano leaves Olga a series of small presents on her doorstep, each of which restores something she has lost—a hair clip, a button, a lid. She falls in love with him because of what those tokens demonstrate, which is his capacity to knit together the minor bestowals of the everyday with the "intense life" that passes through him on stage, and because of what they promise, which is that as a writer she might be able to do the same.[51]

It is well known that at the beginning of her career, Ferrante made the decision to publish under a pseudonym and to decline interviews or appearances that would expose her identity. Other female writers have chosen to publish under names that conceal their gender, from George Eliot to J. K. Rowling, but Ferrante's aims are different. In a letter to her Italian publisher, written just before the publication of her first novel, *Troubling Love*, she defended her invisibility by explaining that the "intense life" contained in books is "a sort of nighttime miracle, like the gifts of the Befana," a witch-figure in Italian folklore who delivers presents to sleeping children on the eve of the feast of the epiphany.[52] In an interview more than fifteen years later, Ferrante writes that this life is "the product of skill, and that can always be improved. But in large part that energy simply *appears, happens*."[53] Unlike Carrano, Ferrante does not find it possible to invite that energy into the everyday, and neither does Olga, who recovers her sense of propriety and ceases to be haunted by the *poverella*, but then stops writing. She can govern herself or she can live by the left hand, but she cannot do both. There "is no woman who does not make an enormous, exasperating effort to get to the end of the day," writes Ferrante in one of the weekly articles she published in the *Guardian* throughout 2018. We "can't fully be ourselves, don't belong to ourselves," she continues, and therefore must maintain in every moment "a ruthless vigilance" over every aspect of our existence: our bodies, our words, our gestures, our ways of complying with a vast network of rules, both tacit and explicit, and propitiating those who enforce them, including ourselves.[54] So much of Olga is claimed by the roles of mother and woman that there is nothing left of her to sleep so that the Befana can come. It's not an uncommon problem.

For this reason, Ferrante's women erase their tracks. None is quite as successful as Rafaella Cerullo, known as Lila, who is the elusive center of the Neapolitan Quartet, and the fullest expression of the ideas that Ferrante has been exploring since *Troubling Love*. The first thing that we learn about Lila in the Prologue to *My Brilliant Friend*, called "Eliminating All the Traces," is that at the age of sixty-six she has realized her lifelong ambition to disappear—not to commit suicide, or to begin a new life under a different name, but to vanish so completely that nothing of her will ever be found. All of Ferrante's novels are about the attempt to recover a woman who is lost—a mother, a daughter, a friend—and in a sense they are all co-authored by the pressure exerted by that missing person, just as Lila invests Lenù with the power to invent the Neapolitan Novels by withdrawing from life so that she is part of the night, on the side of the gift.

Paradoxically, what characterizes Lila above all is *presence*. Even as a six-year-old, the shoemaker's daughter is the most charismatic child in the impoverished postwar neighborhood where Lila and Lenù grow up. Over a period of six decades, she is the incandescent light to which all the characters in the Neapolitan epic are drawn, from the local pastry maker to the vegetable vendor, the housewives, the professors, the politicians, the union organizers, and the neighborhood Camorrists, the elegant Solara brothers, who spend their murderous lives trying to figure out how to buy her. Everyone agrees that Lila is incurably lawless, but they also agree that she can accomplish things that others cannot even imagine. She is variously described as an alchemist, a holy warrior, a goddess, a fairy, a magician, and a devil, and she energizes almost every commercial and creative enterprise that takes place in the 1500 or so pages of the Neapolitan epic, including the writing of the epic itself, and then arranges her own deliberate disappearance into "one of the many dimensions that we don't know yet but Lila does."[55] Lila is a flesh-and-blood woman, but her presence is otherworldly. There is something magical about her, whether she is the affluent and leisured wife of a successful grocer or a single mother living in two rooms, working eight hours a day emptying pigs' intestines while being groped by her boss, threatened by Fascists, excommunicated by her parents, and afraid that the brutal husband she married at the age of sixteen and then left for another man will find her and cut her eyes out before slitting her throat.

Over the last few years, I've noticed that every time I walk into a national chain bookstore, the volumes of the Neapolitan Quartet are prominently displayed on a table marked "Recommended for Book Clubs." This clever marketing, along with the romantic book covers, is obvious shorthand for "Recommended for Women." I have never seen any of the volumes of *My Struggle* displayed on this table, and I wonder why, given that both Knausgaard and Ferrante are primarily interested in creative power, and that their multivolume epics became global sensations at roughly the same time. Forgive me, I am being disingenuous. I know perfectly well why: the assumption is that a man's struggle to balance domesticity with creativity is of interest to everyone, but a woman's struggle to do the same is of interest only to other women. The other day I was talking to my neighbor, an avid reader and amateur historian, who told me that he is particularly interested in the history of Naples, and has visited the city more than once. I asked him whether he had read the Neapolitan Novels, and he looked at me warily. "Aren't those books mostly about female friendship?" he asked. "No," I snapped. "Absolutely not." I could have said, "Absolutely, yes, just as the *Iliad* is mostly about marital infidelity, the *Aeneid* is mostly about a bad breakup, and the *Oresteia* is mostly about a series of domestic disputes."

Make no mistake, the Neapolitan Novels are not just about the emotional tides of Lila and Lenù's lifelong relationship. They are not just about the social and political struggles of postwar Italy, either. They are also about the creative power of women who gain access to emancipatory zones of being, and this desire is signaled at the very beginning of the series with the epigraph to *My Brilliant Friend*, which comes from Part One of J. W. Goethe's play *Faust*. Professor Faust wants to act and to *feel*—to feel "a new world grow" in him, as he once did in prayer, because a decade of rigorous scholarly research has not shown him what he seeks: the "secret force / [that] Hides in the world and rules its course."[56] Enter Mephistopheles with his blood contract. A glimpse of the secret force does not come cheap, nor without help. If this is true for Goethe, who sends help in the form of divinities and demons, it is equally true for Ferrante, who sends help in the

form of Lila. When I teach *My Brilliant Friend*, I ask my students to track
the number of times the word "secret" is used in association with Lila. We
lose count very quickly.[57] But it doesn't take long for the word to become
attached to Lenù as well, especially in the later volumes of the epic. From
earliest childhood, when she designs a pair of shoes that seem to come from
"some world parallel to ours," Lila is always associated with hidden stores
of vitality, but in her hands that vitality becomes mobile and contagious.[58]
Even I feel it, as a reader. When I come to the end of the final volume in the
series, I immediately feel heartache and homesickness. I crave the company
of these ingenious women. From time to time, I glance over at my bookshelf
just so that I can see the spines of the books in which they live.

Lila is a woman of great fragility as well as ferocity, self-erasure as well
as hyperbolic presence, and in Ferrante's telling, these qualities are in no
way antithetical. Quite the opposite. One of the most discussed aspects of
the Neapolitan Novels, particularly in academic circles, is what Ferrante
calls *smarginatura*, which Goldstein translates as "dissolving margins."
These are frightening episodes in which Lila sees people and things lose
their stable outlines, and in which she too seems to dissolve, "moving for a
few fractions of a second into a person or a thing or a number or a syllable,
violating its edges."[59] As in Ovid's poem, these metamorphoses are always
brought about under the pressure of extreme emotions: Lila's father throws
her out of a window when at the age of ten she begs him to allow her
to continue going to school; her brother Rino and the other men of the
neighborhood exchange gunfire with the Solara brothers at a New Year's
Eve party, endangering everyone's lives; Mount Vesuvius erupts, and all of
Naples is thrown into chaos.[60] Lila is terrified when she sees matter melt into
unstructured energy, and there are times when her own mind collapses so
that she can no longer function. But these episodes also show her the force
that hides within forms that appear to be finished, hardened by custom and
use, and when she is able to expose this force to others she changes the way
they live, the way they think, the way they are.

Lenù's writing is always an attempt to express the intense life that her
friend taught her to see, and she soon decides that academia is no place for
it. As an undergraduate, she gets stalled while working on her thesis, on
Book IV of the *Aeneid*, "The Passion of the Queen," which tells the story
of Aeneas's abandonment of Dido. In the eyes of gods and monarchs, the
Queen of Carthage is a distraction from Aeneas's political destiny, which is
to rule over Italy and to "bring the whole world under law's dominion."[61]
When Aeneas prepares to leave, Dido berates him and begs him to stay, but
he fights "down the emotion in his heart" and gets back in his boat.[62] Lenù
takes a break from her thesis about the conflict between law and emotion to
write her first novel, which is an attempt to evoke "a dark force crouching in
the life of the protagonist, an entity that had the capacity to weld the world
around her," but also to destroy it at will.[63] This force, which so closely

resembles Lila, is the real subject of the story. Beginning in childhood, Lenù applied herself with brutal discipline to the task of becoming an intellectual, studying until midnight and then rising before dawn every day in order to learn to speak in refined Italian rather than in dialect, read books and newspapers, translate Greek and Latin, memorize textbooks, pass exams, write articles, and most difficult of all, to hold her own with people from wealthy and cultured families where these achievements are not considered a heroic repudiation of desperate circumstances, but a basic condition of life, like breathing. But as she grows up, Lenù begins to worry that her hard-won education has taught her to master "words to the point of sweeping away forever the contradictions of being in the world, the surge of emotions, and breathless speech."[64] She fears that she has achieved nothing more than to learn to manipulate scholarly conventions that make it impossible to express what matters most to her: her "bare and throbbing heart."[65]

As a scholar, it is painful for me to contemplate Ferrante's scathing assessment of the intelligentsia in general and academia in particular. None of the educated people in the Neapolitan Novels, including Lenù's aristocratic husband Pietro Airota, a prominent legal scholar, share her belief that one should "learn everything about the world with the sole purpose of constructing living hearts."[66] These people are trying to change the class system, raise the status of women and workers, and wrestle the state out of the hands of criminals, and they do not believe that the heart, whether pulsing on a page or in a human body, has anything to contribute to this important work, nor that there is a mysterious force crouching in their lives, waiting to make or dissolve meaning upon caprice. They believe that the forces at work in the world are fully subject to law's dominion, and they describe them in a jargon-filled voice of authority that puts Lenù to sleep. In her youth, she is intimidated and aroused by their erudition. In adulthood, she is bored by it, and by them. Of everyone she knows, including all the esteemed scholars and intellectuals, she feels that only Lila is able to be fully present within writing, so that when you read her words you hear *her* voice and no one else's.

When asked to comment on all the disappearing girls and women in her novels, Ferrante said, "There are many reasons to disappear. The disappearance of Amalia [in *Troubling Love*], of Lila, yes, maybe it's a surrender. But it's also, I think, a sign of their irreducibility."[67] After Lila vanishes, Lenù worries that she has surrendered to despair, particularly after the disappearance of her beloved four-year-old daughter, Tina. Of all the losses that take place in the final volume of the epic, *The Story of the Lost Child*, this one is by far the most appalling. Tina's body is never found, and no one knows whether she was abducted by strangers, murdered by the Solaras in retaliation for Lila's attempts to expose their criminality, or met with an accident on the neighborhood's busy *stradone*. And then, in the final pages of the novel, Lenù receives a package in the mail. Inside she finds Tina and Nu, the two dolls that six-year-old Lila and Lenù threw into a cellar used by the Camorra as a test of their own courage. When the girls descended into the darkness to recover them, the dolls had vanished. Long before Tina was the name of Lila's daughter, it was the name of Lenù's doll; long before Nu was the name of Lila's doll, it was the name of her own mother, Nunzia. In these dolls, three generations of women are entwined, just as throughout their lives Lila and Lenù always mirror one another; they loved the same man, raised each other's children, borrowed each other's names, and faceted one another's intelligence. The lost dolls are held in dark reserve for decades, like invisible guarantors of bravery, until Lila sends them to her friend, her other self, to prove "that she was well and loved me, that she had broken the confines" of humanity.[68]

When my daughter finished reading *My Brilliant Friend* she had two questions for me: what is a dissolving margin and what happens to the dolls? I explained *smarginatura* as best I could, and then told her that to find out what happens to Tina and Nu she will have to read to the end of the series. I was boring and talked for too long, so she interrupted me in mid-sentence and said, "That's enough, I already know where the dolls went." "You do?" I said, shocked. "Of course," she told me, and then explained: the dolls climbed the stairs out of the basement and stabbed Don Achille, the head of the local Camorra, whose murder shifts the balance of power into the hands of the Solara brothers. This is how you read when you jump between Elena Ferrante and *The Vampire Diaries*. I tell my daughter that there is not a scrap of evidence to support her crazy killer dolls theory, but that I like it anyway. In Ferrante's writing dolls are often surrogate selves, and in this sense alive, but what if they were never lost? Instead they dissolved in the darkness of the basement, and then spent the next sixty years doing whatever they could to shift margins and release energy for the taking. Having assassinated Don Achille, maybe it was Tina and Nu who gunned down the Solaras, decades after they gained control over the neighborhood. And if I credit the dolls with killing, I can also credit them with a lifetime of creating, whispering inspiration from a parallel world into Lila's ear. After she dissolves her own body, it makes sense that she would find the dolls again and restore them to their solid form, sending them back to Lenù like gifts from the Befana. Now Lila can take up their invisible work, and they can help Lenù to tell the story of her vanished friend.

Suddenly I remember a detail: as a child, Lila writes and illustrates a book called *The Blue Fairy*, which Lenù cherishes for many years as evidence of her friend's ability to bring ideas to life. Although we never learn anything about the story this book tells, I recognize the story it refers to: Carlo Collodi's nineteenth-century classic of Italian children's literature, *The Adventures of Pinocchio*, about a puppet who finally, after many entertaining disasters, becomes a real boy. The power to turn wood to flesh is wielded by the Blue Fairy, an immortal child: Lila, Tina, Nu. Pinocchio's transformation from toy to boy is not a metamorphosis, exactly. On the final page of Collodi's tale, Pinocchio emerges from the puppet he once was and then stands back, looking down at the wooden version of himself with derision. The doll somehow generates the living boy; it is no longer animate, no longer able talk and act, but it is still there, like a husk or a shell, or like a model from which the livelier version emerges.[69] Now I'm thinking about Ferrante's dolls in a similar way. I see them as generators not of one little boy, but a force field of women, a secret and composite force, unleashed by Lila and her lost daughter. So I was wrong, there is evidence to support my daughter's theory; enough to satisfy me, in any case.

In the fall of 2016, a news story broke in the global media, claiming to reveal Elena Ferrante's true identity. I will not repeat the name or summarize the evidence here. Google the story if you must, but you'll get nothing from me. Any reader of Ferrante's work will understand that the name changes nothing about the books themselves, because the part of a person that is responsible to the world is not quite the same as the part that meets the Befana. I think this is what Lenù means when, at the end of the Quartet, she realizes that what distinguishes Lila from the other talented people she has known is her "gratuitousness." She "possessed intelligence and didn't put it to use but, rather, wasted it, like a great lady for whom all the riches of the world are merely a sign of vulgarity …. She stood out among so many because she, naturally, did not submit to any training, to any use, or to any purpose."[70] It is true that throughout her life, Lila moves restlessly from task to task—writing stories, designing shoes, setting up a business, organizing a union, programming computers, researching the history of Naples—and that as soon as any aspect of her creativity is claimed by others, she withdraws or collapses. I don't see this as either a waste or a defeat. Whenever a form hardens, Lila detonates it and moves on. Reflecting on his own struggle, Knausgaard speaks of the need "to step out of society, almost out of humanity."[71] As Lenù says, her friend never wanted to commit suicide or start over under an assumed name, but to escape the confines of humanity. Like Ferrante herself, she wants to step into the secret and stay there, sending irreducible life back into the world. Why do we make this so much harder for women? It's a stupid question, I take it back.

* * *

When my father left Canada and moved to London in the mid-1960s, he took temporary lodgings in a rooming house and began to look for a flat. He and my mother had just graduated from high school and she was to join him in a few months, so he needed to find somewhere for them both to live. He heard about a place in the North West of the city, near Primrose Hill, and was told that the landlady, who lived in the house, for some reason charged rents lower than the going rate. My father hurried to the address he was given, 5 Fellows Road, where he met with the owner, an elderly woman named Francesca Mary Wilson, who received him in her living room, which was crammed with books and clearly doubled as a study. After some conversation, she invited him to move into the small apartment located in the basement, although it got far more natural light than might have been expected, thanks to a large bay window overlooking the front garden. Along with this invitation, she issued a caution: while my father was free to move in right away, today if he wished, she had not yet decided whether he would be permitted to stay on as a permanent member of her household, which included four or five other flats. It would take her several months to reach that decision. During this probationary period, she would like to meet with my father for a few hours every Sunday afternoon. At each meeting they would discuss a book, which she would lend him from her personal collection. "Here," she said, pulling a thick volume from a nearby shelf, "you can start with this." It was a copy of *The Idiot*.

It gradually became clear that before she made a final decision about whether to offer him a conveniently located apartment at a reduced rent, my father's landlady did not want to know that he was a quiet and responsible tenant, nor that he was either financially solvent or in particular need; she wanted to know what he thought about the canonical nineteenth- and early-twentieth century novels on the reading list that she had prepared for him. At this point in his life, my father had not yet read a book from cover to cover—any book. He had undiagnosed dyslexia and was expelled from junior high. He then acquired a police record, and eventually attended a high school for the visual and performing arts, where traditional academic subjects were not emphasized. He had moved to London to apply to art school, not university, and in the 1960s there was still a big difference between the two. Nevertheless, he picked up *The Idiot* and accepted the keys to the basement flat. Over the next few months, he had no time to furnish his new apartment or apply to any of the schools where he hoped to be admitted because he spent all of his waking hours sitting on a bare mattress on the floor, devouring 500-page novels and trying to formulate some thoughts about them, or at least keep track of the plots. On Sunday afternoons, he presented himself to Francesca Wilson, book in hand. They sat together and she asked him questions. What did he think of Steinbeck's depiction of the Depression? Some people believed Tolstoy was a more important writer than Dostoevsky. Having recently read them both, what were my father's views on the subject?

When my father describes these colloquies more than fifty years later, his face glows. He shows me how Francesca tilted her head to one side as she listened to him speak, leaning forward and watching him intently, as though his ideas about, say, Tergenev's *Fathers and Sons* were revelatory to her. At the time my father did not know that she spoke fluent Russian, had done relief work during the Russian famine of the early 1930s, and a decade earlier had helped the scholar Nicolai Bakhtin—brother of Mikhail Bakhtin—to emigrate to England from exile in Paris, where she found him penniless. He also didn't know that she spoke at least five languages in addition to Russian, and had written half a dozen books about the thousands of refugees and displaced people she had helped during every major European humanitarian crisis of her lifetime, from the 1919 Vienna famine to the liberation of Dachau. Nevertheless, I think my father sensed that his assessment of Turgenev was not really what mattered to this woman. She had spent her life being interested in strangers, and having now read a few of her books, I see that she constantly talked to the people she helped—on trains, in DP camps, on the streets, and in the hospitals and orphanages that she helped to establish throughout Europe. In her book *Aftermath*, which begins with her arrival in Germany forty-eight hours after the end of the Second World War as Principal Welfare Officer for UNRRA (The United Nations Relief and Rehabilitation Administration), she writes about the importance of remembering that the masses of displaced people flowing through Europe in need of food, shelter, and medical care were comprised of individuals, each with a story that could only be known to someone who spoke their language and took the time to listen.[72]

My parents lived with this remarkable woman for over a decade. It took them some time to begin to understand their good fortune—they were only teenagers at the outset. After I was born, a few years after their arrival at 5 Fellows Road, my mother gave birth to a second daughter, Louisa, whose internal organs were fatally malformed. Shortly after the birth, she was taken away so that my parents would not have to watch or hear her as she died, which took almost a week. At the time, this was believed to be a kindness to parents of a child that could not survive, although it is impossible to imagine the cruelty inflicted on an infant whose senses were unimpaired and must surely have registered the agony of her abandonment. I know that these doctors were kind, because when they learned that my parents could not afford to bury their daughter, they took up a collection and paid for the funeral themselves. A year later my mother had a third, healthy child. She is named Francesca Mary Brittan. On the day of her birth, Philippe Petit performed his high wire walk between the Twin Towers.

For me this is like one of those moments of gratitude in a fairy tale when someone who is invisible or taken for granted surges back into the story. All is dark, empty, and then saturated with presence. Or I picture the way birds suddenly assemble to form a flock that swoops this way and that with such swift choreography that it seems to be a new living thing with its own intelligence. I have learned that this phenomenon is called murmuration, and that it is a defensive maneuver designed to elude a predator, similar to shoaling behavior in fish. Murmuration is a beautiful word, but it is so quiet, so *murmuring*, that it cannot express the explosive velocity of this attempt to survive. And I think that is how both of their Francescas made my parents feel: newly alive. My father says that Francesca Wilson was one of the most important mentors of his life, not because she turned him into a lifelong reader of great novels—she did not—or invited him into a social circle that included Harold Pinter and Lucien Freud, and not because for over ten years she never raised the rent and sometimes tactfully refrained from collecting it, but because she listened to him as though his thoughts mattered deeply to her, for the simple reason that she found other people inherently worthy of generous attention, and apparently believed that a wholehearted if inexpert conversation about *Anna Karenina* was as good a way as any to get a glimpse inside the blind alleys and trick drawers of another's person's mind.

By the time I graduated from high school I too had read all the books on Francesca Wilson's syllabus. This was a requirement in our family, and so were the Sunday meetings in which we gathered to try to express our thoughts. Our purpose was not to learn the techniques of literary criticism, which none of us knew anything about, or to prepare for university, which none of us had yet attended; it was to learn to reveal something of ourselves, as though we lived in a world in which crucial judgments about a person's existence might suddenly hang on an impromptu conversation about Theodore Dreiser. Decades later, when I read Jonathan Rose's monumental book, *The Intellectual Life of the British Working Classes*, I recognized our family's reading habits in his accounts of the "mutual improvement" societies that began in the eighteenth century and flourished well into the twentieth, created by laborers who wanted to educate themselves and one another. I was not surprised to read this: "When mutual improvement alumni graduated to the ancient universities, they were likely to be disillusioned" by the rigid structures and narrow aims of professional intellectualism.[73]

My sisters and I entered the academic humanities, and three of us became professors. Yet for some years now, I have been troubled by the differences between the way writers talk about their work and the way professional scholars do. In the three decades I have now spent in universities, I have never once heard a scholar describe their writing as a bare and throbbing heart, or recommend that an argument should strive to resemble a spirit in its mystery and distinctiveness. When I have chaired my department's graduate programs and taught mandatory seminars on professionalization, I confess that I failed to mention the need to draw the essence of what we know out of the shadows: not the shadows of the archive, but of ourselves. I have also begun to be troubled by how often writers allude to the deadness of academic thought, as Hannah Arendt does in her introduction to a collection of Walter Benjamin's essays, where she accounts for his failure to secure a professorship in Germany by referring to "the customary academic suspicion of anything that is not guaranteed to be mediocre."[74] She says this calmly, as though it were so obvious as to be beyond dispute. I suppose I could overlook this judgment, given Arendt's stratospheric standards of excellence, if I did not hear it echoed in so many places, including my own students.

In a small Honors seminar last year, I assigned David Constantine's short story "The Loss," which is about a prosperous British banker who one day discovers that he is lighter by twenty-one grams. His soul has left his body and flown to one of the outer circles of hell. The loss is devastating, of course, but no one notices it and so he keeps on working and living as best he can. From time to time he crosses paths with other soulless people, who silently acknowledge one another. Aside from the banker, Constantine describes only one other member of the walking dead, and he is a "successful academic:" a Dante scholar, who knows a great deal about the circles of hell and gives our banker a brief lecture on the topic.[75] Here I should mention that in addition to being a celebrated poet, novelist, and translator, Constantine taught modern languages for many years first at Durham University and then at Oxford. There is nothing anti-intellectual or satirical about his work; it tends to be meditative, alert to the buried workings of life and to the rare circumstances in which they rise up to shatter complacent self-awareness. In the final scene of "The Loss," the banker imagines that his head is encased in a thick helmet of ice and that he might need to take a pickax to his face, and particularly to his eyes, in order to "give exit to the tears that were, so he believed, welling up in there, hot melting tears welling up and not allowed to flow."[76]

After more than twenty years of teaching, I am reasonably good at leading a conversation about a piece of writing. I have a sense of where the sightlines are likely to be and how to ask the questions that gradually illuminate the blind spots, just as I know how to listen carefully to the answers, because fresh readers will always see things that I miss, and I want nothing more than to be surprised. When I opened our discussion of "The Loss," I assumed that the primary difficulty would be to make sense of the connection between the soulless international banker and the successful literary scholar, and I gave a preamble suggesting that we should begin with the strangeness of their alliance. After I was done speaking, my otherwise lively class was silent. I looked around at blank faces, but foolishly pressed on, as one does. Finally someone spoke, the conversation flowered, and I realized that for these students there was no shock in the comparison between a global financier and a successful humanities professor. I was asking them to name the obvious: in Constantine's telling, both men value persuasion, measurable achievement, and mastery. Both are willing to subordinate themselves to institutions; both are alienated from their emotions and those of others. Both are, in effect, dead. And isn't it the truth? I tried to conceal my alarm at the ease and speed with which my class reached this consensus.

To be fair, it probably wasn't a consensus. This discussion took place on a dark evening in mid-winter on the North Atlantic seaboard, during that interminable season of the year when nature tries to kill us every day, and I suspect that several people in the room were so tired that they would have preferred to lie face-down in a frigid puddle of slush, or have their skin flayed by a wall of driving sleet, rather than conjure up suitable thoughts about "The Loss." I often felt the same way that term. Nevertheless, the words "I want to write like an amateur," which had been circling around in my head for some time, grew louder. I tried to ignore them. I have spent my life learning to be a scholar; to be an amateur is more dangerous, something I will have to figure out for myself. A friend, to whom I had not mentioned this voice in my head, gave me a copy of Saikat Majumdar's essay, "The Critic as Amateur," in which he distinguishes the critic from the professional scholar like this: "The scholar is defined by his commitment to his archive of study. His subjective sense of self is subordinated to (though not effaced by) this commitment. The critic, on the other hand, celebrates and foregrounds his subjectivity; the archive, in his case, is subordinated to the self, through which it is processed and presented."[77] And of course an amateur is a person who does what they love, and does it in their own way. Majumdar goes on to suggest that "the critic, especially of aesthetic discourse, may have something to gain from a *lack* of scholarship."[78]

This heresy reminds me of Michel de Montaigne, the first amateur, who in the preface to his *Essays* on matters as various as cannibals and clothes, idleness and friendship, warns the reader, "it is myself that I portray." Although a learned man, he often calls attention to the incompleteness of his knowledge and the haphazardness of his methods, allegations confirmed by the translator and editor of my Penguin edition, whose footnotes reveal the places where Montaigne misquotes or misconstrues his sources. There is never a sense that these imperfections mar his writing, because mastery is not his aim and intellect is not his only tool. In Montaigne's hands an essay is an experiment, and its purpose is not just to develop ideas but to capture the vivid particularity of his own way of being in the world. He claims to be the first to address a reader with his "whole being, as Michel de Montaigne, not as a grammarian, a poet, or a lawyer."[79] In my favorite of his essays, "On Experience," he writes, "the lessons we derive from the examples of others will hardly serve to instruct us, if we profit so little from those that come to us from ourselves."[80] He is convinced that his life is good to think with, not just the contents of his library, and so are a growing number of scholars in our own century.[81] A few years after the publication of "The Critic as Amateur," Saikat Majumdar and Aarthi Vadde edited a book-length collection of essays under the same title. Each essay explores what Majumdar and Vadde describe as "the entanglement of passion with knowledge," of messy life with professional learning.[82] At one point they half-jokingly suggest that the collection might have been called "Criticism for the Whole Person," even those elusive twenty-one grams.[83] And they ask the most important question of all: what will happen to scholars in the humanities if we cannot invent ways to speak with our whole selves? Cultural death, I suppose; or obsolescence.

Now I too find that I want to return to the amateur conversations that shaped my early life. More and more, I notice that as I travel through a city, my eye goes to the vacant lots and boarded up houses, anything empty or abandoned. In part, this is nostalgia for my childhood in a neighborhood of broken things, which for me were filled with as much magic as failure. This is testament to the storytelling power of my parents, who every day convinced us that we were like royalty in disguise, gathering our resources unobserved in the hinterland, soon to step forward in shining and undeniable majesty. All around me I saw a dark force crouching in our lives, just as Lenù says, gaining strength and waiting to discharge it—the same force that I felt in myself. Sometimes we broke into buildings that had been reclaimed by the city and slated for demolition, and I felt the same way about them, even though within a day or two they were gone. Now when I walk by an empty lot filled with weeds that heave up the asphalt or split the concrete, I have the uncanny sensation that if I hopped the chain link fence I would vanish as soon as my feet hit the ground, and I stand there for a moment, thinking about how good that would be. I wouldn't disappear forever, just long enough to find what I'm looking for; long enough to forget what I know so that I can feel stupid and alive. Then I'll come back and tell you about it, and maybe you'll find it helpful, if I can find the words and you're still listening.

4

Shame

*He who has absolutely no belongings of any kind around which
social consideration crystallizes does not exist.*

SIMONE WEIL[1]

A few years after the financial crash of 2008 but before the election of Donald
Trump in 2016, I saw a white man in New York City who was sitting on
the sidewalk, head bowed and shoulders slumped, in front of a handmade
sign that read, "Unemployed, Sad, Embarrassed, Ashamed." I grew up in
a place where a lot of people felt this way, although not all of them were
unemployed. There were tidy little homes like the one my father built, and
orderly lives unfolding within them, but there were many other houses with
sagging roofs, half-painted exteriors, or floors with holes in them through
which you could see dirt and sand, like the one in my best friend's kitchen.
An eight-year-old might come out of one of those houses and arrive at the
bus stop to go to school wearing nothing but her older brother's oversized
T-shirt accessorized with her mother's silver stilettos and several knee-length
strands of Mardi Gras beads, no pants or packed lunch. The beach was the
end of the line, and here it was not necessary to pretend that any aspect
of your life was intact. There was a woman I used to see on the bus in the
morning, the mother of one of my sister's friends, and I remember the winter
when the front door to her house blew open and the porch filled up with
snow. There seemed to be no question of shoveling it out or even of closing
the door. She had platinum hair like Debby Harry and a brisk way of sliding
into a double seat behind the driver, where she sat very still looking out the
window as we drove into the city past the slag heaps and the factories. A
few years later she was stabbed to death in the neighborhood, leaving three
young daughters, and at this point in my life I find that I think of her often.
I can't account for the persistent vividness of my memory of her.

When we moved to the beach strip my father's parents came to live with us. They had helped to finance the building of our house, so I suppose it's more accurate to say that we lived with them. Either way the arrangement became unendurable, so they bought the cottage next door, where my grandfather faced each day in a three-piece suit and my grandmother raged. Like most people who grew up during the Depression, she had to turn her mind early to how to make a living, and she had spent her life working to put distance between herself and the crumbling disarray of a place like this. As a teenager her first plan was to become a mortician, because funeral parlors always had steady work, but when it turned out that she was not strong enough to lift a dead body, she apprenticed herself to a hairdresser instead. She was disappointed, but I've always been relieved that I had a grandmother who knew how to trim my hair and pierce my ears rather than embalm my corpse.

When my grandmother bought her first salon, in the 1940s, she named it *The Astoria*, after the Waldorf-Astoria Hotel in New York, which was the most opulent place she knew. Like all beauty parlors, hers was a place where women came to spin a dream. For some, that dream involved nothing more than tightening the rivets on a suit of armor, especially in those decades of the mid-century when a woman's hair resembled a helmet; yet I'm sure there were other women who left my grandmother's hands feeling like a turned kaleidoscope. In either case, my grandmother was proud of the upscale clientele she built over the years, and of her own ability to understand what these women wanted from her even when they did not. "*Never* agree to dye a woman's hair red in February," she told me firmly. "She'll only come back in March furious with you." I don't have any use for this advice in my current line of work, but I do bear it in mind, especially in February.

At the height of my grandmother's career she owned five salons, although I never heard her call them that. She always referred to them as "the shop." The James Street shop. The Main Street shop. Beauty was a business and she was a merchant, along with my grandfather, who did most of the interior design work. He had wanted to go to art school, but after his father was committed to a psychiatric hospital, where he soon died, my grandfather got a job at one of the biggest steel mills in the country. In this unpromising environment, he too began to spin a dream. For forty-five years he travelled to the mill each day in a suit and tie, carrying his lunch in a brief case, not a metal domed-top lunch box like the other men used. When he got to work, he changed into his boiler suit and reported for duty on the shop floor. Some of the other men found this behavior laughable and said so, but according to my grandfather, they slowly came around to his view that a steel worker need not be slovenly or undignified or use foul language. Instead he could dress with refinement and use polysyllabic words. It was my grandfather's idea to display an open copy of the concise Oxford English Dictionary in our living room on a wooden lectern ordinarily used for a bible. He liked words and encouraged us to like them too, and he had such strong ideas about optimal silhouettes and ideal hemlines that he eventually opened a boutique for women's clothes in the same building as my grandmother's flagship salon. By night, he worked at the mill; by day, he designed dresses and helped my grandmother to run her beauty business. It's not clear to me when he slept.

As a child, I thought my grandfather was dressing for the white-collar job he must have wanted. He became a foreman, but he never got a job in management and he never put anything in his briefcase except a tuna fish sandwich. That was his choice, I later learned. His own father had worked in Stelco's offices before his psychiatric collapse, and from the beginning my grandfather was offered positions within the company that would have allowed him to sit behind a desk and wear a suit and tie all day. He refused. By working the night shift as a laborer, he kept his days free for art—clothes, interior design, painting—and he put distance between himself and the memory of his tyrannical father. Yet by mid-life, my grandfather too had become a tyrant, a violent alcoholic who terrorized his family to such a degree that my grandmother stashed empty bottles around the house in case she had to knock him out, and my father learned how to barricade himself against physical attack or fight back. When my father turned seventy, we organized a family party at a stylish new restaurant opposite the original *Astoria*, which has long been shuttered, and over lunch he told me how he sometimes hid there all night to escape my grandfather's rampages at home. These were the years when he was beginning to siphon money out of the businesses that he helped to build, secretly taking out loans and mortgages that my grandmother did not discover until there was very little equity left. The bank did not require her signature on any of these loan documents or inform her of their existence, and the police did not believe her when she told them that her husband was trying to kill her.

By the time we moved to the beach, my grandfather was sober. Retired from the steel company, he now taught portraiture and still-life painting to adults, including the residents of a retirement facility for nuns, who regarded him as a local treasure and soon included him in many of their leisure activities, even though he believed that the dictionary contained the true gospel. My grandmother could not bear his transformation from scourge and spendthrift into twinkly old man flanked by the wimpled Sisters of Mercy. Everyone admired my charismatic grandfather, but it was largely his fault that she now lived in a winterized cottage at the scrag end of town, downwind from the smokestacks, a few feet from the train tracks, and directly underneath industrial powerlines, when some of the women she had trained in the arts of gentility had married pennywise men and lived in spacious brick homes in the city's leafy old neighborhoods, or in generously proportioned modern houses in the new suburbs. *Her* former apprentices, whose prospects she had helped to transform! One of them told me that until she knocked on my grandmother's door, aged sixteen and desperate for a job, she had never seen a woman wear a tailored dress and heels in her own home on an ordinary week night when she was not even expecting visitors. Half a century later, she had not forgotten the shock of it. First the opened door, and then the studied elegance of my grandmother, who had the power to offer a young woman a new life.

When my grandmother lost that power she became vicious. My grandfather took us out for ice cream while wearing a straw boater and coordinating ice-cream suit cut from blue-striped shrunken seersucker, à la Tom Wolfe, and she stepped into the role of domestic terrorist that he had vacated. Over the years, she repeatedly brought everyone in the family to tears by the skillful cruelty of the comments that she pretended to offer as sage and loving advice for how you might fix up the shambles of your failed life, or mend the cracks in your broken character. She turned on my mother and me first. Her attacks always began with a sunny tone and an inviting smile, as though everything she was about to say was intended to be kind. Then her lips hardened and her eyes froze. The light in the room shifted, exposing her teeth as sharp protrusions of bone, and her lacquered nails as talons. Sometimes she poked me with them as she told me how stupid I was. "Dumb, dumb, dumb," she would whisper, one of her pink nails beating a tattoo against my temple. Even at the age of twelve or thirteen it was clear to me that she had forfeited whatever place in the world she once held, and that it was now mine for the taking.

On the first anniversary of my grandmother's death, I had a dream in which she approached me with outstretched hands, which I ignored. I put my own hands on her shoulders, gave her a very sharp shake, and said, "It's time for you to die now." My father says she hated me because of her six granddaughters I am most like her, and that she loved me for the same reason. As a child I didn't understand how love and hate could be so close, although I understand now. It's true that I have her white-blonde hair and some of her gestures, and I do believe in the magic of a beautiful dress, but these are superficial similarities. In truth I see the legacy of my grandparents in both of my parents—my mother by affinity rather than inheritance, of course—and in all my sisters. We are the kind of people who one August instantly agreed that the best way to celebrate my mother's birthday that year would be to host a party in which all the guests would be invited to borrow from her closet and jewelry box and come dressed *as* her, down to her signature graphic stroke of liquid black eyeliner on the upper lid, which she has been wearing since the age of fifteen, and her beloved beaded hoop earrings, which she collects by the dozen. When my mother arrived at this surprise party she was greeted at the front door by my grandfather, aged eighty, who was wearing one of her ankle-length floral skirts, an off-the-shoulder white eyelet blouse, and a nametag that read, "Hello! My Name is Cora."

Why do we love this sort of thing? It's got something to do with the sensation of being here but not here, myself but also some other version of myself that might include a version of you, which together open onto glimmering depths where it is impossible to feel trapped or small. I imagine that this is the billowy feeling that my grandfather was chasing when he shaped a life of contradictions and quick changes, and that it is the feeling my grandmother lost in the last decades of her life when she scarcely left her bedroom and made it her business to inform all of us that we were too damaged or inept to know what opportunity looked like. During one especially dismal period, we gave her a broomstick as a birthday gift. It was the kind of joke that my grandmother would once have enjoyed, because it would have reminded her that she was powerful and everyone knew it. This time the joke did not land, and the temperature in the room became hypothermic.

In giving my grandmother a broomstick we told her what we thought of her, but we also inadvertently revealed what she thought of us. If she was a witch, we had helped to make her one. I'm sure that's how she saw it. At an age when she was testing her strength against dead weight, my three sisters and I were encouraged to pursue our dreamy interests in novels and photography and eighteenth-century keyboard instruments, and no one ever asked us how we planned to make a living. Because of where and when and who we were born—agreeable white girls with excellent test scores—we went on to earn eleven university degrees in three countries, almost entirely at the expense of taxpayers and private endowments. We were nurtured by public healthcare and education, by revised banking and policing practices, and we were not grateful. We gave no more thought to these advances than to indoor plumbing and electricity. We did not understand what it meant that our grandmother had willingly employed young women with children born out of wedlock, "fallen women," in years when those words did not reek of mothballs but of fatal scandal, or that later in her life she opened her house for months at a time to teenage girls who for various compelling reasons could no longer go home, including our own mother. We did not recognize our grandmother as one of the wise women who quietly brings new life into being; and so, like the thirteenth fairy, she withdrew her support and cursed us all.

In her ninth decade, she announced that she was done being a wife, mother, and grandmother, and no longer wanted to be addressed by those titles or to carry out any of the responsibilities associated with them. In her tenth decade, she stood firm. We were not welcome to visit her without making an appointment in advance, even though through her front window we could see her sitting alone. She might be drinking a glass of whisky while doing the cryptic crossword, her hair in an elaborate chignon. Whenever I called to make a booking she greeted me with the frosty tone of voice you use on a telemarketer. She wished only to be herself, Mary Aylard. I don't know whether my grandmother was sad, embarrassed, and ashamed like the man I saw sitting on the sidewalk in New York. I do know that she was angry, and that she devoted much of her solitude to devising increasingly bizarre money-making schemes that no one in our family had the aptitude or inclination to bring to fruition, which enraged her even further. Anger is often the first line of defense against shame, although it's possible that my grandmother would have been angry under any circumstances. She lived with grievances deeper than any I have ever felt, including an abusive mother and the sudden death of an infant daughter. No matter how many of her sorrows I list or how deeply I study them, there will always be a region of darkness around my grandmother, as there is a region of darkness around me, because that is what it means to be a person.

Often when I'm talking one of my sisters will interrupt to tell me how much I sound like our grandmother. The older I get, the more it happens. "You looked just like grandma when you said that," they tell me. "That was exactly the kind of thing she would say." We pause for a moment, and I press for details, but I never get any. This is a woman to whom we gave a broomstick. Do I want to be like her? Do I have a choice? "Be more specific," I say. "Is it the words or the pitch of my voice?" "Is it my facial expressions or my intonations?" My sisters just shrug and smile, and I understand: it's everything. If she comes to me in a dream again I will not ignore her outstretched hands or tell her that it is time for her to die. Now that I am older I can begin to be faithful to her, but only because I know that I will never have to see her again, and also that this is exactly the kind of thing she would say.

* * *

At the end of the Depression and the beginning of the refugee and humanitarian crises created by the rise of fascism across Europe, Simone Weil wrote, "he who has absolutely no belongings of any kind around which social consideration crystallizes does not exist." Belongings are one of the ways in which a human being becomes visible as a person, in the fullest sense. This is obvious in the case of gifts, whose purpose is always to clarify where people stand in relation to each other, the gods, and the ancestors. In the indigenous cultures of South America, gifts arouse "the greatest human passions" and expose "the very nature of being a person," argues the anthropologist Michael Taussig.[2] The same is true of consumer cultures, and of those profane things we buy with overburdened Visa cards and lines of credit. Even Marcel Mauss believed that "things sold still have a soul."[3] Granted, he was writing about objects handcrafted by rural French artisans using heirloom techniques that predated Napoleon, but even in the era of Walmart and Dollarama, his point stands: things are made by people, with the resources of this earth, and they change life itself, especially if they end up in landfill or an ocean trash gyre. We yearn to adorn ourselves so that within the brief span of our strange lives there are moments when everyone can see that we are noble and sacred, or at least fully human, no matter that the adornment in question is not a priest's white robes or a king's purple raiment, but a pair of shoes bought on sale or a house whose doors are tightly affixed to their hinges. In this way we push against the limitations of what we are given or struggle to preserve it, sometimes with a family costume party or a visit to the beauty parlor, but other times with brutality so extreme that it reorganizes history for centuries.

There is a moment in Greta Gerwig's debut film *Lady Bird* that made me gasp in recognition. A woman named Marion berates her teenage daughter for throwing her school uniform on her bedroom floor, where it is sure to crumple by morning. "You can't look like a rag because that makes us look like rags," Marion yells.[4] Her daughter only hears the anger in her voice, but I hear the panic too. The film opens with mother and daughter driving back to their modest home in Sacramento while listening to an audiobook of *The Grapes of Wrath*, so we know that poverty is on Marion's mind, and perhaps in her history, given that Steinbeck's novel is about the mass migration to California of people who lost their houses and farms during the Depression. Now it is 2002, the new dot-com economy is deflating, and Lady Bird's father has lost his job, along with the family's unsteady foothold in the middle class. "Some of your friends' fathers could employ your father and they won't do that if it looks like his family is trash," Marion says as she tells her daughter to pick up her uniform and hang it up nicely.[5] Like my own mother, she spends a good deal of time in thrift stores and in front of a sewing machine, crafting appropriate formal wear for her ambitious daughter. To relax, Marion and Lady Bird like to attend viewings of houses for sale in the rich neighborhoods, where they marvel at the furniture and table settings. I think of my grandmother, holding court in her favorite chair, which was custom upholstered in plum velvet secured along the frame by shining brass studs.

In the final scene of Gerwig's film, Lady Bird is standing in tears outside the church of St. John the Divine in New York City. We can hear the choir singing in praise and worship. At Lady Bird's insistence, her parents have refinanced their house to help pay her excruciatingly expensive tuition at a selective liberal arts college, although her father is still unemployed. She calls her parents on the cell phone they bought her and identifies herself by her given name, Christine. "Thank you," she says, "thank you."[6] For much of the film she is ashamed of her parents, with their clapped-out car and their house in a shabby suburb of a second-tier town, and terrified that these limitations will trap her in a life that cannot match the inner spaces of her heart and mind. Her mother is infuriated by her daughter's demands and by her scorn for everything she has been given, including her name. The rift between them deepens, and Marion struggles to express her love for the daughter who was born years after she had stopped hoping for a biological child, a child who came to her as though from within the pages of a fairy tale. Only now, as Christine's horizons are opened by a cross-country move and access to the elite education that confirms her special potential, can she begin to feel and give thanks for these bequests.

After I saw *Lady Bird*, I read an interview in which Gerwig cites Simone Weil as an influence, and this made sense to me.[7] So many stories and experiences attest to the truth of Weil's meditations on the quality of the attention that we direct at other people, including ourselves. At around the same time, I was reading the German writer Jenny Erpenbeck's novel *Go, Went, Gone*, which follows the lives of refugees from several African countries as they try to navigate the laws that govern their ability to live and work in Berlin, a city that in recent years has done more than any other to shelter people in flight from countries that are no longer habitable because of war or environmental damage. As they wait for their asylum cases to be reviewed, the men live in tents in Alexanderplatz, a public square that until the Wall came down was located in the Russian zone of the German Democratic Republic. Like her protagonist, a recently retired classics professor named Richard, Erpenbeck was raised in the East Berlin of the GDR, and the wisdom of her novel comes in part from her ability to connect the twenty-first century refugee crisis in Europe with the internal displacements of the last century, when her own family involuntarily became citizens of a new country that was created by military conquest and then, some forty years later, dissolved almost overnight.

In the West, we tend to remember the fall of the Berlin Wall as a triumph. In her fiction and in her life, Erpenbeck is equally alert to what was lost, especially hope for an alternative to capitalism. Despite the violence of the GDR, it was a "mode of being," and although Richard and his friends still marvel at their freedom of movement and their buying power, they also mourn the loss of hopes that were inseparable from the daily constraints that once held their lives together.[8] "That's another thing he could write about sometime," thinks Richard, "the gravitational force that unites lifeless objects and living creatures to form a world."[9] "Has time come to a standstill?" he wonders as he contemplates a towering fountain built by the Soviets, "Is there anything left to wish for?"[10] When the refugees in Alexanderplatz stage a hunger strike beside a placard that reads, "*We become visible*," Richard knows that this is a fact as well as a plea.[11] We come to exist within a field of attention, and these men live outside its vanishing points.

How to change this? Like J. M. Coetzee, Erpenbeck reaches for ancient traditions of gift. Richard undertakes to help some of the refugees, visiting them every day in their new lodgings and eventually inviting a few men to live in his home and arranging for others to live with his friends. Retired and widowed, he has time for these men: time to listen to their stories over a period of several months, time to come to know them as more than ciphers of agony, time to give them the uncalculated attention that allows them to become visible. Richard discovers that they know as little about the history of Berlin as he knows about their own countries of origin. He drives down a street in the former East with a young man from Burkina Faso, Rufu, and sees familiar remnants of the Reich, a monument to the Soviet "liberation" of Berlin in which 80,000 Russian soldiers died and countless German women were raped, and traces of the Wall and its armored watchtowers where soldiers shot fugitives trying to return to the West. Rufu sees none of this. He looks at the passing landscape and says, "Beautiful."[12] He has never heard of the Wall. The name Hitler means nothing to him.

"We're not giving away anything for free," says the German media, irate at the notion that men like Rufu are reliant on state charity. The elderly lawyer who represents many refugees pro bono laments that Germans believe the law to be strong only when it is "unrelenting and hard as iron."[13] "Zero tolerance" is another way to say this. The lawyer reminds Richard that in the first-century *Germania*, the Roman senator Tacitus praised Teutonic generosity to strangers. Again like Coetzee, Erpenbeck acknowledges the dangers as well as the necessity of bending the law to make space for exceptions. She writes about a refugee from Niger named Osarobo who becomes friends with Richard and in desperation may have broken into his house to steal whatever money and valuables he could find. Instead of feeling angry or betrayed, Richard imagines that Osarobo's soul is "now flying out into the universe, flying somewhere where there are no longer any rules … completely and irrevocably alone."[14] He weeps for him as he wept at his wife's funeral.

Erpenbeck tries to imagine an attitude to refugees that is not based on guilt or moral obligation and does not calculate value exclusively in relation to GDP. To do this she draws on Homer and Hesiod, Tacitus and Seneca, the Bible and fairy tales, sources in which gifts are never reducible to material wealth and a person who comes to you empty-handed may well transform your life. These are difficult ideas to put into practice in the secular democracies of the twenty-first century, particularly because most of the men Erpenbeck writes about are from former European colonies. Here the gift has a far less gracious history than in Greek and Roman antiquity. When Portuguese merchants first began trading with the peoples of coastal West Africa in the fifteenth century, they gave the name fetish (*fetisso*) to the strange things that people wore close to their bodies and would not sell at any price. These things were gifts, probably the kind that the anthropologist Annette Weiner calls "inalienable possessions," which must at all costs be kept "transcendent and out of circulation" because they open the pathways to the ancestors and divinities.[15] Without them a person has no social or metaphysical substance. Frustrated and a little afraid, the Portuguese got back in their boats and went home, importing fetishism as a byword for illness and error in the modern European imagination. Hence we have Marx's analysis of the value transfer that makes commodities conceal the workers who made them, which he called commodity fetishism, and then Freud's explanation of the libidinal transfer that makes objects (or body parts) stand for bodies: sexual fetishism. In every case, attention is misdirected or blocked and the human being disappears.[16]

In the history of modern colonialism, gifts never revealed presence. They denied or tried to control it. When in 1770 the distinguished cartographer Captain James Cook steered the *Endeavour* into a place whose marvelous fauna will earn it the name Botany Bay, on the coast of the continent that will come to be known as Australia, he waited for the surf to quiet and then assembled a landing party and rowed ashore to offer the native inhabitants some trinkets.[17] The scene could be taking place in any of the British colonies, at any moment of first contact, but what happened next was unprecedented: for the first time in Cook's long career he encountered people who had no interest in anything he had to give them. It was not that the Aborigines were bargaining for more or better gifts, which would have been understandable and easily remedied. When Cook found his first offerings untouched on the ground after two days, he responded by leaving things "of somewhat more value," including cloth, mirrors, combs, and beads.[18] The Aborigines left them in a heap, along with the clothes that the ship's botanist, Joseph Banks, had tried to give them. In their journals, Banks and Cook record these failed transactions in detail and with mounting distress. Both are mystified by the indifference of the Aborigines to everything they are given, their refusal to reciprocate, and the fact that they appear to want absolutely nothing from the European visitors other than their speedy departure. Both write that the Aborigines have "no idea of traffic, nor could we communicate any to them."[19] Cook concludes that they are "like other animals," in part because they do not wear clothes or live according to any system of social organization that he can discern, but also because "they did not touch a single article of all that we had left in their huts."[20] Nakedness and disorganization suggest animality, but the inability to take an interest in European goods confirms it.

Before both of Cook's subsequent expeditions to the South Pacific in 1772 and 1776, he was pressed by the British Admiralty to "distribute among the Inhabitants such Things as will remain as Traces and Testimonies of your having been there."[21] Why? Because if he cannot persuade the Aborigines to pick up his gifts, he fails to claim New Holland as a British colony. Each European nation claimed legal possession of foreign lands and peoples by enacting distinctive public rituals, and unlike their rivals, the British did not rely principally upon speeches, declarations, processions, or religious icons to export their authority. They relied upon household objects.[22] The Aborigines quickly figure out that the best way to get rid of their unwanted visitors is to set those objects on fire, and they begin the long process of trying to burn the newcomers off the land.[23] With the taste of smoke on his tongue,

Cook gathers his crew and boards the *Endeavour*. Before sailing away, he claims "the whole eastern coast, from latitude 38° to this place, latitude 10 1/2° S" with the name "POSSESSION ISLAND."[24] As a result, in 1786 the government of Prime Minister William Pitt will decide that the colony can do no more than serve the Empire as a secluded prison for criminals and dissidents, and that there is no need to negotiate a single treaty with its native inhabitants. The only wealth that Cook ever succeeds in bringing home is a name: one adjective, a noun, five syllables, and sixteen letters. POSSESSION ISLAND is the gift that the Aborigines refused to give in exchange for Cook's, and the British decided that a place where possessions had to be made from words could safely be declared *terra nullius*, land belonging to no one recognizable as human.[25] Where there is nothing there is no one.

For the next 200 years, the British try to force Aboriginal peoples to wear the same clothes as settlers, buy the same furniture, eat the same food, use the same tools, and relinquish their gift economies for private property and commodities. In the attempt to alter the habits of the body and transform consciousness, no physical detail was too trivial for study or legislation. In early nineteenth-century Tasmania, a missionary named George Robinson required the Aboriginal people who lived on his reserve to practice using money between 10 a.m. and noon each Thursday using decommissioned British coins.[26] In mid-nineteenth century Victoria, a missionary named Dr. Thomson recommended the following cure for nomadism: habituate Aboriginal children to shoes and their soft feet will encourage them to settle down.[27] In his 1939 New Deal, John McEwen, Federal Minister for the Interior, promised that Aborigines would be granted full citizenship when they demonstrated a willingness to sleep inside a house and fill it with furniture. His chief advisor, Adolphus Peter Elkin, expressed a fervent desire that they learn to fold their clothes.[28] This material evangelism prevailed even in places where settlers encountered people who were "deeply embued with the spirit of trade," as David Livingstone wrote during his mid-nineteenth-century missionary travels through the British and Portuguese colonies of Southern and West Africa.[29] When Anthony Trollope visited South Africa in the 1870s, he suggested that the key to civilizing African boys lay in teaching them to build square tables.[30] Nearly a century later, urban planners in Johannesburg believed that by moving from round houses into square ones Africans would more readily embrace private property.[31]

Put on a pair of shoes and you're no longer a nomad. Lie down to sleep in a rectilinear bedroom and wake up with a savings account. In the years that I spent reading the diaries of British colonists in Southern Africa and the South Pacific, this was the kind of magical thinking that fascinated me. The widespread belief was that accessories, furniture, and architecture can change not just how someone lives, but who they are. It didn't take long for despoiled people to understand that this logic might be reversible: if you show people how you live, they might change their minds about who you are. On the whole, they did not. In the first half of the twentieth century, many Southern Africans, including the African leaders of newly formed workers' unions, pointed out that because they owned and used the same things as white people, from teapots to horsehair sofas to shoes and waistcoats, they should be paid the same wages and afforded the same political rights.[32] African miners often used bits of scrap metal to sculpt the bicycles, airplanes, and houses that they saw in Johannesburg, not because these toys represented the sum of their ambitions, but because they wanted a larger share in the economy that produced them.[33] Apartheid was designed to make that impossible.

In the early 1980s, the American anthropologist James Ferguson was doing fieldwork in Lesotho, where he watched an older man build a rectangular house of exactly the kind that nineteenth- and early twentieth-century colonists tried to force his ancestors to live in. "Why do you want to build an expensive and impractical house instead of a traditional Sesotho one?" Ferguson asked. The man responded by posing a series of questions about the size of Ferguson's own family home in the United States. He confessed with some discomfort that it had about ten rooms. "That is the direction we would like to move in," the Sesotho man concluded.[34] Years later, Ferguson returns to this conversation to argue that the building of a European-style house "was a powerful claim to a chance for transformed conditions of life—a place-in-the-world, a standard of living, a 'direction we would like to move in.'"[35] What is really at stake is the "right to be connected, noticed, and attended to" as a fully participatory member of the modern world.[36]

Albert Luthuli, one of the founders of the African National Congress, wrote that under apartheid the Black man's home "is the white man's garbage can."[37] Others called it the white man's second-hand shop, junkyard, backyard, barnyard, or toy store. Everyone from Black leaders to ordinary people described being relegated to a world of broken-down things that turned them into gleaners or animals.[38] The tribal homelands to which the apartheid government tried to deport all Africans who were considered economically disposable— the so-called "surplus people"—looked like today's refugee camps and migrant detention centers. Photographs and verbal descriptions always emphasized their emptiness. They were filled with people but nearly void of buildings, objects, or opportunities to acquire them. And how often has a camera or a pen captured the story of a family carrying its dwindling store of battered possessions from one place to another, or trying to improvise a shelter from salvaged scrap?[39] Again and again, these images reveal that although desperate places are crowded with people, there is nothing to see. Stripping away property and infrastructure makes people more visible, and starkly so, but destitution has always been the mark of the outcast. Writing about Zimbabwe's civil war and economic collapse, particularly after the violence brought about by the election of

2008, the novelist NoViolet Bulawayo describes a shantytown filled with people whose houses were bulldozed and livelihoods destroyed. Many are university-educated members of the former middle class. Now they live in tin shacks, their children are starving, and they are no longer "real people" in other people's eyes or in their own.[40]

James Ferguson calls this "asocial inequality." He writes about the invisibility felt by the poor and unemployed in the former colonies of southern Africa, many of whom will never find stable waged labor in their lifetimes. If social inequality "implies a common membership within a 'society,' and relations of inequality within those members," then asocial inequality describes people who do not exist in any but the most bureaucratic sense, have no place in the economy, and are willing to trade this anonymity for subjugation.[41] "A great deal of poor people's labour," writes Ferguson, involves "trying to convert asocial inequality into the social kind" by "trying to strike up—or assert, or reassert—a social and personal relationship (even a highly dependent one) with those better off than themselves."[42] By way of illustration, he tells the story of a white American friend visiting Johannesburg who was shocked and embarrassed by the steady stream of African men who called him *Baas* and offered to perform some small task in exchange for a tip. It's not just the need for income that is being expressed here, although that need is real. There is also a need to be recognized for performing a service, no matter how minimal. Even in rich countries, panhandlers often want more than money, which is one of the reasons why they make most people uncomfortable, including me. Dropping coins into a cup or a hand is far less demanding than making eye contact or conversation. Recently, I gave a few dollars to a man collecting change from passengers in cars stopped at a red light. He looked at me intently and said several times, "You have a good heart, ma'am." The man needs my money, but he also needs to strike up a conversation and assert a bond, however weak and ritualized. For a moment I look back at him, although in truth I would rather not. Then the traffic light changes, and I drive away.

To some degree, Ferguson's argument that the desire for belonging is more powerful than the desire for autonomy is specific to the history of southern Africa, where social identity has long been understood to be contingent on networks of relationships, and where formal employment, even under apartheid, was often inextricable from patronage.[43] But his broader claim is that asocial inequality is a growing global problem, not a regional or even postcolonial one, and that relief efforts and government programs that attempt to address it only through financial aid do not understand the loneliness at the heart of extreme poverty, especially that of people who have travelled far from their homes to look for safety and work. If it is humiliating to call a white man *Baas* and beg to wash his car for spare change, it is even more debilitating to be paid by the state to do nothing at all.

Some governments have considered implementing a Basic Income Grant (BIG) or Universal Basic Income (UBI) to address what South Africa's former Minister for Social Development, Zola Skweyiya, called a "deep social crisis ..., a time bomb of poverty and social disintegration [which] has the potential to reverse the democratic gains made since 1994."[44] The need to create a basic or universal income for all citizens is gaining traction among some economists and politicians even in affluent democracies with robust social infrastructure, including public health care and tertiary education. Beginning in 2014, the German entrepreneur Michael Bohmeyer crowdfunded an unconditional Basic Income pilot project that gave a group of randomly selected Germans one thousand Euros a month for a year, regardless of their financial circumstances, and then studied how this gift affected them. No matter what they did with the money or how much they needed it in the first place, Bohmeyer found that all the recipients reported that "the monthly payments just made them feel better." He concluded that an unconditional stipend tells people, "We are all equally worthy of existing," and, "We as a society believe you are OK."[45] Yet in some cases, the people who stand to benefit most from the BIG are resistant to it. Ferguson speculates that in South Africa some of the hesitation is linked to the proposal to make the grants directly available via bank machines equipped with iris and fingerprint scanners, which would be convenient and reduce the risk of fraud, but also eliminate even the most rudimentary human contact. In the case of people who already feel disposable, this reduction of the individual to biometric data seems to produce what the Italian philosopher Giorgio Agamben calls "identity without the person," a merely bureaucratic and utilitarian identity.[46] Even if the BIG were disbursed face-to-face, it's not clear that it would make the recipients feel that their value as human beings was being acknowledged. As Ferguson argues, Western liberalism tends to equate both state and individual sovereignty with self-sufficiency—hence the foundational importance of national declarations of independence—which can make it difficult to understand that what the world's most vulnerable people seek is not just to be financially self-sufficient, but to be "connected, noticed, and attended to."[47]

This is true of less vulnerable people too, as Michael Bohmeyer's experiment suggests. In the mid-1980s, the British historian Carolyn Kay Steedman published a landmark study of the white working class, *Landscape for a Good Woman*, in which she writes about her own postwar childhood in order to challenge the existing frameworks for understanding the aspirations of poor people in England. Steedman's mother was born into several generations of textile mill workers in Lancashire, and before the Second World War she fled south to London, in search of education and a higher standard of living. She never managed to obtain either, although her clever daughter did. Steedman emphasizes that her mother's aspirations centered on specific things, especially clothes: a New Look skirt, which

required twenty yards of fabric at a time when fabric was so scarce that
some postwar brides fashioned their wedding gowns out of rain coats; a
particular pair of suede heels. "Politics and cultural criticism can only find
trivial the content of her desires," writes Steedman, "and the world certainly
took no notice of them."[48] The unobtainable New Look skirt was not just
a symbol of glamorous postwar femininity, but proof that a woman was
included in the society that produced it. Steedman attributes her mother's
lifelong shame and rage to her feeling of exclusion from that society, from its
"structures of care and affection," and from all that is good in the world.[49]
I think of Lady Bird and Marion scouring the thrift shop for the right dress
to wear to meet her affluent boyfriend's family, and of my best friend, who
grew up in a rented house with four rooms and a hole in the kitchen floor
and now buys eighty dollar lipsticks, which we examine with the fascination
usually afforded to sacred relics. Why exactly is a tube of pigmented resin
this expensive, and why does a professor of economics who understands
pricing and scarcely wears makeup choose to buy it?

I can ask myself a similar question, given my modest collection of
immodestly priced shoes, including the heeled lavender spats and the
400-dollar floral suede sandals, which draw admiring stares and comments
from strangers everywhere I go. These shoes come from my favorite designer,
John Fluevog, who promises "Unique Soles for Unique Souls." I appreciate
the frankness of this appeal to metaphysical vanity. He names most of his
shoes after real women, groups them together into "Families," and embeds
inspirational messages in the soles and inner linings. "Old Friends Are Good
Friends," says Erika, the updated saddle shoe in black and ivory with hot
pink detailing, member of the Fellowship Family. At an Emergency Medical
Clinic the other day, Erika engaged three people in extended conversation
with me and then with one another.

"If you don't buy these boots you'll regret it for the rest of your life," a
friend once told me with fevered intensity, having chased me down the street
and dragged me back into the store I had just walked out of. She is not a
frivolous woman. It was the morning of my sister's wedding, I had things
to do, and I couldn't afford those sensational red lace-up ankle boots even
though they were on sale. I bought them anyway, and every time I wear
them they make good on the message on their sole: "Your Love Makes Me
Sing." It really does, Mr. Fluevog. During one deeply exhausted period in my
life, I ended every day by looking at these and other shoes online, and had
several avid dreams in which I pursued John Fluevog through dark streets,
and in one instance through the hallways of a hospital emergency room, to
discuss the retroflexion of a heel or the contouring of a T-strap.

When I wake in the morning from this or any other dream, the first thing
I see is one of my mother's many paintings of jewel-like shoes. She pictures
them hanging on a washing line, or perched on a pedestal, or standing
magisterially alone in the corner of a room where they can command all

the attention. The ones in the painting that hangs on my bedroom wall are golden, in styles spanning several hundred years, and they grow on the branches of an ornate golden tree that glows against an indigo sky. These shoes are *alive*. They were not built by a human or elfin shoemaker on a wooden last, but by rain and photosynthesis. You know how it is when you put something new on your body, earrings or a dress, and for a time it changes you and then it doesn't? It gets used up, it dies, and there may even come a moment when it becomes impossible to wear the earrings anymore because to do so would be a foolish regression to an obsolete self, a part of your life that is over now and should not be revisited. My mother's imaginary shoes aren't like that. They never stop growing, and every time you put them on it's the first time. These tree-shoes are made by earth and sky, and to slip your feet into them would be to feel your body and your bearing and perhaps even your soul subtly adjusted, brought into fresh bloom not just by the maker's singular vision but by the renewable energy of the world itself. Any artisanal object implies—truthfully or not—that it was made by someone who sees the life within you and has given you a piece of theirs. Such a person certainly might wish to appear in your dreams to discuss the finer points of your impending metamorphosis. Surely this is the desire to be touched and transformed that drove two generations of women into my grandparents' dress shop and beauty salons. Whatever else they do, these bodily adjustments are intended to show that you have earned the right to surround yourself with things made by people with a revelatory perspective on how to handle fabric or leather or hair, and that you in turn are a person who deserves to be attended to with the same caliber of care.

One summer an emaciated woman moved out of the local motel and in with the old man who lived at the top of our laneway. A few weeks later she walked down to our house with a present for my sisters and me: two pairs of shoes, which she had decorated with designs drawn in black Sharpie. The shoes looked as though they had been rescued from a dumpster and then scribbled on by a child. We politely accepted this peculiar offering, and then returned it a week later when she knocked on the door again to tell us she needed her shoes back. In lieu of a dress, our new neighbor wore a large grey rag tied over each shoulder, which was so torn that we could see she owned no underwear. My sisters and I had no scruples when it came to throwing out ugly or stupid gifts from our relatives, so I wonder now why we kept the shoes rather than putting them straight into the garbage. I don't know why, but it must have been the experience of being given something by a person with no teeth, no clothes, and no fixed address. We were teenagers, and not inclined to piety on any topic, but we knew that this interaction was about more than shoes. It would be shameful to get rid of them; shameful to do anything but line them up in the front closet and pretend that someone might wear them someday. The woman's dignity was at stake, and so was ours. She lived in a blind spot, an attention deficit, and every single thing that happened in our household, from before dawn till past midnight, was designed to ensure that we would never end up like her. We were learning all the things you need to know, all the ways you need to be, in order to become visible without also being a target. My mother sometimes sent food and clothes to our poorest neighbors, but that's not what this woman wanted. She wanted us to answer the door when she knocked and to hold onto the magic shoes until she needed them back, and we could do that.

In her novel *We Need New Names*, NoViolet Bulawayo writes about the food and clothes delivered by the "expensive white people" of an American NGO to the inhabitants of a shantytown in economically devastated Zimbabwe.[50] The children are humiliated as well as delighted, especially when the employees of the NGO take publicity photos of them even though their clothes are rags and their feet are bare. In Bulawayo's novel, every time someone looks through a lens or at a screen, the people they are looking at disappear. They become brittle symbols of suffering or they are dismembered by pornographic images that focus on parts, never the whole. When the novel's narrator, a young girl named Darling, becomes an illegal immigrant in the United States, she continues to believe that real people own Lamborghinis and wear beautiful clothes, and I admire the way Bulawayo shows how expensive white people become invisible within their prosperity just as Darling and her friends vanish into poverty. Bulawayo gives Darling a voice so filled with exuberant life that it bounces when it hits the page, but as a teenager she rarely recognizes an equivalent life in people who aren't like her. At one point the daughter of Darling's employer tries to commit suicide, and when Darling looks at this upper-middle class white girl with an eating disorder, she thinks, "just exactly what is your real problem?"[51] She sees her designer clothes, her big house, her fridge full of food, her pure-bred dog wearing a pink leather jacket, and she thinks about the staggering cost of her annual tuition at Cornell. Then she concludes, "I already know all there is to know about her."[52] The rich white girl is wearing an "Invisible Children" t-shirt, so we have a good idea what she sees when she looks at Darling. There is no chance that these two girls will look at each other and ask Simone Weil's question, "What are you going through?"[53]

Magicians try to persuade us that it is difficult to make a human being disappear, a feat requiring great skill and stagecraft. Art, life, and any number of scenes from the history of human encounter suggest the opposite. We see the vanishing act in Bulawayo's descriptions of the fraught relationship between a Nigerian-born girl and an African-American one, who both think they know everything there is to know about one another and feel mutual contempt as a result; we see it in the phone conversations between Darling and the childhood friends she left behind in Zimbabwe, who assume that like all Americans she is now on friendly terms with Kim Kardashian and therefore can understand nothing of their difficult lives at home.[54] On a smaller and far less catastrophic scale it was there in the neighborhood I grew up in, whose mostly poor white residents were generally considered trash and sometimes publically referred to as such. And I hear it when I talk to aging women who tell me that the whole world looks right through them now that their skin is falling down. If I had a dollar for every time a man yelled out his car window at me when I was young I could put a down payment on the Rockefeller estate, so I don't spend a lot of time mourning my lost collagen. If middle age prevents me from being grabbed by the pussy by a total stranger again, then I am content with the bargain. Sometimes I imagine that there is a ledger that stipulates a minimum number of sexual threats that a woman has to endure in her lifetime, allowing for extra layers of prejudice and bad luck. I have decided that I met my quota by the age of fifteen: so, enough. Some people might dispute this calculation, but after careful consideration I have decided that I am not open to feedback on this matter. (Now *that* is exactly the kind of thing my grandmother would say, in a tone of frozen politesse that a foolish person might mistake for actual politeness). The endless blow job requests were not a testament to my beauty, you understand, simply to the way things worked in that time and place.

"Menopause will be a blessing for you," my doctor says gently. He is referring to the estrogen-fed disease that causes me so much pain, despite the surgeries and the drug that recalibrates my endocrine system, but there may be other benefits too. The only woman I've ever heard talk about aging in a way that I instantly understood was the Mexican-American writer Sandra Cisneros, who says that as her youth faded she felt as though someone "put a knife away."[55] Yes, that is how it is, but then the knife just gets pointed somewhere else, and there's no comfort in that. Walking down the street with my daughters or my startlingly beautiful niece, I feel male attention slide off me and toward them, and I'm afraid. Last year my teenaged niece got up from the dinner table to demonstrate how she avoids being groped on the Montreal subway, showing how she blocks her body with her backpack or leaps away from hands, and because she played the scene for laughs, my daughters thought it was hilarious. "It's normal," my sister murmured as her daughter showed us her defensive strategies. I looked at my own daughters and thought, "You have a lot to learn." It would be better if a woman didn't have to choose between being hunted and being ignored, but the truth is that we don't have a choice. My sister says "normal," but what she means is *given*. It's what we are given.

* * *

Of the many definitions of grace that Marilynne Robinson has offered over the years, today I am struck by this: "it means the understanding of the wholeness of a situation, so that everyone is understood in her humanity, the perceiver extending no more respect to herself than to others, understanding any moment as a thing that can bless time to come or poison it."[56]

An expanded sense of time and the ability to perceive wholeness often go together. For this reason, time is one of Jenny Erpenbeck's governing obsessions as a writer, and it is also one of Richard's. He has retired from his job as a classics professor, but being a scholar is not the kind of job you retire from. Despite no longer being on a university's payroll, he continues to read and write, and as he does so he comes to understand the Greek pantheon differently. He learns that the ancient ancestors of the young Taureg man whom he calls Apollo were among the first to worship Athena, a goddess who is said to have been raised in the country now known as Tunisia. He learns that the Greeks were taught to steer chariots by the Berbers, that Medusa hailed from Libya, that the Tuareg once lived in Syria, that for thousands of years people, stories, and gods have moved across the earth, and that classics cannot rightly be considered a merely European or even Mediterranean field of study. "How many times, he wonders, must a person relearn everything he knows, …, and how many coverings must be torn away before he's finally able to truly grasp things, to understand them to the bone? Is a human lifetime long enough?"[57]

No, it is not long enough. This is why throughout her body of writing Erpenbeck always thinks in generational or even geological time. In his attempts to understand the wholeness of his situation, Richard finds himself reading about the emergence of space-time itself from undifferentiated matter. When he describes Germany as a "country of bookkeepers" whose citizens suffer from "emotional anemia," he is complaining about their refusal to pay attention to any qualities of body or mind or economy that cannot be quantified, and about the loneliness, the fragile illusion of self-sufficiency, that this refusal creates.[58] Some of what Richard does for the refugees he befriends is pragmatic: he arranges legal and medical help, he finds housing, and eventually he decides that instead of buying himself a tractor lawnmower he will buy a plot of arable land in Ghana for a man named Karon, whose family will be saved from starvation as a result. But much of what Richard does comes from the widening of sightlines, even into the primordial beginnings of the world, that allows him to stop seeing himself as an almsgiver, just as he stops believing that the Greek pantheon is narrowly Greek. He learns that there are things people need from one another that our money cannot buy and protections that our nations' laws cannot guarantee, no matter how justly conceived and stringently enforced they are. And although Richard and his circle of friends from the former GDR are all professionally successful and economically stable, they realize that they too need to feel the presence of this life outside of life, and that what they give to the refugees helps to reveal it. Perhaps this is because Richard's friends are all getting old and facing grief. It is increasingly difficult for them to pretend to be self-sufficient, and those who are willing to drop the pretense come closer to something like the time of the angels, where it is possible to pay one's respects to everything.

It occurs to me that most of the writers I love treat time as Jenny Erpenbeck does. They pry it open to show the layers, not to conduct experiments in historiography or other tired forms of irony, but to reveal as much as possible of the wholeness behind human particularity. The first writer who taught me this was Michael Ondaatje, who has gone on to influence a generation of novelists. When I first read him as a teenager his prose gave me vertigo. I felt that I was being given a view of my familiar Southern Ontario surroundings that was so vast I couldn't get my bearings but never wanted to leave. I hope never to recover from my first reading of *In the Skin of a Lion*, a novel in which the building of Toronto's Bloor Street viaduct in the 1920s rhymes with the building of the walls of Uruk, and time opens until we can see all the way back to the *Epic of Gilgamesh*. I had a sense of what to think about this novel, and later as a scholar I learned to write about some of those thoughts, but I had no vocabulary to express what it made me feel or why. Even if I quoted sentence after sentence or entire paragraphs here, I wouldn't be able to explain the joy it gave me. I once spent the better part of a year reading all the sources quoted or mentioned in *The English Patient*, which was a fine education and a great pleasure, but didn't help me understand the joy at all. It emerges from a total aesthetic, more like a fragrance than an object.

In Ondaatje's writing, a human life can traverse centuries and millennia, cross oceans and races. If your name is David Caravaggio and you live in four novels by Michael Ondaatje, then your life spans 400 years and two continents. You are an early modern Italian painter, an Italian-Canadian thief, a Second World War spy, and a Roma man living in postwar France under an assumed name.[59] If your name is Commissioner Harris, then at a moment of absolute crisis you can be a civil servant in 1930s Toronto who speaks in the voices of ancient Mesopotamian scribes. It is possible to navigate the deserts of mid-twentieth-century North Africa with the help of Herodotus, and for a Sikh soldier to recognize his own face in fifteenth-century paintings by Piero della Francesca and Michelangelo.

At the end of *Anil's Ghost*, Ondaatje writes, it "was a long time since he had believed in the originality of artists ....You slipped into the old bed of the art, where they had slept."[60] The man whose thoughts are being described here is Ananda Udugama, and he is helping to rebuild an ancient 120-foot-high statue of the Buddha that was blown up and looted by thieves in the middle of a killing field in late-twentieth-century Sri Lanka. Before his wife, Sirissa, was murdered in the ongoing civil war, Ananda was an eye painter in a village of stonecutters. His job now is to reassemble the Buddha's face from the pieces of the obliterated statue and then to perform the sacred ceremony in which he paints the eyes that bring the stone icon to life. He is not interested in trying to invent a new or original face. He believes that a face is brought to life by its similarity to other faces, and he strives to reveal those similarities so that in his statue of the Buddha everyone in his warring country will recognize something of themselves or of the people they love, but never see an exact and limiting likeness. The god is sacralized by these shifting resemblances, and so are the people who see them.

Every human being is also someone else. Every face is made of other faces, including those of strangers and enemies and gods. These are the beliefs that shape Ondaatje's writing, beginning with his seminal first novel, *Coming Through Slaughter,* about the legendary New Orleans jazz trumpeter, Buddy Bolden, of whom only one photograph survives and no recordings. Ondaatje looks at this image of an African-American man who died in the mental ward of a hospital in Louisiana years before he was born in Sri Lanka, and the photograph "becomes a mirror" in which he sees himself.[61] He sees Bolden cut his face open with a razor blade to bring "his enemy to the surface of the skin," and remembers doing the same thing.[62] "Why did my senses stop at you?" Ondaatje asks. "Did not want to pose in your accent but think in your brain and body" no matter "your nation your colour your age."[63]

Empathy is one of those words we sugar until it makes your teeth hurt. Ondaatje takes the sugar out. In his writing empathy comes with a razor blade or a bomb or through cross hairs. It is an emergency response to the pressure of unendurable states of mind, which are so isolating that a person will do almost anything to feel less alone. To help these suffering people, for whom he feels great tenderness and in whom we might occasionally recognize ourselves, Ondaatje exfoliates time so that he has the history of the world and the breadth of humanity to work with. If this is intellectually thrilling, it is also so deeply moving that it is as though a door opens in my own life, and it opens onto the future as much as the past. It is not an escape to long ago or far away. Sometimes Ondaatje puts himself in the story—a name, a photograph—to make this point as clearly as possible, and he describes his characters as people who have things to do when his back is turned and go on living when he is finished writing about them. This sounds fanciful, even precious, but I think it's a way to express the mysterious aliveness of things, including those we make, which to some degree come from beyond our control and in the end always elude it. If we are to "bless time to come," as Robinson urges, rather than poison it, then a good part of our attention must be directed toward that hidden aliveness.[64]

Fairy tales and children's stories have always pointed us in this direction. Outside of sacred texts and contemplative practices, they offer a formative encounter with mysterious forms of life. In middle age, I find myself returning to these books for reasons I can scarcely explain even to myself. First I read them as a child, then I read them to my children, and now I read them again, much to my children's bemusement. They wonder about my apparently arrested development. Should I not have advanced to vampire romances by now? I think it's the inertia of midlife that sends me back to these primary stories about the invisible reservoirs from which renewal springs. I notice that many of the moments I'm drawn to are the same ones that excited me as a child, although now they sometimes move me to tears, perhaps because they no longer confirm what I feel, but remind me of what I once felt. Above all, I find myself turning to the scenes in which one world accordions open to reveal another. This happens in the first chapter of each of the Narnia books, when a child crosses from ordinary life into Aslan's kingdom, but it can also happen even within magical worlds.

On a dreary Tuesday morning, when the day feels like Mount Everest, I might turn to the opening chapter of *The Voyage of the Dawn Treader*, where a painting of the ocean hanging on a bedroom wall suddenly liquefies and swells, pulling three children onto a boat. Or I might turn to a later scene in this same book, one from the last chapter, in which Lucy Pevensie looks down into the ocean and meets the eyes of a little Sea Girl, who is tending a school of fish in the shallows. They look at one another with curiosity, one girl in the air and the other underwater, certain that under different circumstances they would be friends. Lewis writes, "Lucy will never forget her face," although she cannot stop to talk to the Sea Girl and will never meet her again, because she is on her way to the "World's End," where the saltwater grows sweet and blanketed with aromatic lilies, and time comes to a halt.[65] Here the air is so rich and the water so nutritious that no one needs to eat or sleep, and the older sailors begin to grow young again. There is always this sense in the Chronicles of Narnia that if you look in the right place a friend will look back at you from a neighboring reality, especially if you have charted a course to the place where your own reality ends.

It is always the case that Narnia becomes accessible only when someone is in trouble. The children need sanctuary from the Blitz or a bully or a fatal railway accident, and the need is reciprocal. It is as though pressure is being exerted on both sides of the wardrobe or the painting or the railway station, or whatever place must thin so that different kinds of life can meet to help one another. *Help* is key here. The children are rescued from one emergency in order to resolve another, often of far greater severity. Someone needs to help expel the White Witch and free Prince Rilian from the Lady of the Green Kirtle, and it seems that some of this assistance must come from beyond Narnia's borders and outside its bestiary, just as the fruit that cures Digory's dying mother in *The Magician's Nephew* only grows in Aslan's kingdom—on the very tree that Digory himself planted on the day when Narnia was born. When the children die at the beginning of *The Last Battle* it may be because they have been called to help resolve a crisis of such gravity that it brings Narnia to an end, its energies exhausted. For Lewis, worlds are as mortal as any living thing, and his Sons of Adam and Daughters of Eve come to understand this mortality because in Narnia they are able to live for many years in a matter of moments, so that with each visit they witness the unfolding of generational time, and on the last day they watch the end of time itself, as the sun burns out and darkness engulfs the land they loved.

When this happens, Aslan builds a doorway to a new life, as he often does. Paging through the Chronicles, I see how often Pauline Baynes, whose lovely pen and ink drawings are as indelible in my memory as Lewis's prose, draws images of people standing at thresholds, doorways or edges.

It is well known that Lewis's books are steeped in medieval and early modern poetry, but they also look forward. They are always peering over a verge where it is possible for something to turn into a better version of itself. Yes, Eustace Scrubb is transformed into a dragon because he is a selfish brat, but how wonderfully improved he is when Aslan skins him! Reepicheep, the most valiant of talking mice, launches his coracle across the Silver Sea toward the thirty-foot wave at the World's End, and although he is never again seen in Narnia, we do not fear for him. We can be sure that whenever anyone crosses a threshold with an open heart they eventually become more capable than they were on the other side of it, until in the final pages of *The Last Battle*, after their beloved Narnia has died, the Pevensies and their friends discover that in Aslan's new country they have turned into creatures that can run as fast as the wind and never grow hungry or tired or afraid. They are like gods now, in an infinitely expanding universe, and this "was only the beginning of the real story," Lewis writes, although he admits that it is not one he knows how to tell.[66] It takes place in an unknown future.

Having been raised with the Bhagavad Gita rather than the Bible, and being more conversant on the topic of the chakras than the incarnation, I was shocked to learn as an undergraduate that the Narnia series is widely regarded as a Christian allegory. I did not see this as a child, and as a young adult it seemed to me that the books were much reduced when read for symbolism, even if it was what Lewis intended. It is said many times throughout the Chronicles that Aslan is a wild lion, not a tame one, and allegory seemed to domesticate him. The moments in the series when I hear the clanging hammer and tongs of allegory are the least interesting for me now, but they are few, and I feel at liberty to think about Lewis's books in any way that is consistent with what I understand to be their view of life: namely that it is governed by an inclination toward generous yet ferocious largesse, and that the good—perhaps the divine—is the name we give to actions that reveal it.

Violence is one of those actions, whether carried out by an intergalactic witch or a schoolyard bully. Rage pushes against solid states so that they either collapse or open, sometimes both. The novelist Mohsin Hamid makes this premise literal in *Exit West*, in which children's books are allowed to stay up past bedtime and come downstairs to mingle with the adults. As far as I'm concerned, this is as it should be. Much is lost when we sequester our primary stories in the nursery or in Children's Literature courses. Hamid names *Charlotte's Web* among his favorite books, and it is impossible to miss the influence of Narnia on *Exit West*, in which ordinary doors become "partially animate" under the pressure of the refugee crisis, instantly transporting people from one part of the globe to another.[67] Like others, Hamid imagines a response to this crisis that draws on the old resources of gift thinking, although he looks for those resources outside of human intelligence and institutions. His doors are not created by corporations or governments, traditions of hospitality, exceptions to the law, or acts of imagination. They are created by the lavish energies of the world itself. This idea is central to so much children's writing, and as adults we tend to stop taking it seriously, especially those of us who do not practice a religion or faith.

Hamid has often written about the dangers of nostalgia, which at its worst sends entire countries in pursuit of lost excellence and phantasmal purity, and he has spoken about his belief that we need to imagine futures that are not dusty dioramas of the past. For Hamid, as for so many, that hopeful future begins with a widening of attention. The larger the mind gets, the less fortified and fearful it becomes. Truly, *Exit West* is a book for star gazers! There are many moments when we are given a view through a telescope or thrown flat on our backs to marvel at a night sky. As their unnamed country deteriorates and the streets fill with corpses, Saeed shows his girlfriend Nadia an image on his cell phone of some of the great cities of the world, altered by the photographer so that all the light pollution is gone and the regional heavens are as visible as they would be if New York City or Shanghai were for some reason abandoned. Saeed explains that to achieve this wondrous effect, which is also a kind of annihilation, the French photographer created a composite of two images, one of the city and another of an empty place at the same latitude. It is the "same sky, but at a different time," he says.[68] Each city is two places, two moments, one filled with people and the other deserted. When Nadia looks at these images, which are available to anyone on earth with access to the internet, she cannot tell whether "they looked like the past, or the present, or the future."[69] They represent everywhere and nowhere, always and never, everyone and no one, and this is why they are filled with promise.

In the early 1960s, during the Cold War, Madeleine L'Engle wrote her classic novel, *A Wrinkle in Time*. In search of their father, who has been imprisoned on an ultra-communist planet called Camazotz, the Murray children tesser across the universe. Time wrinkles, space bends, and the cosmos is discovered to be prodigal with invisible forces, some of which are healing and others murderous. It is excruciating to move through the fourth dimension—"an agony of pain," is how L'Engle describes it—but it must be done if other kinds of agony are to be remedied.[70] Mr. Murray must be rescued, and Meg, his daughter, must learn to feel less desolate in her creative precocity, which is of an independent and disobedient variety that is not celebrated in the mid-century American classroom, or in its suburbs. Or in its women. An agony of pain also turns the normal doors in Hamid's novel into special ones, "and it could happen without warning, to any door at all," with the result that everyone looks at every door with new alertness.[71]

The options for doors are no longer limited to opened, closed or ajar, but now include a fourth state: magic portal, tesseract.

Step into such a door and you do not know where you will arrive or how you will be greeted. It depends on the extent to which your host understands that a person who comes empty-handed often bears riches that no one yet knows how to see. It is a matter of knowing how to look, of being alert to potential where others see only a threat to their identity and their tax-base. And not just potential, which is a chilly word, but friendship and help. Like Jenny Erpenbeck, Hamid wants the citizenry of the rich countries of this world to stop seeing ourselves as almsgivers, dispensers of charity that we give out of ethical or legal obligation and for which we receive nothing in return other than a sense of our own moral esteem. Hamid tells a different story, although he does not scant the difficulties of doing so. In the opening pages of his novel, before the reader understands its fantastical premise, he describes a man "with dark skin and dark, woolly hair" struggling to emerge from a woman's bedroom closet in the middle of the night.[72] The sleeping woman is white, the place is Australia. The man is fighting for his life, every muscle straining in a desperate attempt to be born into this sanctuary. He succeeds, and we are pleased for him, but Hamid also wants us to be worried about the safety of the woman. The dark man emerges from "the heart of darkness."[73] He is made of flesh and blood but also of archetypes, which in his case mean that he is someone to be despised and feared, the living nightmare in the closet. He stands over the sleeping woman. What will he do now? He observes that "alone a person is almost nothing."[74] He observes that he is alone, just like the woman. Then he leaps out her bedroom window and makes his way into a new country, alone but hoping for the best.

In a wise children's story, as much hope as danger comes out of the heart of darkness. Meg Murray is almost killed by the Black Thing, but she is also nursed back to life by dark-furred creatures. Charlotte first addresses Wilbur in the middle of the night, after he has been brutally acquainted with the fact of his mortality and left alone to bear it. The Dark Lord threatens Harry's life, but how many times is he covertly helped by Severus Snape, master of the Dark Arts? Whatever form she takes, whether spider or Potions professor, a fairy godmother never arrives for elevenses. She comes in the dark, at the fertile hour of despair. In this she is like the Room of Requirement, whose door only appears to those whose urgent needs cannot be met elsewhere. The Room is not visible on the Marauder's Map, and neither are the people who enter it in search of the castle's most dangerous and essential reserves. It is where Draco Malfoy finds the broken Vanishing Cabinet that he repairs and uses to spirit Death Eaters into Hogwarts, thus bypassing the protective enchantments that prevent Apparition onto school grounds and leading to the murder of no less a man than Albus Dumbledore. Yet the Room is also the headquarters of Dumbledore's Army and of the resistance movement.

"Wild nights are my glory," says Mrs. Whatsit, the interstellar being who tessers space-time.[75] They are Hamid's too. He imagines a near future in which refugees who magically arrive in England, including Nadia and Saeed, are concentrated in a neighborhood that comes to be known as "dark London."[76] It is dark because the city cuts off the neighborhood's utility and transportation services, because most of the people who live there have dark skin, because they are feared by nativists, and because, by night, violence erupts on the ground and government drones patrol the air. It looks very much as though a war is about to erupt in which the newcomers will be slaughtered, much as they were attacked by militants in their home countries. Then something surprising happens on both sides. Migrants in dark London begin to organize themselves into councils, some along ethnic and religious lines and others according to more flexible principles, and not always in agreement with one another, but all with the aim of figuring out how destitute people from around the world who do not speak the same languages might live together with minimal conflict and agree on how to survive the hostility of their new home. This is "something new," thinks Nadia, and also something primal and wild.[77] Saeed looks at her and sees her "animal form," and they both see the "strangeness" of the other's face, which they find intensely erotic as well as alienating.[78] At the same time, light Londoners decide that they do not have it in them to carry out a massacre; after a series of skirmishes, the police and the army withdraw, and negotiations begin.

This must be acknowledged as a courageous choice, Hamid writes, not resignation or strategic retreat. It must be understood as a gift, not an obligation; freely given, not required by law. You cannot bully people into true generosity any more than you can force gratitude. "Courage is demanded not to attack when afraid," and established Londoners are afraid of the newcomers for many reasons, not least that they will overwhelm social infrastructure that has taken several generations to build, including public health care and education.[79] Hamid imagines a "London Halo" housing development for refugees in which migrants and natives work side by side, and describes a moment in which Saeed approaches the foreman to thank him for his work.[80] The foreman is an aging white man of good will, and suddenly he reminds Saeed of soldiers in his home country, who when asked to describe the battles they have fought, "looked at you as if you had no idea how much you were asking."[81] This man is being asked to give, as soldiers are asked to give up their lives if necessary. He is being paid for his labor, and in that sense compensated, but he must be willing to concede that his life and his country will change, which means that he must confront his own fears and those of the displaced people on whose behalf the changes are being made. These displaced people are *ashamed*, Hamid writes.[82] It is shameful to have nothing, to be nowhere at home, to hold out an empty hand. If the foreman is anything like Richard, in *Go, Went, Gone*, he may slowly come to understand that his nation's prosperity comes at the expense of other people's suffering, and that this global history of exploitation is hundreds of years old, often invisible, and yet built into the very fabric of who he is. No matter how difficult his life has been, no matter how precarious his place in the economy, the foreman has to acknowledge this shame and feel it echo in himself. Aside from an immediate threat to physical safety, is there anything more frightening? How hard do we work, each of us, not to feel ashamed?

Hamid writes beautifully about "the foundation of a human life, waiting there for us between the steps of our march to our mortality, when we are compelled to pause and not act but be."[83] Some people call this meditation or prayer; others call it the empty space of creativity. When children enter it, they play; when adults enter it, they become capable of honesty and courage. In the hopeful near-future that Hamid imagines, that courage is expressed as a "migrant compassion badge," featuring a "black door within a red heart."[84] Like the thresholds of Narnia, this one opens only when there is trouble so deep that it sends people in search of one another, each exerting pressure on either side of the crisis, so that as a man pushes his way out of the heart of darkness another man walks into it, each hoping to feel less alone. On one hand, great distances have been crossed; on the other, the transit is intimate, interior, more a case of acknowledging what is right here, in our own families and neighborhoods. Even C. S. Lewis, the most Christian of modern fantasists, gave his messiah a Turkish name, Aslan, which he borrowed from Edward Lane's early-nineteenth century translation of the *Arabian Nights*.[85] It is prophesied from the beginning of time that Narnia and the Pevensies need one another, but Aslan's creation contains many worlds, not just the one familiar to the schoolchildren of English Christendom.

My own children have an uncle from India, another born in Canada to Pakistani immigrants; they have white cousins from the American Midwest, Jewish cousins from Toronto and New York, and Canadian cousins of South Asian and African descent. At some family festivities there are men who wear yarmulkes, at others there are women in headscarves, and the only thing that alarms my daughters in either setting is the embargo on bacon. They have grown up with a range of skin tones and accents, religions and ethnicities, and are not troubled by the differences because it is clear that they are less consequential than the similarities among the members of our family. These are all middle- or upper-middle-class households with the usual aspirations and methods of realizing them. My children feel at home here, whether there are gilded excerpts from the Koran on the walls, a mezuzah in the front doorway, or a quasi-Buddhist meditation shrine in the living room. But when we visit the neighborhood where I grew up, I can see that it frightens my children and they don't know how to explain why. I watch the way they recoil from the most vulnerable people in our own family precisely to shield themselves from shame.

Despite gentrification, there are still many tumbledown houses and struggling people in the neighborhood, including members of my immediate family. This remains a place where problems with mental health and addiction are not handled discreetly in a doctor's office or treatment center, but play out in public, right here on the sidewalk. Here it is not strange to drop out of high school, as three consecutive generations of women in my family have done, and become a grandmother before forty. If you are drunk, you fall down for all to see; if you are clinically depressed, you come over at midnight and cry openly, because everything is just so hard and you don't understand why. My children cannot believe their eyes or ears. They have never seen adults behave this way and want nothing to do with them. We rarely invite these relatives to our family gatherings any more, and they never invite us to theirs, because, as one of my cousins once said, we make them feel like losers. They represent all the constraints my sisters and I fought to leave behind. We had some of the right talents for the time, and parents who understood how the meritocracy works and what will happen to you if you can't figure out how to make yourself useful. With each generation, the distance between us grows, but my children are afraid that it will suddenly shrink and that they will be trapped in a life where there are few choices and no illusions of sovereignty. I know this fear well. It never leaves me.

I remember the year in which my children, then very young, insisted that we watch *The Wizard of Oz* every Saturday night. That's fifty-two consecutive viewings, not including the two live stage versions we also attended during this period. Sometimes the girls were too tired to watch the whole film, so they would ask to fast-forward to the parts they most wanted to see, which always featured the Wicked Witch of the West. They could take or leave Glinda the Good, with her sweet voice and her bedazzled gown, and they didn't care whether the Tin Man got a heart, but the Wicked Witch was critical viewing. They watched this green-faced villain who hated little girls, trembling with urgency. The important thing was to confront fear in the safe space of a story, and to grow stronger by that confrontation. On screen, their surrogate, Dorothy, had to learn that Glinda's saccharine goodness is not strong enough to send her home until she has repeatedly done battle with the bad; only then can she click her heels together and return to the Dustbowl, where she will trade the technicolor Mary Janes for the scuffed oxfords, which are more suitable for a life spent in the bosom of her impoverished family, chasing chickens and slopping pigs. My daughters became interested in fairy tales only when I stopped reading the sanitized versions and picked up the Brothers Grimm, in which Aschenputtel's conniving stepmother hands her daughters a butcher's knife and obliges them to cut off parts of their feet—a toe, a heel—to fit into the prince's glass slipper. Each in turn rides away with him on horseback, hemorrhaging. "Let's read that again," my daughters would say, aghast but fully alert.

Stories like these suggest that love and loyalty are more important than the magic shoes, and that if you take them by force, you will be found out and punished if you don't bleed to death first. But the beautiful shoes are also part of a world in which there is almost no chance that either of my daughters will drop out of high school to have a baby with a drug dealer and then end up working a series of minimum wage jobs. The beautiful shoes are part of a world in which there is almost no chance that either of my daughters will drop out of high school to become a drug dealer and then end up in jail, although in my experience that trajectory is more common among men. I have done everything in my power to create a life, and a set of resources and protections, in which I can prevent that from happening. My mother painted golden tree-shoes; now they are in my closet, and I will not give them up or exchange them for the second-hand shoes of my childhood. I can't go home again; my children don't want to and neither do I.

No, that's not true. In fact, I constantly dream of going home. I like to imagine that when my sisters and I are very old we will move back into the house that my father built, four bespectacled old ladies living on the edges of the neighborhood, but by choice, and with all our creative powers intact. We'll be like Mrs. Whatsit and Mrs. Who, and nothing at all like my grandmother. I don't know what we'll do with our time, although I feel sure that we'll be quite busy at tasks of our own devising, because no one will be watching and we'll have nothing to prove any more. "We have come so far," I will say sententiously. "It is over." Last night I was talking to my mother and she mentioned a local news item that referred to trash, and she said, "I guess they're talking about us." "Don't be ridiculous," I said forcefully, "Not us." This too is a response to the wholeness of what is given: the poison is inextricable from the blessing, the courage cannot be parted from the shame.

5

Patience

How enormously long the lifespan of a planet is compared to the life and breath of any one human being.

JENNY ERPENBECK[1]

To my knowledge, Antoine de Saint-Exupéry's *The Little Prince* is the only fairy tale to emerge from the Second World War. It was written after the fall of France, when Saint-Exupéry went into exile in the United States before returning to Europe in 1943 to fly with the Allied forces. He was soon shot down, although it was decades before the wreckage of his plane was recovered. A few years ago, the National Ballet of Canada premiered a ballet based on *The Little Prince,* and at the same time an animated version of the novella was playing in movie Theatres around the country. Naturally, these events sent me back to my bookshelf. As I read the story for the first time since childhood, I remembered the rose and the baobabs, but I had forgotten the parable of patience, if I ever knew it. Saint-Exupéry's pilot lands in the Sahara with a broken plane and enough drinking water for a week, a situation that calls for expedience and a tight focus on the essentials, as Saint-Exupéry knew very well, having survived a similar disaster in his youth. Instead, the aviator is confronted by a little caped man who asks for a drawing of a sheep and then wants to have a meandering conversation about it. For the next eight days, the prince teaches the pilot that to love or understand anything—a fox, a flower, a stranger, the desert, the universe—takes more time than you wanted to spend and considerable tolerance for detours, even if you are about to die of dehydration. In one overheated moment, the pilot points out that what he really needs right now is a better wrench and a large glass of water, not another story about plant life on Asteroid B-612. Not so fast, says the prince. Why should a man listen to a story when he should be looking for a well or turning a bolt? Because the time that he wastes on the little boy is precisely what will save the aviator's life.

"It is absurd to look for a well, at random, in the immensity of the desert," the pilot says.[2] Yes, it is. But when he holds the prince in his arms it does not feel absurd. Suddenly the pilot looks across the sand and is confident that its hot shimmer conceals water nearby. He picks up the boy and carries him all night, and at daybreak finds a well more sumptuous than any he has ever known. Its water is so sweet and plentiful that it reminds him of a Christmas gift or the music of Midnight Mass. "It was good for the heart, like a present," he thinks.[3] He and the prince both drink deeply. Then, and only then, is the aviator able to fix his plane. The heartbreak comes soon after when he realizes that the little prince intends to die so that he can return to his asteroid. His job is to tend his rose and sustain the hidden reservoirs that keep us alive on earth. Our job is to climb out of our machines and look for them. The story ends with an invitation to do so: an empty landscape, where the prince once stood.

Can you see him? If not, "please do not hurry on," writes Saint-Exupéry. "Wait for a time, exactly under the star."[4] Those too busy to wait might end up like the hero of that other wartime fable about a man coping with sunstroke and absurdity, Camus's Meursault, who believes that the stars have nothing to offer but indifference. This idea was powerful in its day, but I don't find it helpful anymore. I am prepared to keep waiting.

* * *

Holding out empty hands to passersby or raising them to a divinity is a perennial gesture of supplication. Add a little more energy to the gesture, and it expresses outrage or astonishment. *What? Why? How?* Curl the fingers over the palm to form a fist, and it says, *No more.* Lewis Hyde writes that "the gift moves toward the empty place," but it is also true that the gift somehow comes *from* the empty place.[5] Saint-Exupéry's aviator leaves us waiting in front of a drawing of a deserted landscape from which the person he loves has vanished, which is a terrible forecast of Saint-Exupéry's own disappearance and that of millions of other people. Mark Osborne's film adaptation of *The Little Prince* wisely depicts the prince and his friends as fragile hand-made paper puppets brought to life by the old and painstaking techniques of stop-motion animation.[6] Here we enter not just a different world but a slower kind of time.

Let's consider another war story, far more drastic and not for children. Euripides wrote "Herakles" during the Peloponnesian War between Athens and the city states it ruled, which began in 431 BCE, lasted for almost three decades, and eventually brought Athens to its knees. In this play, Herakles returns to Thebes after completing the last of his twelve labors. At this stage, he might be hoping for a hot bath and a welcome home party, but that's not

FIGURE 5.1 *The Little Prince as a hand-made paper puppet. Source: Mark Osborne. The Little Prince. Performed by Jeff Bridges and Mackenzie Foy. 2015; Paramount Pictures.*

what Euripides has in store for him. In his absence, Herakles's family has been imprisoned and condemned to death by a usurper named Lykos. Foolish Lykos is no match for a man who has been to hell and back, and Herakles swiftly liberates his wife, father, and children, and takes back his throne. However, while he is doing all of this, the goddess Hera conceives yet another plan to punish him for being the child of her husband's infidelity: she sends

Herakles into a delirium in which he slaughters his wife and sons. He awakens to find himself lying beside their dead bodies, a physical posture that immediately told the ten to fifteen thousand people in the audience that Herakles is a casualty of the massacre he has just perpetrated. His life as a hero is over, and he's not sure that he can figure out what comes next. Now the twelve labors look easy. In despair, Herakles casts about for ways to kill himself, but is interrupted by the arrival of Theseus, who has heard the bad news and hurried to Thebes to help his friend. "I owe a debt of gratitude to Herakles," he explains, because "he brought me up alive from underground–/ so in case he has need / of my hand or my allies, / I've come."[7]

Gratitude is as important for Euripides as it was for Homer before him. Theseus urges Herakles to start afresh by leaving Thebes and returning with him to Athens, where Theseus can offer him wealth, citizenship, and ritual purification from the crime he has committed. Herakles stands beside the bodies of his wife and sons and declares himself a corpse, urges the citizens of Thebes to bury him with his family. "We are all dead," he says; "Mourn us all in one."[8] "I'll share your bad luck" now, Theseus says, because "I shared your good luck once, / when you brought me from the dead world back to life."[9] By "this grace," says Theseus, "I repay you for saving me."[10]

Grace is a form of excess, which is why it is always an experience of refreshment and increase. We think of gifts as adding to what already exists, but now I want to explore a different possibility, which is that a gift can give by taking away. A gift can subtract some of what already exists, and in doing so reveal potential that was for some reason obscured. Picture Herakles, awakening in a pool of his children's blood; and then Theseus, lately of Hades. He's not just going to prevent Herakles from committing suicide, he's going to help him become someone new. When Herakles arrives home, he is a hero, a father, a husband, and a king. Who is he now? This question is likely to have resonated with the members of an Athenian audience dealing with the deaths of husbands and sons and the possibility of wholesale military defeat. The most valuable form of gratitude that Theseus offers Herakles is not what he gives but what he offers to alleviate: grief, rage, shame, fear, and despair. This alleviation somehow emerges from Theseus's recent experience of having nothing at all, including a substantial body. Like the little prince, he comes from life outside of life.

The relationship between subtraction and generosity is visible in the transition from *charis* to coinage, which is where my story about grace began in the first chapter of this book. Now I'd like to return to the rituals of animal sacrifice from which the idea of money developed. The Homeric *Hymn to Hermes* describes such a sacrifice, carried out by Hermes after he stole fifty head of cattle from Apollo. After the theft, Hermes immediately slaughters two cows and carves their flesh into twelve equal portions, one for each of the Olympian gods, as ritual requires. He is very hungry after his exertions but knows that he should not eat the sacrificial allotment, so he hides it in a barn "as a token [*sêma*] of his youthful theft."[11] In reading the *Hymn,* Lewis Hyde emphasizes the importance of the fact that the hidden portions are called a *sêma,* a "marker, sign, or token," and he speculates that in the process of moving the food from the fireside to the barn Hermes changes its meaning.[12] The roasted meat is no longer just a ritual offering to the Olympians, but a sign of something new, we're not sure what, although it is likely connected to Hermes's desire to be an Olympian himself, which is why he stole Apollo's cows in the first place. Hyde goes on to consider what it means for Hermes to turn twelve skewers of barbequed beef into tokens of his youthful theft, but I'm more interested in the connection between the meat and the development of the particular kind of token called coinage.

In a book called *Money and the Early Greek Mind,* the classicist Richard Seaford writes that before the invention of money, "citizenship and entitlement to participation in the sacrificial meal seem to be one and the same."[13] Unlike gift exchange, which was restricted to the elite, an animal's body had to be equally divided among all members of a polity, just as the gods were provided with equal portions. This principle is so fundamental to the social order that the word for law, *nomos,* derives from *nemein,* meaning distribution.[14] Distribution *is* law. The earliest forms of Greek currency showed their symbolic and material origins in the shared feast because they were made from leftovers, from what remains after an animal's body has been butchered, cooked, and eaten. They were metal roasting spits (obols, drachma), the tripods that suspended the cauldrons above the cooking fire, or animal bones cut into discs of equal size, polished, and engraved with the legend "ΒΙΟΣ θΑΝΑΤΟΣ ΒΙΟΣ (life death life)."[15]

The idea of modern money begins with what is left when the sacrificial meal is over and everyone's belly is full. From these ceremonies of equal distribution, the Greeks abstracted the principle of citizenship in a *polis* much larger than a group of men gathered around a campfire, as well as the related idea that a coin should be worth the same in every hand.[16] As Jeremy Trevett argues, coinage and Athenian democracy were inextricably linked, which helps to explain the "hostility to money found in the writings of anti-democratic political theorists." The *polis,* Trevett concludes, "was a world of coins."[17] This was pragmatically true, because service to the state was paid in money, and it was also symbolically true, because in "the democratic city, all coins, like all citizens, were made of the same stuff, and all were pure and precious matter."[18] Tampering with currency was a capital offense, and counterfeiting was understood to be a form of murder. This imaginative symmetry between the value of citizens and of coins certainly does not mean that money remained true to the ritual that inspired it. No one would be so rude as to gobble up another man's dinner, but I hardly need to say that the further we get from the fireside and the feast the less money is associated with fair shares and the more with individual greed.

Nevertheless, in the fourth century, when monetization was well established, Aristotle praises money's capacity to create the "proportionate exchange" or "give-and-take" that he deems essential to virtue.[19] He writes in *The Ethics* that money expresses the desire for equivalence, which "is the need which holds all things together."[20] It is also the need that holds all citizens together, "for if man had no needs at all or no needs of a similar nature, there would be no exchange or not this kind of exchange" and therefore no "association of men."[21] Coinage facilitates the political unity made possible by common desires, which are more powerful than the differences among individuals or among the goods that they make. In this sense, a coin's value is guaranteed by the shared appetites that allow a shoe to turn into a house or a flagon of oil or into anything else that people want. Far from running counter to ethics, which for Aristotle is the study of how individuals might best pursue happiness, money draws attention to what is the same in people and objects, and by extension to the importance of social as well as material equivalence. For Aristotle, coinage reveals the equality of presence, just as it allows an architect and a shoemaker to price their dissimilar wares using a common measure.

Yet money does not make every aspect of *charis* obsolete. Aristotle approvingly observes that men continue to "give a prominent place to the Temple of the Graces"—a public place—because the need for grace is one of the collective needs that money expresses.[22] However, that need is not fully met by money any more than it is fully met by law, a dilemma that has come up many times in this book. To be fully equitable, Aristotle argues, a state must bend its laws, no matter how just they are, because a rigid universal standard can never render justice to an individual. In fact, he makes the remarkable claim that an equitable man is "not overly just."[23] Such a man does not always enforce the law even when it is on his side, but is willing to cede his rights out of charity to his neighbor. The Temple of the Graces is a reminder of what eludes coins and the law: the gratuity within people and things, which cannot be measured but must be attended to if people are to be happy with each other and the state they have created. Aristotle makes it clear that money does not fully meet the need for grace, but it is also true that money meets a need that was not fully satisfied by *charis*, namely to expand the idea of equality beyond the elite.

Part way through the *Iliad*, Achilles complains to Odysseus, the "same honor waits / for the coward and the brave. They both go down to Death, / the fighter who shirks, the one who works to exhaustion."[24] To die in a blaze of glory that will be celebrated for all time is the only way to defy the humiliating gruel dished up by Pluto, "the divider into equal portions."[25] Aristocratic Achilles would have hated money as much as he loathed the underworld, which seemed to standardize the soul. Years later, people found much to admire in this standardization, especially those who wanted to redistribute power so that it was no longer concentrated in the hands of kings like Achilles. One of the most common early coin types minted in the ancient Greek cities bore an image of the *astragal*, the knucklebones of a sheep or goat, long associated with the Graces and with aristocratic games of chance.[26] Despite these restrictive associations with *charis*, Leslie Kurke speculates that the *astragal* was popular as a coin face because it "naturaliz[ed] coinage by linking it to the eternal order of the gods, the dead, and the body."[27] In the Homeric epics, *astragalos* is "the normal word for a human vertebra, always in the contexts of a hero sustaining a mortal injury."[28] The *astragal* is human as well as animal, and if it naturalizes money it also democratizes it by subtracting everything but the manifest equality of bone.

Ideas that come from the bone are often more generous than the ones they replace. I think this is what Marilynne Robinson means when she describes grace as "a sort of ecstatic fire that takes things down to essentials."[29] In the scene that prompts this insight, there are two people being burned down, one a Christian minister and a man of faith, the other a sinner by his own and general reckoning. They share the same name, John Ames, because the minister is godfather to his namesake, but all their lives they have been bitterly at odds. The two men sit together in the dark, half asleep. Ames is dying, and his godson is so consumed by shame at the things he has done in his life that he feels beyond the reach of any community. The kind of grace that gives by taking away pain only seems to become available under conditions like these, when people are already reduced to a minimum. In a later essay called "Realism," Robinson writes that grace always entails the "lifting or easing of a burdensome weight."[30] She imagines that this buoyancy is part of creation, which is why we have a moon that periodically relieves gravity of its duties and lightens the vast waters of the oceans enough to raise the tide. What a gorgeous thought. Do you think it could be true?

I don't believe in God, but I do believe in the mysterious bond between less and more that I see in the Abrahamic traditions, beginning with the foundational scene in which Abraham makes all the necessary preparations to take his only son onto a mountain to sacrifice him. The knife has to touch Isaac's throat before—**NOW!**—the angel appears and calls Abraham twice by name. The covenant is restored and Isaac lives, but he came so close to dying that it is as though his departing spirit lifted the angel's wings as he flew to grant the reprieve. As a sacrificial victim, Lazarus is not so lucky. When Mary and Martha send word that their brother is seriously ill, Jesus deliberately waits for two days to go to his home in Bethany, and after he arrives he tells the disciples that he is *glad* Lazarus has died, because only now can Jesus reveal the full glory of God.[31] When I try to understand what glory means to Jesus, I always think of the severed ear of the centurion's servant. I should probably be paying attention to the bigger picture of what is happening in Gethsemane, but instead my mind snags on a detail: when the Roman soldiers arrive to arrest Jesus, the disciple Peter picks up a sword and angrily hacks off the ear of one of their servants. The ear falls to the ground, and Jesus stoops to pick it up out of the dust. By the lobe or the flange? Then he walks over to the bleeding man and reassembles him, almost absentmindedly, as though to show in this small way that the purpose of his life on earth is to reveal the secret adhesive that holds everything and everyone together.[32] As is so often the case in the Gospels, something appears in a place where there was nothing: not enough sentience, not enough food and drink, not enough energy left to keep the body alive. And the raising of Lazarus is the limit case, the full revelation of presence that galvanizes those who oppose Jesus and leads to his crucifixion, and then to the second resurrection witnessed by Mary Magdalene.

In a meditative novel called *Nora Webster*, the Irish master Colm Tóibín stages a more modest scene of revelation at a mid-twentieth-century vigil for a Catholic woman in the small Irish town of Enniscorthy. The revelation is brought about by several different kinds of pain. Nora Webster is mourning the agonizing death of her husband from tuberculosis, and she is taking heavy medication for injuries caused by her attempt to paint a room in her house. This minor renovation is one of several ways in which she tries to enlarge her life, but she is caged by her responsibilities as a middle-aged mother and widow, and her day's work with a paintbrush is so arduous that she feels as though the muscles in her chest are closing in around her heart. Under the influence of strong painkillers, she falls asleep and has a dream-vision in which she is returned to yet another scene of pain: her mother's wake. In life, the two women were often in conflict, and there was no peace between them. In her dream, Nora sits through the night beside her mother's dead body, studying her face. At first Nora thinks that without life in her "her mother was nobody."[33] But as the hours pass, she begins to feel that in death her mother becomes everybody, or at least everybody Nora knows. "It was as though her mother in this long night alone became all of them," she thinks.[34] Her mother's "natural life" is gone, replaced with "something else."[35] Nora has no name for this something else, but she feels sure that it is older and larger than individuality. It is "a long time in the making," Tóibín writes, and it only becomes visible when the temporary energy of a particular face is gone.[36] What remains when that energy vanishes seems to Nora truer and more important than anything she thought she knew about her mother while she was alive.

This larger life has its own pulse. We sense it by moonlight or firelight, or whenever the conscious mind is in abeyance and physical details recede. If it is a long time in the making, it also takes a long time to see. "We barely manage, all of us ... to see what's there," writes Tóibín. "That's the hardest thing, although no one would tell you that. If we could just look at what's there!"[37] Surely this difficulty explains why Jesus let poor Lazarus die in the first place, and why he has to spend four days in the tomb before he is called forth. The miracles have to be staged again and again in each of the Gospels in order to give people the time they need to see that presence overflows its container, whether it is a basket of food, an ear, or a human body. And Lazarus has to be immersed in the earth long enough for his temporariness to be washed away. It might be better to imagine that he was *planted*, not buried, and thus brought into contact with the lifespan of the planet itself. Little is said of what happens to him after his resurrection or about the life he went on to lead, but I cannot imagine that he was the same man he was before he died. That is the point, I suppose. After Lazarus arises he is clearly marked as a vessel for a kind of energy that is not particular to him, and it is not the same as the natural life his parents gave him. Most of the time people move too quickly to see the life that is made visible only when individuality ends, and we hold too tightly to our working theories of themselves. When other than a wake would a daughter spend ten hours staring at her mother's still face? And when would she ever look at a stranger or an enemy with such unbroken intimacy?

* * *

Exactly halfway through *The Odyssey*, King Odysseus embarks on a dangerous journey to the underworld to visit people who no longer exist. Having narrowly escaped Circe's pigpen, he has wasted a year in the witch's bed, a goblet of mulled wine in one hand and a drumstick in the other. Finally he is confronted by his men, who remind him that it is past time for their journey home to resume. Circe agrees to release him from her enchantment on one condition: he must "go down to Hades," a phrase that in the Homeric epics is always a synonym for death. "You will be twice dead, / when other people die only one time!" promises Circe: a strange enticement.[38] She tells Odysseus that when he gets to Hades he needs to seek travel advice from Tiresias, the blind prophet of Thebes, but Tiresias offers very little guidance that it is actually within Odysseus's power to follow. The prophet warns him that he will have to suffer for blinding Poseidon's son Polyphemus, "but you can get home, / if you control your urges and your men."[39] Can this be a joke? Odysseus is notoriously unable to control either, and you'd think a seer would know it. Tiresias's first instruction for a safe homecoming is to avoid the island of Thrinacia, because anyone who kills the divine cattle of the Sun who live there will surely die. A little later, Circe repeats the instruction almost word for word: if you land on Thrinacia, do not kill the cattle of the Sun. Still later, Odysseus repeats the warning to his men: do not kill the cattle of the Sun. In due course, the men land on Thrinacia and kill the cattle of the Sun.

In practical terms, it is hard to see why Hades was worth the trip. During his visit, Odysseus exchanges news with many people, beginning with his crewman Elpenor, dead only a few hours, followed by his mother Anticleia, Agamemnon, Achilles, and Herakles. Having drunk from the trench of sacrificial blood, each knows him at once, and rushes forward to talk. There is a sense in which Odysseus is fortified by their recognition, but another in which he is learning to be weak and silent, to bide his time as the dead must. Circe calls him a fool, and says, "Your mind is still obsessed with deeds of war. / But now you must surrender to the gods."[40] If he is to survive the journey to Ithaca, and then liberate his kingdom from the rapacious suitors who are plotting to marry his wife and kill his son, then the man who has always lived by his wits must learn how to be Nobody without crowing about it. Tiresias does not mention that before he takes revenge on the suitors Odysseus will need to spend weeks in disguise as a frail old beggar, clothed in rags, keeping company with slaves, dependent on handouts, and subject to all manner of insults in his own home. The purpose of a temporary death does not seem to be foreknowledge, but a dress rehearsal for the surrender that will eventually make survival possible.

Exactly halfway through the *Aeneid*, Aeneas's dead father Anchises appears to him. A partial list of the disasters that Aeneas has weathered at this point would include the sack of Troy, the murder of his wife, the death of his father, a typhoon, famine, plague, Harpies, the suicide of Dido, and the attempted arson of all his ships by the travel-weary Trojan women, who are driven to pyromania by vengeful Juno. Marooned on a beach and surrounded by the charcoal remains of his fleet, Aeneas begins to lose confidence. He wonders whether he should "forget the destiny foretold" and put someone else in charge of leading the Trojan refugees to their new home.[41] Then he is visited by the ghost of Anchises, who tells him to hold fast to his quest, but first to visit Elysium, where "you will hear of your whole race to come / And what walled town is given you."[42] Anchises guides his son through the Blessed Groves, a waiting room and training ground where spirits prepare to be born, already armored for battle. Over thousands of years, the dead are cleansed of who they were, and once "unmemoried" they are ready to be born again.[43] These shades will become Aeneas's sons and grandsons, the "souls of the future," and their purpose is to show him his destiny as the founder and patriarch of Italy.[44] Unlike most of Homer's ghosts, Anchises can come and go from Elysium, and when he appeared to Aeneas on the beach he could simply have told his son about his whole race to come. But again, it isn't really foreknowledge that matters. In order for his despair to lift, Aeneas has to immerse himself in the underworld where the past slowly turns into the future, and where what is empty becomes full again. It is not information that he seeks from the ancestors, but a lesson in patience that has to be learned with the whole body.

The first word of Homer's war epic is "rage." The word refers to Achilles, although everyone in the opening book of the *Iliad* is enraged by Agamemnon's refusal to return Chryseis to her father, even the gods. The difference is that Achilles holds on to his anger much longer than anyone else. His most common epithet is swift or fast runner, but for three-quarters of the epic he is so paralyzed by pain that he is literally motionless. After the public insults he receives from Agamemnon, Achilles famously refuses to go anywhere, hunkering down in his tent and insisting that he won't fight until the Trojan army comes to *him*. Yet there is no journey to the underworld in the *Iliad*, because in this epic the cure for paralysis happens above ground, among the living, who learn to surrender as time bends and slows.

When Agamemnon comes to his senses, he twice tries to compensate Achilles for Briseis with a "priceless ransom," and Achilles's reasons for refusing it are as strange to the Greek heroes as his refusal to fight.[45] Like Agamemnon, they assume that he is devoured by anger and pride, and to some degree they are right. "My heart still heaves with rage," Achilles tells Ajax.[46] Ajax understands this, although like everyone else he thinks it is time for Achilles's heart to settle down. What none of the Greeks can understand is that during his sabbatical from battle, Achilles has begun to question the purpose of a decade-long war in which breathing men are turned into bloody corpses over whom other men will fight and become corpses in turn, until they all meet as equals in Hades: heroes, cowards, and middling warriors alike. Once Achilles finally enters the fray he kills more people than anyone else, Greek or Trojan, and with far greater ease and cruelty. However, he also accomplishes what no one else can even imagine, which is to join with his enemy to bring the war to a temporary peace.

Achilles poses his questions about the value of the war in a torrent to Odysseus and Ajax, to whom Agamemnon has given the unenviable task of trying to change Achilles's mind with the help of an enormous pile of treasure in which he is not at all interested. 'Why have we made this "insane voyage" to Troy to restore Helen to her husband, King Menelaus?' Achilles demands.[47] "Are *they* the only men alive who love their wives, / those sons of Atreus? Never! Any decent man, / a man with sense, loves his own, cares for his own."[48] 'Agamemnon took Briseis from me,' Achilles says, 'just as he has separated every Greek warrior at Troy from the woman he loves. Why are these injustices less serious than Paris's abduction of Helen?' And why does Agamemnon think that Achilles—or anyone, for that matter—should risk his life in exchange for slaves and gold? "I say no wealth is worth my life!" shouts Achilles.[49] 'Therefore,' he continues, 'I recommend that you tell everyone to get in their boats and sail home while they still can, which is what I am planning to do in the morning. I care nothing for your contempt or praise, much less for your loot, because "I say my honor lies in the great decree of Zeus."'[50] It is generally agreed that clever Odysseus is the great mind of the Homeric world, but in moments like this I find Achilles far wiser. He could never invent the Trojan horse or outwit a cyclops, but here he asks questions so fundamental that Odysseus's jaw is agape and his mind awhirl.

"A stunned silence seized them all, struck dumb."[51] When Ajax and Odysseus return to the other Greek leaders to report this conversation, they are struck dumb too. Achilles has this effect on a lot of people. When he finally appears on the battlefield in Book 18, a dozen of the Trojans's best soldiers are so stunned by his blazing presence that they lose their wits and accidentally commit suicide, "crushed by chariots, impaled on their own spears."[52] No one else in the *Iliad* can kill men just by showing up, and no one else kills with such merciless efficiency that the river Xanthus, which flows through the plains of Troy, rises up in a great bloody wave to try to drown the warrior who has fouled its waters with so much gore. Men cannot "think as one" with Achilles, and neither can nature.[53] Yet even as he massacres his enemies and runs from a river, he carries the shield made for him at his mother's request by the immortal metal smith, Hephaestus. The smith is married to the goddess Charis, one of the Graces, and the world he depicts on Achilles's shield is a world of circles. Hephaestus begins with images of the earth, moon, sun, and all the celestial bodies that wheel through the firmament, and underneath them he forges the other cycles of social and natural life. There is the "sacred circle" of the city elders who sit to judge a murder and repair a family,[54] the deadly circle formed by a divided army laying siege to a walled city, the "dancing circle" where girls and boys link arms and dance together for their own joy and that of the crowd that rings them, and the cyclical story of the seasons, planting and harvest, birth and death, all girdled round by the ocean.[55] For me, the lines in which Homer describes this shield are the most exquisite in the epic. They lift us into the air, far above the killing grounds, so that we see the earth and everything that happens on it from the soaring and timeless perspective of a god.

Why should Achilles be given this gift by the god of fire? He is not a man whose heart lifts or turns in time; it runs on the spot, lashed by fury at Agamemnon, grief at his blood-brother Patroclus's death, and a desire to avenge him by killing Hector. The intensity of that grief moves Achilles's mother Thetis to protect Patroclus's dead body from decay, just as it moves Achilles to chase Hector around and around the walls of Troy and then to pull his unblemished body around and around Patroclus's burial mound. Patroclus dies wearing Achilles's armor and fighting for him, and Hector dies wearing his armor (stripped from Patroclus) and fighting against him. Their bodies and fates are married to Achilles's, and when in the final books of the epic their corpses burn, they are at once themselves, each other, and Achilles in effigy. Nevertheless, Achilles will not acknowledge any human connection with Hector, even though when they finally meet the Trojan prince is dressed from head to toe in Achilles's own outerwear. In the moments before they begin to fight, Hector proposes that they agree to return the dead body of the conquered man to his family for proper burial, but Achilles spits on this proposal just as he ignored Agamemnon's gifts and the "binding oaths" that would have united them in common cause.[56] If Achilles does not want to be bound to his friends, he certainly does not want to be bound to his enemies. "There are no binding oaths between men and lions," Achilles sneers at

Hector, just as "wolves and lambs can enjoy no meeting of the minds."[57] 'If I could,' he gloats, 'I'd love to carve your flesh and eat it raw!'

Achilles does not eat Hector's flesh, although he desecrates it with such savagery that even the gods are shocked. In response to his gratuitousness, Zeus decrees that Achilles must accept a ransom from King Priam and allow him to return Hector's body to Troy. Both men agree to this plan, although when Priam sets out from Troy alone by night in a wagon loaded with treasure, he is mourned by his wife and family "as if he went to his death."[58] They don't know that he is given safe passage through the battleground by Hermes, who lightens Priam's heart, just as he breathes fresh spirit into his tired horses and waves open the heavy locked doors to Achilles's shelter. Hermes tells Priam that his son's dead body remains unblemished because he is so very dear to the gods, and the King is filled with joy. As patron of trade and the dead, Hermes is uniquely qualified to preside over the purchase of a corpse, but by the time Priam arrives at Achilles's table the god's work is done. Zeus has ordered this meeting, but in lifting the King's sorrow and fear Hermes prepares the ground for what happens next. Simone Weil calls it the "grace of war."[59] Bernard Knox calls it a "mystery, a thing unprecedented."[60] Homer calls it a marvel. Priam falls to his knees in front of Achilles and kisses his hands, and a "sense of marvel runs through all who see him."[61] Achilles marvels; his men marvel. Even Priam marvels: "I have endured what no one on earth has ever done before," he says. "I put to my lips the hands of the man who killed my son."[62]

In this moment Achilles looks at Priam and thinks of his own aging father, weeps for the suffering he has caused him and for the pain he has inflicted on the King of Troy and his people. It is hard to believe that this is the same man who threatened to flense Hector's corpse with his teeth. But it is the same man, as we are reminded shortly when Priam oversteps by suggesting that Achilles take the ransom and sail home. Achilles shoots him a "dark glance" and says that if further angered he may not be able to stop himself from breaking Zeus's sacred host-laws by killing his guest.[63] Priam is terrified. When he risks his life and flouts tradition by kneeling before his enemy, he achieves what Agamemnon and his allies could not, which is to turn Achilles from an outlaw into someone with whom a man can "think as one."[64] After weeping with him, Priam thought he knew him well enough to send him home to his father. Then Achilles glanced, and Priam realized his mistake. That flicker of rage shows that even now Achilles remains unbiddable. Yet the two men continue to gaze at one another in awe, and Achilles offers to stop the war until Priam has had time to bury Hector with the honor he deserves. Neither man doubts for a moment that Achilles alone has the power to make good on this promise by holding thousands of men at bay.

Anne Carson reminds us that at his trial for treason Socrates aligned himself with Achilles. She calls them both "eccentric gentlemen who find themselves defying the rules of life of their society and disappointing the hopes of a circle of intense friends."[65] Eccentrics: people who step outside the loop that turns into a noose unless it loosens. Both men become eccentric by the strangeness of the way they value their own lives. Socrates appears to value his too little; Achilles, too much. Socrates's students cannot understand why he accepts his death sentence with such equanimity; Achilles's allies cannot understand why a warrior-king decides that treasure and the admiration of his peers do not justify risking his life. Carson writes that Socrates and Achilles make choices that bewilder everyone around them because Plato and Homer want to "convey a hero in his *difference* from other people, a hero whose power over other people arose in part from something *incognito* in his very being."[66] What is *incognito* isn't just hidden, but "something worth hiding," Carson says.[67] It's something we want and need to know. One of the functions of grace is to coax what is hidden into the light, but the secret doesn't respond to predictable overtures. The *incognito* is always "coming from somewhere else," and to beckon it, you have to come from somewhere else too.[68]

Priam did, when he knelt to ask Achilles for mercy; and Achilles did, when he granted it. This is why he has surprising admirers like Socrates and Simone Weil, a woman who was devoted to compassion and charity, which are not causes that are usually linked with the King of the Myrmidons. It's not that she covets Achilles's ability to slay men with a look or praises his heart-stopping excesses. What attracts her to him is exactly what makes him baffling to everyone around him: that *incognito* quality that comes from stepping outside the circle and slipping some of the strangeness out there into your pocket. Weil's own pockets were filled with it, and in the letters she wrote after the occupation of France she often describes her unwillingness to be "adopted into a circle, to live among people who say 'we' and to be part of an 'us,' to find I am 'at home' in any human *milieu* whatever it may be."[69] She refused to be baptized or take sacraments because she distrusted the institutional thinking and collective emotions of the church as much as those of the state, and blamed both for the rise of totalitarianism. God "likes to use castaway objects, waste, rejects," she writes, because human judgments are so flawed that what looks like waste to us may well be closer to the sacred than we know, and also because "the love of Christ is essentially something different."[70] Different than what? Different than the love of the house of Atreus that drives Agamemnon to exact vengeance on the people of Troy by murdering their men, raping their women, plundering their vaults, and burning their city to the ground. Closer to the love that Achilles feels when he looks at Priam and for a moment sees his own father. Weil understood that this is no less a marvel in our time than it was in Homer's.

* * *

In a play called "Hekabe," Euripides imagines the scene at Troy after the city has been taken and Achilles and Priam are both dead. The Greeks are ready to return home victorious, ships loaded with prisoners and loot, but they can't move because there is no wind to fill their sails. Achilles seems to be to blame for this paralysis. His ghost has appeared to demand one last gift before he will allow his former comrades to leave: he wants Priam and Hekabe's daughter Polyxena to be sacrificed on his tomb. Hekabe has already forfeited her husband, many sons and daughters, and her kingdom, and she does not want Polyxena's throat cut to gratify the spirit of the man who helped to bring about these losses. Moreover, she has a competing claim on Greek gratitude, which she puts to Odysseus when he comes to lead Polyxena to slaughter. 'Remember when I found you inside the walls of Troy and you begged for my protection?' Hekabe asks him. I saved your life then, "Now let me tell you what you owe me."[71] Odysseus admits that he is in her debt, but cannot overrule the decision made by the Greeks to give Achilles what he wants. They all know what happens when he doesn't get the girl.

Polyxena goes bravely to her death, telling her mother that she prefers to die than to live as a slave. Just as Hekabe is preparing to bury her daughter, a servant brings her the corpse of her young son Polydoros, who has been murdered by Polymestor, the Thracian King and Trojan ally to whom he had been sent for safekeeping at the beginning of the siege, along with a large quantity of gold. Once Polymestor learns that Troy is lost, he takes the gold and kills the boy, throwing his body in the sea lest the Greek army come looking for a surviving son of Priam and destroy Thrace in the process. Presented with the body of her son, Hekabe cries, "I do not exist. There is nothing left. Not even evils."[72] This is not exactly true—Hekabe still has her wits and a powerful new claim on the Greeks, which she now puts to Agamemnon himself. She pleads with him to help her to punish King Polymestor, because if men are allowed to murder their guests in defiance of Zeus's holy laws "then there is no justice among human beings."[73] She sharpens the point by claiming that Agamemnon owes her for the nights he spends with her daughter, Kassandra, who is now his slave. "Out of the dark, out of love in the night, / come all our greatest grace and gratitude," she says.[74] This has to be understood as a petition, not a statement of fact.

Agamemnon agrees to help, mainly because Hekabe has him cornered. "God sends no wind," he says, "and we must wait / and watch."[75] Or more exactly, wait and take revenge. He sends for King Polymestor, who arrives at the Greek camp with his young sons. Having assured him that he is safe as her guest, Hekabe lures him into her tent where she murders his children and gouges out his eyes. Now *she* is in violation of the host laws, although she does not seem to be interested in this irony. Polymestor appeals to Agamemnon to avenge her crimes, but no one credits his story about killing Polydoros to avoid an invasion, and no one has sympathy for the murder of his children. Besides, the winds have changed and it is time for the Greeks to go. Blinded and aggrieved, Polymestor hurls out a series of prophecies while they are packing: Hekabe will soon be turned into a red-eyed dog and die alone on the shores of Troy, and her daughter Kassandra will be murdered along with Agamemnon as soon as they get to Argos. "Take and throw him on a deserted island / since he wants to run his mouth," says heedless Agamemnon.[76] So much for blind prophets.

Nothing comes out of the dark in this play except more darkness. Everything is taken and nothing is given other than news of future debits. Perhaps this is because Hekabe repeatedly demands gratitude, believing that it is hers by right; perhaps it is because she repeatedly confuses vengeance for justice, believing that it is hers to adjudicate. Or perhaps it is because everyone in this play believes that the best way to pass the time while you wait for the wind to change is to murder a child. Then again, it may be the case that after ten years of war the empty place is just empty, void. The gods are nowhere to be found, and people no longer trust anything they cannot see or touch, even prophesy. Despite Polymestor's prediction, Agamemnon appears to believe that he and his men will find "all things happy in our houses, / released as we are, from this ordeal."[77] He is desperate and stupid enough to believe this, but no one in the Athenian audience does. By the end of the fifth century, Agamemnon's story is a myth so well established that it cannot be changed. Everyone knows that Clytemnestra is already plotting revenge for her husband's sacrifice of their daughter Iphigenia the last time the winds were blowing the wrong way and the Greeks couldn't get where they needed to go—to Troy, at the beginning of the siege.[78] Everyone also knows what it feels like to be on the losing side of a very long war. Where there is no grace there is only vengeance, and although the Greek ships set sail in the end, Hekabe is exiled from the human species, Polymestor dies unheeded on an island, and Agamemnon will soon be cut down by his wife.

W. G. Sebald wrote about situations like this, minus animal transfiguration. His subjects were usually survivors of modern wars, particularly the Holocaust. When I walked into the Holocaust Void in Daniel Libeskind's Jewish Museum in Berlin, I felt in my body something of the disabling emptiness that Sebald conjures throughout his writing. At the center of converging corridors whose walls house recessed displays of photographs, documents, household goods, suitcases, and musical instruments, each telling the story of a particular Jewish individual or family, I open a heavy door and enter a slim shaft several stories high, its bare concrete floor and rough walls lit only by a small skylight. The thick door shuts, and I am in silence and near-darkness. Why does this empty space produce such visceral terror? Is it because it evokes other enclosures where life ends—a bunker, a train car, a gas chamber, a crematorium, a grave? It does, but in another context it might feel like a sanctuary or retreat, an anchorite's cell. There may be people who experience it this way, but I did not, and neither did my companions on a gray November afternoon. On the strength of a passport photo and a scuffed violin, I can know very little about a stranger who lived and died more than three-quarters of a century ago, but as I peer through the glass at these artifacts, I feel that I have been permitted to know or at least to imagine something. Within the museum I have something to do, something to look at and think about. But when I walked into the Void, I felt obliterated, as though the entire world had ceased to exist.

In the summer of 2010, thirty-three Chilean miners were trapped more than 2000 feet beneath the ground when a mineshaft collapsed. The miners spent sixty-nine days waiting to be rescued and very nearly starved to death, but they never felt that the outside world had ceased to exist. According to Héctor Tobar, who has written a book about their ordeal, they decided that their burial alive meant something. They felt increasingly sure that the darkness that surrounded them was filled with divine intelligence, and that they were being watched and cared for by something "bigger than us."[79] The fact that they numbered thirty-three reminded them of Jesus in the tomb, and they began to pray together every day in the conviction that God was planning their resurrection and that their prayers could somehow comfort their families, who had been camped for weeks at the entrance to the mine. When the rescuers' drill finally broke through the enormous rock blocking their exit, the miners looked at it and said, "God exists."[80] From this moment forward, their faith waned. They began to quarrel among themselves and stopped praying together. As soon as their rescue became likely, they lost the need to believe in a presence larger than their own and the bond among them frayed. They went back to being individuals with their own interests to think about, and turned their minds to the lives that they would eventually resume.

I thought about this during the solar eclipse of August 21, 2017. I was in Ottawa on that day, and although more than 60 percent of the sun was blocked by the moon, the daylight never dimmed. It was very strange to look through protective glasses and see that a giant bite had been taken out of the sun without any diminishment of its radiance. Some French tourists were sunbathing on the grass beside me, and they had no idea than an eclipse was in progress at all. Now I regret that I didn't make an effort to witness totality, especially after reading essays about it by Helen MacDonald and Annie Dillard, who both, decades apart, write about what it is like to stand in a crowd of people and feel the world end for a few minutes. People and animals scream as the sun disappears and the earth's magnetic fields are disarrayed; Helen Macdonald falls to her knees and weeps, and Annie Dillard steps out of time. When they look around, they both sense that they have been transported to an underworld without even moving. As the sun comes back, everyone returns to a life that they can understand, and for a few moments—perhaps a few hours—it is a larger life than the one they felt before. MacDonald describes a "wordless solidarity" among strangers that resembles that of a "religious congregation."[81] Dillard writes that when the star that sustains life on this planet goes dark we come into rare and fleeting contact with "what our sciences cannot locate or name, the substrate, the ocean or matrix or ether that buoys the rest, that gives goodness its power for good, and evil its power for evil, the unified field."[82] This unified field, she continues, is what allows "our complex and inexplicable caring for each other, and for our life together here." Caring is "given," she says. "It is not learned."[83]

Thousands of people travelled great distances to watch the world go dark in the summer of 2017, and I don't think these pilgrimages can be fully explained by a fascination with astronomy or a hunger for spectacle. There is a collective intuition at work here about the way totality brings us into the gift zone, but total eclipse is an exceptional event, and there is no force of will or flourish of legerdemain by which we can put out the sun when life becomes unbearably small, nor any guarantee that caring will last more than a few moments, if it happens at all. No one chooses to be buried alive, alone or with thirty-two other people, although I have read about the extreme cavers and "cataphiles" who risk their lives to explore the underworlds of our planet, and sometimes die in the process, buried within deep time.[84] No one can reach into her own body, pull out a vertebrae, and say, "Let's cut this up and use it as our common currency," although when I look at my friend's anorexic daughter a few days before she is hospitalized with impending heart and organ failure, I can see every tiny bone in her spinal column, and it is as though her skeleton speaks the pain that she is hiding even from herself. In the absence of a celestial rarity or ecstatic fire, the things people do to bring about totality on their own terms are often dangerous and violent.

In the worst years of his addiction, my grandfather squandered most of the equity in five hair salons, a dress shop, an apartment building, and the family home, no matter that this money was not his to give but belonged in equal or greater measure to my grandmother. In old age, when he was broke and sober, he used to spend hours on public transit travelling to the center of the city, where he stood at the busiest intersection and chose a stranger out of the crowd. Then he handed over his bank card and PIN, and asked the stranger to withdraw money from his account. The pretext for my grandfather's request was that he was legally blind and could not read an LED screen, but in the early 1990s it was easier to find a brick-and-mortar bank than an ATM. Downtown Hamilton had been hollowed out by the decline of the steel industry and poor urban planning, which meant that my grandfather was standing alongside homeless people on a main street whose once upscale stores were now Bingo halls and pawnshops. In half the time it took to get downtown he could have reached the branch where he banked all his life and safely made a withdrawal with a teller. Unfortunately there was no chance that this teller would decide to drain his bank account, pocket the cash, and run down the street, and because there was no danger in the transaction there was also no intimacy, no path out of loneliness. My grandfather handed his trust to strangers for the same reason that he gave them all his money years earlier: he gave in order to risk getting taken. He was willing to be taken down to nothing because for reasons I do not fully understand his life was always too small for him, and he could not bear the claustrophobia of it.

There is a shockingly intimate murder scene that takes place toward the end of David Malouf's novel *Ransom*, which is about the meeting of Achilles and Priam in the final weeks of the Trojan war. Unlike Homer, Malouf does not end his story with temporary peace and funeral games. He ends when Troy is a heap of stones, its splendor forgotten, its monarch dead, and its people at the mercy of roaming brigands. He imagines that when Achilles and Priam meet they experience violent flashes of clairvoyance in which they foresee this devastation: Priam's son Paris will murder Achilles, and then Achilles's son Neoptolemus will catch Priam in his palace, wrestle him to the ground, wrench his head back, and saw through the cartilage at his throat, slipping in a widening pool of the old man's blood. With mixed triumph and shame, Neoptolemus will cry, "Father," dedicating the murder to Achilles and seeking his approval.[85] Instead it is the dying Priam who will respond, taking on the role of father for his teenaged murderer as though in homage to Priam's own bond with Achilles, the man who killed so many sons of Troy. I am a father too, Priam seems to say to Neoptolemus, and even as you kill me I can make you my son. Or perhaps it is only as you kill me that I can make you my son.

"I am responsible for the other insofar as he is mortal," wrote Emmanuel Levinas more than half a century ago.[86] In the intervening years, many have agreed. Variations on Levinas's thinking are to be found everywhere that vulnerability and precariousness are identified as the impetus to caring. Mortality is universal, which is why the Greek god of the underworld portions equal shares, yet we know that most of the time this idea of equality is as bloodless as a shade, and so is the abstract intellectual language of ethical obligation or duty of care. Responsibility is far too weak a word for what Priam feels for the teenager who is cutting his throat. What he feels is not a thought or commitment; it is what is left when thoughts and commitments are gone.

Priam knows what it is like to be intimately bound to a killer because he has had this experience before. Malouf reveals that the King's name means "the price paid": the man who brings the ransom has already been ransomed.[87] Priam was born Podarces, but as a child was renamed by Herakles after an earlier war in which Troy was razed. During that war Herakles killed most of the city's royal family, but on a whim offered Podarces's sister Hesione the right to choose one gift from amid the wreckage, and she chose her six-year-old brother from a crowd of orphans destined for slaughter or slavery. Priam tells his wife that all his life he has felt that some part of him is in the underworld with Podarces, the little boy whose identity Priam surrendered to Herakles in exchange for survival, and another part is in the slave compound, where for sixty years he has "known only drudgery and daily humiliation and blows."[88] Without the gift that binds him to Herakles, his father's killer, Priam could be that slave—some part of him feels that even though he is king he *is* that slave, and Malouf suggests that it is this ongoing experience of contingency and terror that makes it possible for Priam / Podarces to get in a broken-down donkey cart and go to find Achilles.

This vulnerability is sometimes figured as bodily injury, and not just because the body is used to represent inner processes that we cannot see. There is a disturbing sense that we learn vulnerability through the body, as through the body of Jesus, first by his crucifixion and then in his encounter with Thomas, who will not believe in the resurrection until he puts his own finger into the wound. In Michelangelo Caravaggio's voluptuous painting of this scene, *The Incredulity of Saint Thomas*, Jesus grasps Thomas by the hand and pulls his forefinger into the cut up to the middle joint, far enough to confirm that the opening is real. We are to understand that when the apostle withdraws his finger his incredulity is gone and he is ready to believe that a new calendar has begun. Jesus would have preferred Thomas to believe without touching, but it is also Jesus who invites the skeptic to put his hand into the wound, and Caravaggio makes sure that we see the physicality of both the hand and the opening. For me, the scene is far more compelling than the instant belief of the other apostles. According to the Gospel of John, Jesus reprimands Thomas for doubting and praises those who can believe without seeing, but long before Jesus's death is abstracted and disseminated in words and images that can no longer be verified with a forefinger, Thomas's literalism connects the founding of a new moral order with the afterlife of a real body.[89]

Because this is a painting by Caravaggio, who loved to profane biblical iconography by using prostitutes and roustabouts as models, Jesus does not wear a halo or exude a golden nimbus. Outside the frame of the painting there is an invisible source of light, which pours from the upper left hand corner over the four men who are pictured, but it does not come from the Nazarene. There is nothing particularly holy or ethereal about him. His body looks strong, especially his hands, which are like those of someone used to a hard day's labor, and he stares down at the wound in his side as though he is almost as shocked by it as Thomas and his companions are. All four men are staring at the cut that is the focal point of the image, but elsewhere there is a curious detail that seizes my attention: a tear in the shoulder seam of Thomas's shirt, through which a sliver of illuminated skin glows. Thomas's left shoulder and elbow are at the very front of the picture plane, even closer to the viewer than Jesus himself, and so it is no accident that my eyes are drawn to the narrow rip in his garment. In shape and size it is nearly identical to the cut in Jesus's torso. If you drew a horizontal line

FIGURE 5.2 *Michelangelo Merisi da Caravaggio, "The Incredulity of Saint Thomas." Credit: Reproduced by permission of The Prussian Palaces and Gardens Foundation Berlin-Brandenburg / Photographer: Hans Bach.*

across the painting, it would intersect the cut and the tear at about the same point. The tear is visible because the dark robe that Thomas wears over his shirt has slipped off his shoulder and down his back, just as Jesus has pulled his robe off one shoulder to reveal his upper body. Even the way Jesus grips his robe is similar to the way Thomas braces his hand against his cloak to prevent it from falling to the ground. The two men mirror one another, the messiah and the doubter. It is as though whatever change is about to take place in Thomas's imagination must first take place in his body, which is being reshaped in Jesus's own image.

Hekabe was presented with any number of dead bodies, and then she turned around and made more, just as Achilles did. The murdered or wounded body is not enough to make a man see his enemy as a father or claim his killer as a son. Something marvelous has to happen so that a person's heart is opened rather than broken by agony, and it is unlikely to be a resurrection. In 1940, Simone Weil wrote an essay lamenting the primacy of physical force in the *Iliad* and in human history, although she also draws a line from Homer to the Gospels, discovering in both the principle that "the sense of human misery is a pre-condition of justice and love."[90] She writes, he "who does not realize to what extent shifting fortune and necessity hold in subjection every human spirit, cannot regard as fellow-creatures nor love as he loves himself those whom chance separated from him by an abyss."[91] Malouf's own fascination with the *Iliad* began around the same time as Weil's, in 1943, when he was a child in Brisbane, the headquarters of the Allied campaign in the Pacific. He shares her belief that misery is a precondition for justice and love, but both know that it is just as often a precondition for hate.

In 1908, a Jewish man named Lazarus Averbuch fled the pogroms of Eastern Europe for the United States, only to be murdered as a suspected anarchist by the Chicago chief of police. After his murder, Averbuch's body was used to support anti-Semitic beliefs about Jewish degeneracy, and there are several macabre archival photographs taken by the city of Chicago's coroner's office in which Averbuch's corpse is dressed and posed upright in a chair as though still alive. A few of these photographs are reproduced in Aleksandar Hemon's novel *The Lazarus Project,* in which a Christian and a Muslim, refugees from opposing sides of the siege of Sarajevo, work together to reconstruct Averbuch's life and death. The novel's epigraph comes from the scene in the Gospel of John in which Jesus calls Lazarus from the tomb:

And when he thus had spoken, he cried with a loud voice,
Lazarus, come forth. And he that was dead came forth, bound
Hand and foot with rags, and his face was covered with a cloth.
Jesus saith unto them, Loose him and let him go.[92]

The purpose of this resurrection is not the return of the dead. In Hemon's novel, as in the Gospels, the purpose of resurrection is the revelation of presence that connects people across divides of religion, ethnicity, and time. *The Lazarus Project* is about the strength of those divides, but it is also about moments when a person looks across them and thinks, "That's me."[93]

With funding from an American arts organization called The Glory Foundation, Brik and his friend Rora, a Muslim war photographer, set out to learn all they can about Lazarus Averbuch. Together they travel home toward Sarajevo through Eastern Europe, where traces of the Holocaust, the Soviet occupation, and the Bosnian war are apparent everywhere. "That's me," thinks Brik, as he stands in a Jewish cemetery that was desecrated first by the Nazis and then by the Soviets.[94] "That's me," as he watches a strutting mobster and imagines smashing his forehead with a hammer.[95] "That's me," as he prepares to punch a Ukrainian sex trafficker in the face.[96] "That's me," as he looks at an X-ray of the bones he broke in his own hand as a result of those punches.[97] "We were like everybody else, because there was nobody like us," he realizes.[98] "And everybody was me, and I was everybody, and in the end it didn't matter if I died."[99] First it is the murdered body of Lazarus Averbuch that provokes this realization; then it is the murdered body of

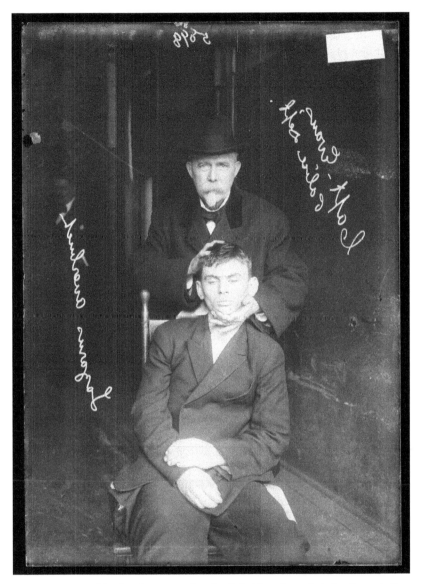

FIGURE 5.3 *Dead body of Lazarus Averbuch held up in a chair by Captain Evans of the police department. Chicago, Illinois, March 2, 1908. Credit: DN-0005898, Chicago Daily News collection, Chicago History Museum*

Rora, who is shot to death in a Sarajevo café by a drug addict who wants to steal his camera. The Lazarus project never ends. It is important that this project always involves reaching back through layers of history, from Abu Ghraib to Sarajevo to Chicago to Kishinev to Bethany. In part this is because it is useful to consult precedents for fresh hatreds, but mainly it is because the part of the mind or the spirit that allows people to look at one another and say, "That's me," is not contemporary. Hemon calls it the "deep face" that is hidden when people are "acting out the person they imagined themselves to be."[100] It is revealed only when people are in so much pain that they no longer know who they are, and it is almost impossible to see in the distracting specificity of the here-and-now or in the strategic faces of the living.

Once again, Thomas has the advantage over the quicker apostles, even though his name is synonymous with shameful skepticism. Now he would probably write a Slow manifesto and be praised for it. He might make a documentary about Fred Rogers, the slowest moving man in the history of American television, and win an award for it. Thomas meets his resurrected teacher for the first time a full week later than his fellow disciples, by which point he has heard the glad tidings twice, first from Mary Magdalene and then from his friends. Even so, he needs to take the extra step of putting his hand into Jesus's side. Everything about Thomas's relationship to the resurrection lags behind. If this delay is presented as a deficiency, it also shows that to make the connection between someone and everyone requires a mind that does not leap to certainty, but stumbles and hesitates, pauses and looks again. The person who is slow to believe may also turn out to be slow to judge.

In her long poem *Memorial*, which she describes as an "oral cemetery," the British poet Alice Oswald turns slowness into a poetic method.[101] Her poem is based on the *Iliad*, but she subtracts Homer's epic heroes and gods, and is left only with the names of the Greek and Trojan dead. Her description of each murder that takes place during the war is followed by a simile-stanza that compares that death with something that happens in nature: wind, rain, darkness, snow, shooting stars, waves on the ocean, seasonal change, one animal hunting another, a mother soothing a child. Some of her similes are drawn directly from the *Iliad*, which she translates from the original Greek, although she deliberately introduces a few anachronisms—a "lift," and a description of Hector as a "man rushing in leaving his motorbike running"—lest we mistake this poem for ancient history.[102] Then, having anchored her memorial in immemorial processes that are the same today as they were when the *Iliad* was composed, she repeats the simile.

Here is how Oswald describes the deaths of Diores, son of Amarinceus, and Pirous the Thracian, who speared each other on the battlefield:

Like through the jointed grass
The long-stemmed deer
Almost vanishes
But a hound has already found her flattened tracks
And he's running through the fields towards her

And again:

> Like through the jointed grass
> The long-stemmed deer
> Almost vanishes
> But a hound has already found her flattened tracks
> And he's running through the fields towards her[103]

The hound and the deer are running for their lives, but we are decelerating, reading the same words a second time. When I first read *Memorial*, my impulse was to skim or skip the repetitions, although I knew that this was not what the poet wanted of me. What she wants of me is what she wants of herself, which is to work with a part of the mind that is not busy figuring things out. On several occasions Oswald has recited the entirety of *Memorial* from memory, and she has described these performances as a homage to the *Iliad* as an oral poem and spoken about the long walks and repetitious tasks that allow her to learn words by heart. If given a choice about her day's work as a professional gardener, she chooses hours of raking, digging, or potting plants.[104] These are the kinds of simple and rhythmic activities that allow a person to memorize hundreds of lines of verse, and they are also the kinds of activities that it might be wise to undertake while listening to those lines, especially to the repetitions I wanted to hurry past. "I already know that," I think to myself, missing the point.

Oswald's shift into the lives of animals is not a way of proposing that killing is natural. That is a fatuous idea. The shift is a way of proposing that the act of remembering needs to be balanced with forgetting the historical and biographical details that pitted Diores and Amarinceus against one another. *Memorial* opens with eight pages of names that evoke contemporary war memorials like Maya Lin's Vietnam Veterans Memorial in Washington, D.C., which engraves the names of fallen and missing American soldiers on reflective walls of polished rock that resemble headstones. But unlike modern memorials, Oswald's poem pays tribute to the dead on *both* sides of the war. She places their names in a common registry that makes no mention of their nationality, a technique that erases the line between past and present, Greek and Trojan, and compels us to forget the very difference that made a memorial necessary in the first place. This is not a conventional memorial or gravestone, which sets out to preserve as much individuality as possible.

When I visit a memorial, I watch the way people interact with it. At the site of the World Trade Center, I notice that people have left flowers, and in one case a small American flag, in the names of the men and women who died there. Each name is cut out of metal, forming a tiny vase that pours into the rectangle of flowing water beneath. When I visited Maya Lin's Vietnam Veterans Memorial, I watched people search for the name of someone they lost and then stand in front of it, often reaching out to stroke the engraved letters, as one might touch a headstone or a face. In their place I would do the same; I would want every lost detail preserved and grieved, and I cannot be sure that I would not become as vengeful as Hekabe and Achilles if I did not feel that this need was being met. I am not a fallen queen or a king in mourning, and I have never fought in a war, but I know what it is like to be seized by terror and rage. There are men I would like to annihilate, not by cutting their throats, but by disassembling every atom of their bodies and every remnant of their minds so that nothing holds them in this world, not even the basic attraction among elemental particles. I had no opportunity to look at my mother's father after he died, so I cannot know whether I might have seen the deep face hidden within the serial child rapist; I have never seen the face of the man who strangled my husband's sister and threw her body in a river, because he is still at large. These men were never brought to justice or even called to account, but I have no choice but to learn to live with them.

My mother's father looked at me and my sisters and he saw prey, ripe for devouring. We were shielded from him, but my mother and other young girls were not. All my life I have watched my mother bear the consequences, including the early death of her younger sister, who was left unprotected in their father's house. The painting you see here, "The Great Escape," is one of my mother's many images of magical alleviation, and it hangs in my house now, right here beside my desk. I grew up surrounded by these iridescent paintings of miraculous flight.

Almost everything my mother paints floats or flies, and all is silvered or gilded. She has been secretly fasting for as long as I can remember, and it has taken me many years to understand that it is because she too wants to be graced, lighter than air. Now her body has lost the capacity to maintain or repair bone, and she is almost weightless. Sometimes it takes a team of paramedics and ER physicians to bring her down to earth. They flood her body with the nutrients that stop her organs from failing and her brain from short circuiting, halt the seizures and the blurred speech, and it is as though they are scraping gold and silver leaf off her body.

"When I was a child, I felt that every day had to be justified," my mother told me recently. This was during a year in which on separate occasions both she and my father had to be revived in Emergency Rooms. "When was it decided that you have no value other than what you create out of nothing every morning?" I wanted to ask her. I too have always felt that each day begins with a pile of rubble and ends with a referendum on the merit of whatever I make of it, but this precariousness is nothing like what my mother feels. Even after we stopped seeing my dangerous grandfather, she called him regularly to tell him about her work and to put me on the phone to detail whatever academic achievements she thought might impress him. His voice on the other end of the line was silky and bored. My mother

FIGURE 5.4 *"The Great Escape," by Cora Brittan. Photo Credit: Robert Bean.*

is a prodigal giver, but her father was not interested in being forgiven. He endured my mother's forgiveness only because he wanted access to the bodies of his granddaughters.

I abhorred my mother's father, and that will never change. Yet one of my sisters is named for his mother, Angeline, who taught my own mother to turn collars and match plaids, along with other vanishing arts of the homestead that my mother still practices, and whose true value comes from the memory of her grandmother's tender attention. Stretched across four generations, I wonder if that love asks something of us: for our great-grandmother's sake, must we trust that her son was once something other than a despicable predator who damaged many lives and should either have been sentenced to life without parole in a federal prison or beaten to death in an alley? Without ever meaning or wanting to, I have posed my oldest daughter a similar question. She is named for her father's sister, Simone. She is too young to be told what happened to her aunt, but already she says that she hates her middle name and will change it when she grows up. I know it's not really the name she hates, but the anguish that surrounds it. She senses those powerful emotions, as children do. One day she will understand why, and what will she feel then? Her name is not just a memorial but a palimpsest in which the presence of a killer lurks. Of course that is true of all memorials. In darker moments, I fear that it is also a beacon to that killer, who might decide to come for my child as he came for her aunt. This is not a reasonable fear, but there it is. Reason has nothing useful to offer under these conditions, and neither does knowledge. Some members of my mother's family knew that my grandfather was a predator, and they knew because they were told in plain language, but they did nothing to stop him because they simply did not know what to do. Lives were irreparably damaged through their inaction, and unlike my mother I do not forgive. She will always be a woman who stands at the tomb, hands open and heart filled with hope. I will always be a woman who stands back, fists clenched and heart filled with fury.

* * *

This is an essay about patience, but children aren't patient. They don't wait quietly for adults to explain the world; they follow the clues and uncover the secrets. Last year my daughters discovered what happened to their aunt. Their discovery was accidental, not the carefully managed revelation I had planned. As soon as she learned the truth, my daughter said, "Now he will come to kill me too." She has said it many times now, and I am shocked, because I never imagined that she would think as I do. "What else are you lying about?" she yelled. "Nothing," I lied. "Good," I think. "She knows how to get angry." My grandmother taught me about rage, and some of what she taught is worth passing on, especially to a girl who fears that she will be murdered. One day my daughter will need to learn that anger is powerful energy because it burns *her* for fuel, but I'll worry about that later, or never.

My grandmother knew how to dye a rich woman's hair blonde without the brassy highlights that would make her look like trash, but she also knew how to knock a grown man unconscious, and she learned this from her own mother. There is a story that my grandmother often told me: one night my great-grandmother was walking home alone on the dark streets of London when she heard a man following her. Block after block, his footsteps quickened as the distance between them narrowed. At first she put on speed, but when she realized that she could not outpace him she whirled around and ran straight into his arms. He was knocked off balance just as she intended, and in that moment of confusion she pushed her hat pin into his eye. My grandmother laughed out loud as she told this tale, waving her hands in delight, but it was clear that there was a lesson here about preparation and ferocity. "Always catch him off guard," she whispered to me. It was assumed in my family that a woman had to fight, and that it was naïve foolishness to imagine otherwise. The fact that we were at war was not an excuse for vulgarity or sensible shoes. A woman must never be brassy, in hair or speech or wardrobe; with every word and gesture she must exude the refinement of a queen, while hiding something sharp and brutal at the center of her character. Late in life, my grandmother took this literally, using her lacquered fingernails like tiny pink bayonets. "Don't be afraid," I need to tell my own daughter, "because you too are a descendant of Hekabe, gouger of eyes."

Euripides tells us that the Queen of Troy ends her life alone, a howling pariah dog in a smoldering warzone. In the last decades of her life, my grandmother turned into a woman who could no longer tell the difference between an enemy and a grandchild; she became cruel, as her own mother had been. These women learned strength, but also viciousness and bitter solitude. I don't want my daughters to have to fight like my great-grandmother, and my grandmother, and my mother, and my aunts, and my sister-in-law, and almost every single woman I grew up with. I don't want my daughters to have to fight like Hekabe, who watched men ignore their own laws to close ranks against her, and who felt so alone that rage became her only food. I have a close-up understanding of what this looks like. It is ruin.

In my family we do not refer to my mother's father by name, and my mother has cut him out of some of her family photos so that we can stand to look at them. You will notice that I have not named him here, and I will not. I leave that patient work to my children, or to theirs, or to no one. I know that it is outrageous to suggest that any memorial should rank the names of the dead alongside the names of their killers. Even in the pages of a book, it is sometimes impossible. But I also know that it is precisely what the Lazarus project asks. This is why Alice Oswald implies that if we are to learn anything from the names of the fallen or about the forces that drive people to harm each other then we have to do more than consider their fleeting particularity. The imperative to think slowly is also why the figure of Lazarus, like the figure of the risen Christ, has such a powerful hold on the imagination, whether or not you have faith in the eschatology that Lazarus embodies. These men step out of life and out of time, and when they come back they are nobody and everybody.

After Simone was murdered, my husband's parents pulled away from their synagogue. They continued to observe the Sabbath and keep kosher, but they found more sustenance in their garden and in volunteer work with new immigrants, refugees, and the homeless. They had full-time jobs and a child still at home, but they joined a group of people who drove around

Toronto in a van late at night, dispensing food and hot drinks to people living on the street, even though the police hypothesized that their daughter might have been killed by a homeless person. At the same time, they joined a counseling circle with other parents whose children had been murdered, which is a specific kind of agony that can only be understood by those who have experienced it. Unlike my in-laws, who lived in a middle-class suburb, many of these parents came from public housing projects or the poor neighborhoods where violence is concentrated in any city. For a few hours a month, differences of race and class were less important than their ability to help one another in a way that no one else could. Twenty-four years after her daughter's unsolved murder, my mother-in-law, Linda Sandler, was cited by the government of Ontario for her exceptional record of service as a volunteer.

When there is serious trouble in a family or community, some people turn their energy toward reforming the corrupt or weak laws that failed to protect them. This is crucial work, and no one can say otherwise. But if there are essential forms of goodness that cannot be legislated, there are also forms of depravity that cannot be prevented by our laws. Step outside the courtroom and you may find yourself in the Temple of the Graces, dancing with the three beautiful young goddesses who wear garlands of flowers in their hair, or you may come face to face with a monster. Whether depravity is uniquely human, or whether it is one of the provisional names we give to those atavistic forces that howl through the world and care nothing for our survival, I do not know. I do know that in my family the people who have best survived it are those who follow an unlegislated impulse to give, including my parents, who are more faithful to the wounded and wayward than anyone I know. If they have a small windfall from the sale of artwork, they send a hefty percentage to the Salvation Army, even though they continue to do a great deal of their own shopping at the Salvation Army. They see no contradiction here. To her great amusement, my mother sometimes accidentally buys the very same clothes that she has donated. Is this an example of giving so that the left hand doesn't know what the right hand is doing, or evidence of an unerring personal aesthetic? Who can say? If old friends or neighbors drop by my parents' house unannounced, they might stay for six hours or for thirty-six, joining any household activities that occur during that period with the conviction that they are fully welcome, even critical to the proceedings. My parents seem to feel that it would be an unspeakable assault on an uninvited guest's dignity to suggest that their presence is not entirely appropriate to the baby shower or birthday celebration that is about to take place. On the contrary, this guest must be given a place of honor at the head of the table, his glass kept full, his stories heard. If he wants to spend the night on the couch or in his car, then blankets will be provided and a hot breakfast made ready in the morning.

Are you currently on a locked psychiatric ward from which you have recklessly decided to discharge yourself against your doctors' orders, only to realize that you have nowhere to live? My father will take your call. Did you once skip bail and become a fugitive in another country, where you now operate within the informal economy, serving clients who are heavily armed? You and your clients are welcome to stay for dinner. Are you a charming smuggler of stolen antiquities and contraband substances who operates under an assumed name? We're having a party, and you are invited. Your skills will prove very helpful once we too are on the run from the police, living in the Mexican semi-desert in a cabin without furniture, electricity, water, or reliable access to food.

Like forgiveness, wanton hospitality can be dangerous. It is often *infuriating*. I see my father only once or twice a year, and during these brief reunions I do not want him to lavish his time on an old friend or a stranger in the Walmart parking lot. I want him to pay attention to me and my children, not play host to all comers. But he is like his own father, who handed his bank card to strangers on a run-down street corner and said, in effect, "Be my guest." My father once assumed full legal responsibility for an incarcerated addict he had known for three days, and often runs errands for homeless people. He has been swindled on more than one occasion. He is an unusually kind man, but I don't think this is ordinary kindness. It is not a principled attempt to be charitable or to implement a theory of social justice, but an uncontrollable instinct to open rather than close, no matter the consequences. Sometimes it looks like giving to get taken, but who am I to know what prayer is? To know when a fist should unfurl, when rage should give way to undefended gentleness, requires wisdom far beyond anything I can summon, even on my best days. And if I often feel that in all this gratuitous giving there is not enough left for me—well, then I have more to learn about survival. In truth, I would rather draw a line under survival and move on to whatever comes next. I am aware that what I want has no bearing here.

In the final pages of *Memorial*, Alice Oswald opens her poem to the ancient time of the heavens. She begins with 200 names and ends with eleven similes that move our minds away from those names and toward the world as it is and has always been, at least in human memory. Leaves fall, chaff blows, birds mass, insects hum, wolves hunt, and water rushes across the earth that feeds us all. Then this last comparison, nice and slow:

Like when god throws a star
And everyone looks up
To see that whip of sparks
And then it's gone

Like when god throws a star
And everyone looks up
To see that whip of sparks
And then it's gone[105]

The whip of sparks is gone, but the glory that holds us together comes out of the darkness where the mind can't reach. This is the oldest and most durable idea about the origin of grace. I keep looking.

Conclusion: Rest

With myths, one should not be in a hurry.
ITALO CALVINO[1]

There are long stretches of time when my mind is so heavy that at almost any hour of almost any day I could sit down and weep. Under these circumstances, my thoughts turn in two directions. In the first, I imagine that I am wearing a fierce and elegant suit of armor. This is not the clanking rusty hardware of a medieval knight, but a radiant bristle of retractable metal spines that emerges from my skin on command and can be thrown a great distance. My weaponry is autonomic, like breathing or peristalsis; it cannot be broken or taken away while I am alive, and it will fight for me even in my sleep. I visualize the materials and mechanics in great detail, as though I might make some drawings and take them to my grandfather's forge or beg Hephaestus for a favor, even though I know that my armor is not something you make. It's something that just is.

Or I walk into a Vermeer painting, where I remove my mind and carefully place it within a white enamel basin that is half filled with cool water. Then, like a mother who has just put her wailing infant down for a nap, I sit on a nearby chair and look at the silver northern light that pours through the opened window. It is this light that makes Vermeer's women look as though they are in the presence of an unremarked benediction, the kind that comes in the middle of an ordinary day's work, and I want to be one of those women. I am not interested in the physical details of how my mind gets out of my skull—does the top of my head pop up like the lid on a shampoo bottle or unscrew like the lid of a Mason jar? This is not important, nor is the question of how my mind is related to my brain or to the rest of my body. In this reverie I don't care about engineering or metaphysics. All that matters is the moment of lightness, of respite.

In the mid-1980s, when Italo Calvino was asked to prepare a series of lectures on the faculties of imagination that he considered most important for the new century, he began with an effervescent essay called "Lightness." This was the first of the six memos that he wrote in the final year of his life for the inhabitants of the new millennium: for us. In this address to the future, Calvino proposes that stories can relieve us of the crushing "weight, the inertia, the opacity of the world."[2] He takes as his first example the mythical figure of Perseus, who with his winged sandals is able to fly toward Medusa and cut off her petrifying head. It takes an airborne man to conquer stone. Readers of Ovid know that Pegasus will be born from Medusa's spilled blood, and that before she was a monster she was a beautiful young woman raped by Neptune in the temple of Minerva. The outraged goddess responded to the desecration of her shrine by turning the young woman's beauty into both a shield and a weapon. Thus we learn that beauty and monstrosity are interwoven, just as astonishment can be creative and light. Perseus's flight is not an attempt to evade this complicated crisis but a different way of approaching it, which is precisely the value that Calvino finds in all stories that lift the mind into a space where it becomes possible to outwit atrophy and despair. "I just want to escape into lightness," says a friend who is battling cancer. I send her fairy tales.

What Calvino calls lightness, Marina Warner calls magical thinking. In *Stranger Magic*, her monumental study of the European reception of the *Arabian Nights* from the early eighteenth century to the present day, she observes that levitation is always associated with strangers, both within the *Nights* and within the minds of its European readers. Only our strangest selves can defy gravity. Flight creates access to a way of thinking that is not from around here but will change the neighborhood, and perhaps for the better; certainly for the better, if the neighborhood is troubled by a Gorgon. Warner writes, the "faculties of imagination—dream, projection, fantasy—are bound up with the faculties of reasoning and essential to making the leap beyond the known into the unknown."[3] Calvino called this leap "thoughtful lightness" to distinguish it from empty frivolity.[4]

Like Perseus and the magic carpets of the *Arabian Nights*, Hermes marries wisdom with levity, and not just because he can fly. He is a thresholder whose natural habitat is the doorway, the window ledge, the property line. It is important not to be too literal about this business of the threshold; edges can appear in unexpected places, including in the very middle of things. People who can fly are particularly good at making this point, and so is a man who traverses the sky on a tightrope, as Philippe Petit did in real life and in the pages of Colum McCann's novel, *Let the Great World Spin*. On the ground, there is the violence of New York City in the nightmare era of Richard Nixon, Watergate, and the aftermath of the Vietnam War. One hundred and ten stories above ground, there is a Frenchman walking between the Twin Towers. As Petit balances on his wire, unperturbed by turbulence, he "felt for a moment uncreated. Another kind of awake," and so do all the New Yorkers who watch from the street.[5] A very similar scene takes place in Teju Cole's *Open City*, another New York novel about the weight of suffering, the gravity of trauma, and men in the sky—several of them, who parachute into Central Park for no reason other than mischief and joy.[6] And then there is Kendrick Lamar on the opposite coast, flying through the poorest streets of Los Angeles in the video for "Alright." He is singing about racism and police brutality in contemporary America, but look at the wonder on the face of every child who watches him soar.[7]

In a book called *Autobiography of Red,* Anne Carson creates this joy in reverse. An ancient monster named Geryon wants nothing more than to change his perspective by getting rid of his wings and living an ordinary life in the contemporary world. He does not want to live alone on an island and then be slaughtered by Herakles, which is the depressing fate ordained for him by several thousand years of Greek poetry. His whole project is to get out of the sky and down to earth, but he is a bright red boy with wings, and it is hard to change the way people see him. In Carson's book, Geryon meets his would-be-killer Herakles in a bus station and asks him for change to make a phone call, although the request is actually a come-on, because Geryon is unexpectedly smitten by the beauty of the man who is destined to be his murderer. This passion is surprising, and so is Herakles's reply to Geryon's request. "I'll give you a quarter for free," he offers. "Why would you do that?" asks Geryon. "I believe in being gracious," says Herakles.[8] This is a coin with more than two sides, and it turns Geryon from a creature of myth into a mortal man. Herakles is not going to become his killer, but his lover, and then the cause of his broken heart.

If this book hasn't offered you a quarter for free at least once then it hasn't done much. In writing, I have of course been trying to prepare the ground for grace, which hardly needs saying, because preparing the ground for grace is what people do. We stroke everything with our senses, constantly feeling for hidden levers and hinges. Like other airborne beings, Hermes embodies the idea that the maintenance of laws, limits, and routines is one of those levers, because gifts always come from within shared practices. For example, if Geryon loads the quarter that Herakles gave him into the payphone at the bus station, he turns a gift back into money, but that doesn't mean that the coin has lost its capacity to create grace, simply that it enters the network of regulated exchanges from which another gift will eventually emerge. Italo Calvino sees similar logic at work in Book Four of Ovid's *Metamorphoses*, where Perseus kills two monsters in quick succession. These murders are worth studying in some detail.

On his way to decapitate the Gorgon, Perseus passes "the forms of men and beasts, made of stone / By one look at Medusa's face," a grisly reminder of what will happen to him if he fails and also that many have failed before him.[9] Their efforts, undertaken with the average resources of average beings, summon Perseus to apply his exceptional resources to the task and remind him of how inventive he will have to be to succeed. He does succeed, and then keeps the snaky-haired head in a bag as a weapon to be used against his enemies. He manages to slay the sea monster menacing Andromeda while still carrying his prize, but then needs to put it down in order to wash the blood from his hands. Now comes the moment that Ovid calls a "wonder" and Calvino, a "miracle."[10] Perseus creates a soft bed of seaweed and twigs to cushion the head, and places it face down on the ground. While he is washing, the seaweed and twigs harden into coral, to the great delight of the sea nymphs, who begin to slip greenery under Medusa's head in order to increase the marvelous harvest.

If this is a miracle, it is also an illustration of how grace works. First, there is the horror of living beings turned to stone and the need for someone who can approach the monster from a different altitude. The statues that surround Medusa teach Perseus that this monster cannot be vanquished by conventional methods. Then, as Calvino points out, there is the startling care that Perseus shows the severed head when he makes a cushion to protect it from injury. And finally, there is the beauty of the coral that the nymphs come to gather. Most important is the fact that the severed head has lost none of its power: even after death it is still fully alive, as Ovid proved a hundred lines earlier when Perseus used it to turn Atlas into a mountain. The head can still petrify, although now Perseus controls it. But not quite, because he has no idea that Medusa will be able to metamorphose her pillow or that the sea nymphs will "use the twigs as seedlings, / Strewing them over the water" so that more of this double-natured plant will grow, brittle as rock when exposed to the air but pliant as a vine when below the water's surface.[11] This is a new life form, and Medusa created it while Perseus's back was turned.

It is possible that Perseus is gentle with the severed head only because he doesn't want to damage his prized weapon, but Ovid offers more complicated reasons to be gentle. The world needs weight, inertia, and opacity, everything that seems to oppose the value of lightness that Perseus embodies and that Calvino celebrates. For millennia, people have admired the magic of human flight and the sudden access of freedom that it suggests. The sky has always been the most prestigious address in the universe. It is not so easy to see merit in a Gorgon, but Ovid will not let us dismiss Medusa or banish her from the scene. The sixth of Calvino's memos for our millennium was to be called "Consistency," but he died before he had time to write it; surely Medusa's severed head represents this value. There are times when we need to fly into a different space, but others when we need to stay put, which is why Medusa is in essence immortal. Lest gravity seem a lesser vocation than lightness, Ovid embroiders a crucial detail on the narrative, namely the birth of coral. Suddenly, and against expectation, Medusa's capacity to astonish creates a gift. When tempered by Perseus's lightness rather than opposed to it, the punishment that Medusa inflicted on everyone who dared to look at her face becomes creative instead of fatal. While Perseus is performing his ablutions, a threshold appears in the middle of things, and a moment of grace.

Perseus did not notice Medusa's miraculous afterlife because he was taking a rest between bloodlettings, and this matters. The next time we meet him, he is fighting off Andromeda's jealous fiancé and his entourage, which leads to a bone-cracking, gore-spouting brawl that leaves dozens of men dead. The invention of coral takes place in the brief interlude in which Perseus is able to put his weapons down. Usually, his hands are so full that we wonder whether he has more than two arms. When he kills Medusa, he's carrying a shield, a sword, and the eyeball that he stole from the twin daughters of Phorcys. At the riot that breaks out at Andromeda's house, his weapons include a scimitar, a javelin, a spear, a firebrand, a mixing bowl, and the Gorgon's head.[12] A novice reader might reasonably conclude that he is an octopus. Perseus is empty-handed only once, and that is when the gift comes.

It is true that coral doesn't seem to change Perseus's violent circumstances, and he is soon back to the miserable business of killing. But we know that the ocean has been transformed and that the sea nymphs live within a new ecology. Ovid chooses not to pursue that plotline, which only serves to increase its hold on the reader's mind. What is taking place in that ocean, we wonder? It is hard to know exactly what the gift will do, or whom it will benefit. For every tale like "The Shoemaker and the Elves," in which a gift solves everyone's problems, there are two about a gift that leads to further difficulties. A woman longs for a child, but then she dies giving birth or has to make a painful bargain with an otherworldly benefactor; Geryon becomes more or less human, but Herakles is a fickle lover and he makes Geryon cry. One story stops, but the one that starts may not be any happier. Yet aren't we always on the lookout for the gifts that take our lives in a new direction, even if it involves heartbreak?

Take away the wings, the monsters, and Ovid's mythic machinery and it is not hard to see ourselves in Perseus, crouching to wash the blood from his hands before staining them again. In the instant when the man is at rest, perhaps imagining that his difficult work is done, the world changes a little as a result of his efforts. Then he picks up his burden and the daily labor resumes. This rest is just as fertile as the labor that comes before and after it, although Perseus does not know that. Like most people, Perseus understands the value of effort, but not of putting his burden down. He does not recognize what has happened any more than the peasants in Pieter Brueghel's *The Fall of Icarus* notice the boy with wax wings who flies too close to the sun and then drops headfirst out of the sky into the ocean, his tiny legs waving frantically on the surface of the water before he drowns.

In the foreground of Brueghel's painting, we see a farmer, his eyes downcast, furrowing the soil with his plow. The farmer, the shepherd, the fisherman, and the men aboard the merchant ships are all so absorbed in the work of cultivation and commerce that they are blind to the remarkable event. Norman Bryson writes of Brueghel's painting, "what runs the world is repetition, unconsciousness, the *sleep* of culture: the forces that stabilize and maintain the human world are habit, automatism, inertia."[13] This is what Calvino called consistency. Yet I don't see this painting as the triumph of sleep over astonishment. The wings fail and Icarus dies unobserved, but in his fall I see an interruption that has not been sensed *yet*. I see a little tremor that may or may not cause Brueghel's farmer to glance up from his plow or the fisherman to glance up from his net, but will almost certainly astonish someone, somewhere, sometime.

Gifts always arrive when people are resting or looking the other way. That seems to be their nature, and ours.

NOTES

Introduction

1   Mary Douglas, "Foreword: No Free Gifts," *The Gift: The Form and Reason for Exchange in Archaic Societies*, ed. Marcel Mauss, trans. W. D. Halls (New York: Norton, 1990), x.

2   I draw the details of Petit's Twin Tower walk from the Academy Award-winning documentary film, James Marsh, *Man on Wire*, performed by Philippe Petit (2008; Magnolia Pictures) DVD.

3   Hermes plays key roles in *The Iliad*, *The Odyssey,* and *The Aeneid*. In Book 24 of *The Iliad*, Hermes guides King Priam to Achilles's camp and facilitates the meeting that concludes the epic and creates the temporary peace in which Hector's body is buried by the Trojans. In Book 5 of *The Odyssey*, the gods send Hermes to rescue Odysseus from Calypso; in Book 10, Hermes intervenes to prevent Odysseus from being turned into a pig by Circe. In Book 4 of *The Aeneid*, Jove sends Hermes to extricate Aeneas from Dido, Queen of Carthage. In these instances, Hermes's role is to make sure that a king survives an encounter with a mesmerizing woman so that the journey and the narrative can continue. As Jenny Strauss Clay argues in *The Politics of Olympus: Form and Meaning in the Major Homeric Hymns* (Princeton, NJ: Princeton University Press, 1989), it is important that Hermes is the last of the gods to be born, because like all youngest children he has to struggle to invent a place for himself in an established order that will be resistant to change. Strauss Clay writes, "the fully articulated Olympian system of divisions and boundaries remains static and lifeless unless it acquires the possibility of movement between its spheres and limits. Introduced only after the hierarchical configuration of the cosmos has been achieved and its boundaries defined, Hermes embodies that principle of motion. Hermes thus allows the cosmos to retain its ordered structure while simultaneously instituting movement between its articulated components." ibid., 98.

4   Lewis Hyde, *Trickster Makes This World: Mischief, Myth, and Art* (New York: North Point Press, 1998), 13. For Hyde, Hermes is above all a figure who transports people, objects, and ideas across spatial and epistemological borders, and is thus a "joint-disturber," or a kind of social and imaginative chiropractor. Ibid., 256.

5   Ibid., 329. Appendix I of *Trickster Makes This World* contains Hyde's own translation of the Homeric *Hymn to Hermes,* 317–31.

6   This composite account of Hermes as patron of discourse (including deception and lies), trade (including theft), and the dead (including the resurrected) is drawn from his role in the myths and epics, but is also indebted to Hyde, *Trickster Makes This World*; Strauss Clay, *The Politics of Olympus*; Michel Serres, *Hermes: Literature, Science, Philosophy*, ed. Josué V. Harari and David F. Bell (Baltimore, MD: Johns Hopkins University Press, 1983); Walter F. Otto, *The Homeric Gods: The Spiritual Significance of Greek Religion*, trans. Moses Hadas (New York: Pantheon, 1954); John Wilkins, *Mercury: Or the Secret and Swift Messenger* (Amsterdam: John Benjamins Publishing Co, 1984), which credits Hermes-Mercury with the invention of cryptography; and *The Cratylus, Phaedo, Parmenides, Timaeus and Critias of Plato*, trans. Thomas Taylor (Michigan: Wizards Bookshelf, 1976).

7   Marilynne Robinson, *Gilead* (New York: HarperPerennial, 2004), 240.

8   Marilynne Robinson, "When I Was a Child," *When I Was a Child I Read Books* (New York: HarperPerennial, 2012), 93.

9   Stanislas Breton, *A Radical Philosophy of Saint Paul*, trans. Joseph N. Ballan (New York: Columbia University Press, 2011), 92.

10 Acts 14:12.

11 Rowan D. Williams, "The Body's Grace," *Theology and Sexuality: Classic and Contemporary Readings*, ed. Eugene F. Rogers, Jr. (Massachusetts: Blackwell, 2002), 317. Williams was Archbishop of Canterbury from 2002 to 2012.

12 Alain Badiou, *Saint Paul: The Foundation of Universalism*, trans. Ray Brassier (Stanford, CA: Stanford University Press, 2003), 77.

13 Gal. 6:15; qtd. in Ibid., 72. Italics added.

14 Mary Douglas, "Foreword," *The Gift*, vii–xviii.

15 Peter D. McDonald, *The Literature Police: Apartheid Censorship and Its Cultural Consequences* (Oxford: Oxford University Press, 2009), 146. See Fig. 2.13.

16 Qtd. in Ibid., 144.

17 Ibid.,146. See Fig. 2.13.

18 For the publishing history of Ravan Press and *Staffrider*, see McDonald, "Publishers," *The Literature Police,* 83–157.

19 Hyde, "The Lucky Find," *Trickster Makes This World,* 128–50.

20 Oliver Sacks, "Altered States: Self-Experiments in Chemistry," *The New Yorker*, August 27, 2012, 40.

21 Dr Seuss, *On Beyond Zebra!* (New York: Random House, 1983), n.p.

22 Ibid., see the illustrations on pages 46, 59, and 61.

23 Gabriel García Márquez, "The Handsomest Drowned Man in the World: A Tale for Children," trans. Gregory Rabassa, *Major Writers of Short Fiction*, ed. Ann Charters (New York: Bedford / St. Martin's, 1993), 450.

24 Anne Carson, *Autobiography of Red* (New York: Vintage, 1998), 44.

25 Ovid, *The Metamorphoses*, trans. Rolfe Humphries (Bloomington: Indiana University Press, 1955), 1.131.

26 Ibid., 1.136.

27 Bruno Schulz, "Cockroaches," *The Street of Crocodiles and Other Stories*, trans. Celina Wieniewska (New York: Penguin Books, 2008), 73.

28 Milan Kundera, *The Unbearable Lightness of Being*, trans. Michael Henry Heim (New York: HarperPerennial, 1999), 5.

29 Karen Armstrong, *St Paul: The Misunderstood Apostle* (London: Atlantic Books, 2015), 6.
30 Simone Weil, *The Iliad or The Poem of Force*, trans. Mary McCarthy (Wallingford, PA: Pendle Hill, 1983), 29.
31 J. M. Coetzee, *Elizabeth Costello: Eight Lessons* (New York: Vintage, 2008), 155.
32 Jhumpa Lahiri, *In Other Words*, trans. Ann Goldstein (New York: Knopf, 2016), 57.
33 Simone Weil, "Forms of the Implicit Love of God," *Waiting for God*, trans. Emma Craufurd (New York: HarperPerennial, 2009), 92.
34 James Ferguson, "Declarations of Dependence: Labour, Personhood, and Welfare in Southern Africa," *Journal of the Royal Anthropological Institute*, no. 19 (2013): 232.
35 Lewis Hyde, *The Gift: Creativity and the Artist in the Modern World* (New York: Vintage, 2007), 29.

Chapter 1

1   Anne Carson, *Economy of the Unlost* (Princeton, NJ: Princeton University Press, 1999), 27.
2   Gabriel Herman, *Ritualised Friendship and the Greek City* (Cambridge: Cambridge University Press, 1987), 69, 43. It is important to note that *charis* only functions among people who are strangers in the limited sense that they have not yet met one another but nonetheless recognize and observe the same social principles. In *The Odyssey*, for example, Odysseus meets plenty of nonhumans who do not honor either the laws of Zeus or the principles of *charis*, including Circe, Polyphemus, and the giants of Laestrygonia.
3   Homer, *The Iliad*, trans. Robert Fagles (New York: Penguin, 1998), 6.142.
4   Ibid., 6.262, 6.263.
5   Ibid., 6.255.
6   Ibid., 6.257–8.
7   Ibid., 6.270–7.
8   My understanding of the political and economic transformation of ancient Greek societies by the invention of modern coinage is indebted to Carson, *Economy of the Unlost*; Leslie Kurke, *Coins, Bodies, Games, and Gold: The Politics of Meaning in Archaic Greece* (Princeton, NJ: Princeton University Press, 1999); Richard Seaford, *Money and the Early Greek Mind: Homer, Philosophy, Tragedy* (Cambridge: Cambridge University Press, 2004); *Money and Its Uses in the Ancient Greek World*, ed. Andrew Meadows and Kirsty Shipton (Oxford: Oxford University Press, 2001). Carson describes the haphazard coexistence of Greek gifts and coins throughout *Economy of the Unlost*, particularly in Chapters 1 and 3.
9   Carson, *Economy of the Unlost*, 60.
10 Ibid., 129. On Simonides's epitaphs and funeral songs, see ibid., 73, 105; on the requirement that the men of Keos drink hemlock at age sixty, ibid., 80–1;

on Simonides's additions to the lyre and alphabet, ibid., 107; on his mnemonic system, ibid., 38–40.

11 Carson uses this phrase in *Economy of the Unlost*, 12; Marcel Mauss used it first in *The Gift: The Form and Reason for Exchange in Archaic Societies*, trans. W. D. Halls (New York: Norton, 1990), 33.

12 Bonnie MacLachlan, *The Age of Grace: Charis in Early Greek Poetry* (Princeton, NJ: Princeton University Press, 1993), 11. On gracious responses to works of art, see ibid., 10–11.

13 Paul Celan, "Speech on the Occasion of Receiving the Literature Prize of the Free Hanseatic City of Bremen," *Collected Prose*, trans. Rosemarie Waldrop (Manchester: Carcanet Press, 1986), 33. Carson quotes a different translation of these words in *Economy of the Unlost*, 41.

14 Celan, *Collected Prose*, 35.

15 Celan, "Letter to Hans Bender," *Collected Prose*, 26. The letter expresses Celan's refusal to contribute to Bender's anthology, *My Poem Is My Knife*.

16 Celan, "Edgar Jené and the Dream about the Dream," *Collected Prose*, 6.

17 Mauss, *The Gift*, 44, 46. Italics in original.

18 On the relationship between failed exchange and bodily harm, including murder, see ibid., 5, 11–13, 40–2.

19 Homer, *Iliad*, 6.282.

20 Ibid., 1.211.

21 Ibid., 1.219.

22 This idea is particularly important to Chapter 1 of *Given Time*, which is also where Derrida critiques Mauss. See "The Time of the King," *Given Time: I. Counterfeit Money*, trans. Peggy Kamuf (Chicago: University of Chicago Press, 1994), 1–33. For example, Derrida writes, "It is thus necessary, at the limit, that he [the recipient] not *recognize* the gift as gift. If he recognizes it *as* gift, if the gift *appears to him as such*, if the present is present to him *as present*, this simple recognition suffices to annul the gift." Ibid., 13. Italics in original.

23 Mauss, "Conclusion," *The Gift*, 70. Throughout the Conclusion, Mauss expresses his belief that twentieth-century European societies need to emulate gift cultures. He writes, "Perhaps by studying these obscure aspects of social life we shall succeed in throwing a little light upon the path that our nations must follow, both in their morality and in their economy." Ibid., 78. He refers to "The Sleeping Beauty" and other folk and fairy tales about uninvited guests on page 40.

24 In 2002, Jean-Luc Nancy gave a series of short talks on philosophy to children aged six to twelve. The talks were followed by question-and-answer periods. These dialogues, as Nancy called them, were later published as *God, Justice, Love, Beauty: Four Little Dialogues*, trans. Sarah Clift (New York: Fordham University Press, 2011). Nancy was inspired by the German radio programs for children that Walter Benjamin wrote between 1929 and 1932. See Jean-Luc Nancy, *Noli me tangere: On the Raising of the Body*, trans. Sarah Clift, Pascale-Anne Brault, and Michael Naas (New York: Fordham University Press, 2008), 68.

25 The Brothers Grimm, "The Sleeping Beauty," *Classics of Children's Literature*, ed. John W. Griffith and Charles H. Frey (New York: MacMillan, 1987), 89–91.

26 E. B. White, *Charlotte's Web* (New York: Scholastic, 1952), 80.
27 Lewis Hyde, *The Gift: Creativity and the Artist in the Modern World* (New York: Vintage, 2007), 19–26. Hyde writes, "Reciprocal giving is a form of gift exchange, but it is the simplest. The gift moves in a circle, and two people do not make much of a circle. Two points establish a line, but a circle lies in a plane and needs at least three points." Ibid., 19. In his own response to Mauss and Hyde, among many others, Derrida also claims that the "figure of the circle is obviously *at the center*" of all cycles of gift-giving. He writes, the gift "opens the circle so as to defy reciprocity or symmetry" and thus it "must not circulate, it must not be exchanged, it must not in any case be exhausted, as a gift, by the process of exchange." *Given Time*, 6, 7.
28 Hyde, *The Gift*, 20, 25.
29 Ibid., 60. For Hyde's reading of "The Shoemaker and the Elves" and his ensuing discussion of gratitude, see "The Labor of Gratitude," ibid., 51–71.
30 Ibid., 64.
31 Ibid., 65.
32 Ibid.
33 Luke 17:21.
34 Mark 12:28–34.
35 Jean-Luc Nancy makes this point in an essay called "Justice," where he asks, "But what is truly just for everyone at the same time as for each person individually? This, one cannot recognize, since it is not given in advance. It must be searched for, invented, and found, each time anew. More is always necessary: one can never tell oneself that things are sufficiently just as they are. One is never sufficiently just. To think in that way is already to begin to be just." Nancy, *God, Justice, Love, Beauty*, 60. In *The Gift of Death*, Jacques Derrida writes, "Guilt is inherent in responsibility because responsibility is always unequal to itself: one is never responsible enough," *The Gift of Death*, trans. David Wills (Chicago: University of Chicago Press, 1995), 51. Slavoj Žižek goes even further, criticizing Emmanuel Levinas, the Laws of Moses, the Gospels, and the Epistles, on the grounds that love for the individual is incompatible with justice for the many. He writes, "the true ethical step is the one *beyond* the face of the other, … This coldness *is* justice at its most elementary." He characterizes the Biblical neighbor as a monster who blinds us to the needs of the people we cannot see. See "Neighbors and Other Monsters: A Plea for Ethical Violence," *The Neighbor: Three Inquiries in Political Theology* (Chicago: University of Chicago Press, 2005), 183.
36 Emmanuel Levinas, *Of God Who Comes to Mind*, trans. Bettina Bergo (Stanford, CA: Stanford University Press, 1998), 75.
37 Simone Weil, "Reflections on the Right Use of School Studies with a View to the Love of God," *Waiting for God*, trans. Emma Craufurd (New York: HarperPerennial, 2009), 64.
38 Ibid., 65.
39 Giorgio Agamben, *Homo Sacer: Sovereign Power and Bare Life*, trans. Daniel Heller-Roazen (Stanford, CA: Stanford University Press, 1998), 27.
40 Qtd. in Giorgio Agamben, *The Kingdom and the Glory: For a Theological Genealogy of Economy and Government*, trans. Lorenzo Chiesa with Matteo Mandarini (Stanford, CA: Stanford University Press, 2011), 49.

41 Ibid.
42 See, in particular, Agamben, "Potentiality and Law," *Homo Sacer*, 39–48.
43 See Agamben, *The Kingdom and the Glory*; Agamben, *The Highest Poverty: Monastic Rules and Form-of-Life*, trans. Adam Kotsko (Stanford, CA: Stanford University Press, 2013); Agamben, *The Time That Remains: A Commentary on the Letter to the Romans*, trans. Patricia Dailey (Stanford, CA: Stanford University Press, 2005).
44 Stanislas Breton, *A Radical Philosophy of Saint Paul*, trans. Joseph N. Ballan (New York: Columbia University Press, 2011), 97.
45 Ibid., 98.
46 Karen Armstrong, *St Paul: The Misunderstood Apostle* (London: Atlantic Books, 2015), 32–3.
47 Ibid., 2.
48 Gal. 3:28.
49 My understanding of Paul's life is mainly indebted to Karen Armstrong, *St Paul*; Reza Aslan, *Zealot: The Life and Times of Jesus of Nazareth* (New York: Random House, 2013), particularly Chapters 13–15; Alain Badiou, *Saint Paul: The Foundation of Universalism*, trans. Ray Brassier (Stanford, CA: Stanford University Press, 2003); Günther Bornkamm, *Paul*, trans. D. M. G. Stalker (New York: Harper & Row, 1969); Stanislas Breton, *A Radical Philosophy of Saint Paul*; and Agamben, *The Time That Remains*.
50 Rom. 5:13.
51 Rom. 4:4.
52 Armstrong, *St Paul*, 32–4.
53 Matt. 7:23. The words "in secret" are used repeatedly in the Gospel of Matthew. See for example 6:4, 6:6, 6:18.
54 Rom. 6:14.
55 Rom. 5:20-21.
56 Rom. 5:15.
57 Badiou, *Saint Paul*, 77. Italics removed from "*without being due.*" Badiou's conception of the relationship between grace and law in Paul's epistles is more complex than the dichotomy that I quote here. Badiou goes on to argue that in Paul law and grace are mutually dependent, and I am indebted to his analysis. I am also indebted to Heinz W. Cassirer, who makes a similar argument in "But When the Commandment Came," *Grace & Law: St. Paul, Kant, and the Hebrew Prophets* (Grand Rapids, MI: Eerdmans / Handsel, 1988), 1–49. Phillip Cary traces Paul's influence on Augustine's understanding of the relationship among law, will, and grace in "Pauline Grace," *Inner Grace: Augustine in the Traditions of Plato and Paul* (Oxford: Oxford University Press, 2008), 33–67. As Cary argues, in the presence of faith, grace "closes the gap between willing and doing" by making it possible to overcome moral and spiritual weakness. Ibid., 46.
58 1 Cor. 15:9, 15:10; 1 Tim. 1:13, 1:14.
59 Rom. 4:13-15.
60 Breton, *A Radical Philosophy of Saint Paul*, 75.
61 Marilynne Robinson, "Givenness," *The Givenness of Things: Essays* (New York: HarperCollins, 2015), 90.

62   Annie Dillard, *Pilgrim at Tinker Creek* (New York: HarperPerennial, 2007), 11.
63   Ibid., 36.
64   Ibid., 139.
65   Ibid., 194.
66   Ibid., 200.
67   Helen Macdonald, *H Is for Hawk* (New York: Penguin, 2014), 275.
68   Ibid., 177.
69   Jane Bennett, *Vibrant Matter: A Political Ecology of Things* (Durham, NC: Duke University Press, 2010), 3. Italics in original. Throughout Chapter 1, Bennett describes this capaciousness as "vital materiality" and "thing-power." See "The Force of Things," 1–19.
70   Ex. 3:3.
71   Henry D. Thoreau, *Walden*, ed. J. Lyndon Shanley (Princeton, NJ: Princeton University Press, 2016), 317, 212.
72   Ibid., 318.
73   Henry D. Thoreau, "Slavery in Massachusetts," *Walden and Other Writings of Henry David Thoreau*, ed. Brooks Atkinson (New York: The Modern Library, 1965), 677.
74   Ibid., 678.
75   Thoreau, *Walden*, 211.
76   Ibid., 217, 318.
77   Ibid., 318.
78   Marilynne Robinson, *The Givenness of Things*, 90. Italics added.
79   Henry D. Thoreau, "A Plea for Captain John Brown," *Walden and Other Writings of Henry David Thoreau*, 683–707.
80   Toni Morrison, *Beloved* (New York: Vintage, 2004), 103.
81   Ibid., 319.
82   Ibid., 323.
83   Morrison, "Foreword," *Beloved*, xv–xix.
84   Barbara Ehrenreich, *Living with a Wild God: A Nonbeliever's Search for the Truth about Everything* (New York: Twelve, 2014), 197. Italics in original.
85   Ibid., 116, 117, 203. Italics removed from "What is actually going on here?"
86   Ibid., 236.
87   Karl Ove Knausgaard, *A Man in Love*, My Struggle: Book 2, trans. Don Bartlett (New York: Vintage, 2013), 401.
88   Ibid., 400.
89   Ibid., 62.
90   Ibid., 63.
91   Karl Ove Knausgaard, *A Time for Everything*, trans. James Anderson (New York: Archipelago Books, 2009), 25.
92   Ibid., 465.
93   Ibid., 467.
94   Karl Ove Knausgaard, "My Struggle with Autobiographer Karl Ove Knausgaard," interview by Eleanor Wachtel, *Writers & Company*, CBC, June 29, 2014, audio 52:55, https://www.cbc.ca/radio/writersandcompany/karl-ove-knausgaard-interview-1.2790787

95   Marilynne Robinson, *Housekeeping* (New York: HarperPerennial, 2005), 19.
96   Ibid., 184.
97   Ibid., 19.
98   Christian Wiman, *My Bright Abyss: Meditation of a Modern Believer* (New York: FSG, 2013), 82.
99   Ibid., 57–8. "From a Window" from MY BRIGHT ABYSS by Christian Wiman. Copyright © 2013 by Christian Wiman. Reprinted by permission of Farrar, Straus and Giroux. The poem originally published in the volume *Every Riven Thing*. Reprinted by permission of Farrar, Straus and Giroux. All Rights Reserved.
100   Ibid., 61.
101   Weil, "Forms of the Implicit Love of God," *Waiting for God*, 101.
102   Rowan D. Williams, "The Body's Grace," *Theology and Sexuality: Classic and Contemporary Readings*, ed. Eugene F. Rogers, Jr. (Massachusetts: Blackwell, 2002), 311, 313, 314. After Williams was elected Archbishop of Canterbury in 2002, this talk became the center of a bitter controversy about the place of homosexuality within the global Anglican Church. Paul Elie describes this controversy and the sense of betrayal felt by many Anglican gays and lesbians in "The Velvet Reformation," *The Atlantic*, March 1, 2009. For a discussion of eroticism as a metaphor for divine grace in Augustine's thought, see Cary, *Inner Grace*, 18–21 and Terrance W. Klein, *Wittgenstein and the Metaphysics of Grace* (Oxford: Oxford University Press, 2007), 43–7.
103   Adam Grant, *Give and Take: Why Helping Others Drives Our Success* (New York: Penguin, 2013). Grant defines takers as "black holes" who "sucked the energy from those around them," ibid., 53. In the workplace, takers are narcissists who refuse to share credit, ideas, or resources with other people. By contrast, Grant argues that givers don't think of wealth distribution as a zero-sum game; they create more wealth rather than grabbing as much as they can.
104   Martin Heidegger, "The Origin of the Work of Art," trans. Albert Hofstadter, *Poetry, Language, Thought* (New York: Perennial Classics, 2001), 73.
105   Derek Attridge, *The Singularity of Literature* (New York: Routledge, 2004), 19.
106   Ibid., 130. For a more recent version of this argument see Jacques Rancière, "The Paradoxes of Political Art," *Dissensus: On Politics and Aesthetics*, ed. and trans. Steven Corcoran (New York: Continuum, 2010), 134–51; For an earlier version, see Jacques Derrida, "Psyche: Invention of the Other," *Acts of Literature*, ed. Derek Attridge (New York: Routledge, 1992), 310–43.
107   Emmanuel Levinas, *Totality and Infinity: An Essay on Exteriority*, trans. Alphonso Lingis (Pittsburgh: Duquesne University Press, 1969), 172.

Chapter 2

1   Marilynne Robinson, *Housekeeping* (New York: HarperPerennial, 2005), 178.
2   Teju Cole, "The White Savior Industrial Complex," *Known and Strange Things: Essays* (New York: Random House, 2016), 340.

3   Mary Douglas, Foreword: No Free Gifts, *The Gift: The Form and Reason for Exchange in Archaic Societies*, by Marcel Mauss, trans. W. D. Halls (New York: Norton, 1990), vii.
4   Matt. 6:1-4.
5   See Marilynne Robinson, "Reformation," *The Givenness of Things* (New York: HarperCollins, 2015), 17–30.
6   Douglas, "Foreword," *The Gift,* vii.
7   Edward St. Aubyn, "Some Hope," *The Complete Patrick Melrose Novels* (New York: Picador, 2015), 301.
8   St. Aubyn, "At Last," ibid., 817.
9   William Shakespeare, *Measure for Measure*, ed. S. Nagarajan (New York: Signet, 1988), 1.3.19.
10 Ibid., 5.1.483-8.
11 Aristotle, *Aristotle's Nicomachean Ethics*, trans. Hippocrates G. Apostle (Grinnell: The Peripatetic Press, 1984), 98. Italics added.
12 Ibid., 99.
13 Franz Kafka, "The Metamorphosis," *The Basic Kafka*, trans. Willa and Edwin Muir (New York: Schocken Books, 1977), 11.
14 See for example Elleke Boehmer, "Not Saying Sorry, Not Speaking Pain: Gender Implications in *Disgrace*," *Interventions* 4, no. 3 (2002): 342–51. Sam Durrant, "J. M. Coetzee, Elizabeth Costello, and the Limits of the Sympathetic Imagination," *J. M. Coetzee and the Idea of the Public Intellectual*, ed. Jane Poyner (Athens, OH: Ohio University Press, 2006), 118–34; Michael Marais, "J. M. Coetzee's *Disgrace* and the Task of the Imagination," *Journal of Modern Literature* 29, no. 2 (2006): 75–93; Michael Marais, "Violence, Postcolonial Fiction, and the Limits of Sympathy," *Studies in the Novel* 43, no. 1 (2011): 94–114; John J. Su examines the political limits of sympathy in Coetzee's work in "Aesthetic Revolutions: White South African Writing and the State of Emergency," *Imagination and the Contemporary Novel* (Cambridge: Cambridge University Press, 2011), 20–54; Shameem Black writes about sympathy / empathy in Coetzee's later novels in "Sacrificing the Self," *Fiction across Borders: Imagining the Lives of Others in Late Twentieth-Century Novels* (New York: Columbia University Press, 2010), 200–54.
15 J. M. Coetzee, "Jerusalem Prize Acceptance Speech," *Doubling the Point: Essays and Interviews*, ed. David Attwell (Cambridge, MA: Harvard University Press, 1992), 98.
16 J. M. Coetzee, "Apartheid Thinking," *Giving Offense: Essays on Censorship* (Chicago: Chicago University Press, 1996), 164.
17 Ibid., 165. I cite and write about these passages from the Jerusalem Prize Acceptance Speech and "Apartheid Thinking" in Alice Brittan, "Death and J. M. Coetzee's *Disgrace*," *Contemporary Literature* 51, no. 3 (2010): 478.
18 Coetzee, "Emerging from Censorship," *Giving Offense*, 35, 36. Many of the essays in this collection take up the problem of what Coetzee calls "introverted censorship." Ibid., 36.
19 Coetzee, "Confession and Double Thoughts: Tolstoy, Rousseau, Dostoevsky," *Doubling the Point*, 261, 290.
20 Antjie Krog, *Country of My Skull: Guilt, Sorrow, and the Limits of Forgiveness in the New South Africa* (New York: Three Rivers Press, 2000), 288.

21 Pumla Gobodo-Madikizela, *A Human Being Died That Night: A South African Story of Forgiveness* (New York: Houghton Mifflin, 2003), especially 117–33.

22 Paul Gilroy, *After Empire: Melancholia or Convivial Culture?* (New York: Routledge, 2006), 13, 70.

23 Claudia Rankine, "The Condition of Black Life Is One of Mourning," *The New York Times Magazine*, June 22, 2015, https://www.nytimes.com/2015/06/22/magazine/the-condition-of-black-life-is-one-of-mourning.html

24 Jacques Derrida, "On Forgiveness," *On Cosmopolitanism and Forgiveness*, trans. Mark Dooley and Michael Hughes (New York: Routledge, 2007), 55.

25 J. M. Coetzee, *Life & Times of Michael K* (London: Vintage, 2004). The quotations in this paragraph come from pages 27, 82, 148, 149.

26 Derek Attridge observes that in Coetzee's work "the racially or socially privileged character can gain virtually no understanding of the inner world of the other who has been excluded from such privilege." Attridge, "Age of Bronze, State of Grace: Music and Dogs in Coetzee's *Disgrace*," *Novel* 34, no.1 (2000): 102.

27 J. M. Coetzee, *Waiting for the Barbarians* (London: Vintage, 2004), 89.

28 Coetzee, *Life & Times*, 179.

29 Ibid., 181.

30 Franz Kafka, "A Hunger Artist," *The Basic Kafka*, 80–90. Kafka's influence on Coetzee's work is well known, and clearly signaled in the title *Life & Times of Michael K*. Derek Attridge discusses Kafka's influence on *Life & Times* in "Against Allegory," *J. M. Coetzee and the Ethics of Reading: Literature in the Event* (Chicago: Chicago University Press, 2004), 51. Coetzee writes about Kafka in *Doubling the Point*, 197–232.

31 See Rita Barnard, *Apartheid and Beyond: South African Writers and the Politics of Place* (New York: Oxford University Press, 2007), 31–4. Like Barnard, Derek Attridge emphasizes K's freedom in "Against Allegory," *J. M. Coetzee and the Ethics of Reading*, 56–7.

32 Coetzee, *Life & Times,* 179.

33 J. M. Coetzee, *Age of Iron* (New York: Penguin, 1990), 21.

34 Ibid., 22.

35 Ibid., 198.

36 Michel De Montaigne, "On Repentance," *Essays*, trans. J. M. Cohen (London: Penguin, 1993), 246.

37 Empathy is a key concept in some recent theories of cosmopolitanism and social justice, including Gilroy, *After Empire,* 13. Martha C. Nussbaum was an early advocate for the political potential of empathy in her influential essay "Patriotism and Cosmopolitanism," *For Love of Country: Debating the Limits of Patriotism*, ed. Joshua Cohen (Boston: Beacon Press, 1996), 3–17.

38 For critiques of the causal link between empathy and altruism see Karsten Stueber, *Rediscovering Empathy: Agency, Folk Psychology, and the Human Sciences* (Cambridge, MA: MIT University Press, 2006), 1–31; Suzanne Keen, *Empathy and the Novel* (New York: Oxford University Press, 2007); and Dominick LaCapra, *History and Its Limits: Human, Animal, Violence* (Ithaca, NY: Cornell University Press, 2009),180–1.

39 Tzvetan Todorov, *The Conquest of America: The Question of the Other*, trans. Richard Howard (New York: HarperPerennial, 1984), 127. In Errol Morris's 2003 documentary film, "The Fog of War," former U.S. Secretary of Defense,

Robert S. McNamara, offers eleven lessons from his own life, beginning with this one: "Empathize with your enemy." "We must try to put ourselves inside their [the enemy's] skin and look at us through their eyes, just to understand the thoughts that lie behind their decisions and their actions," McNamara counsels. The ability to imagine what the enemy thinks and sees might reveal that they are not an enemy at all; on the other hand, empathy makes it easier to manipulate and defeat an adversary, which is what Todorov calls "understanding-that-kills." See Errol Morris, The Fog of War: Transcript, "The Fog of War: Eleven Lessons from the Life of Robert S. McNamara," accessed September 21, 2012, http://www.errolmorris.com/film/fow_transcript.html.

40 See, for example, Stephen Greenblatt, *Marvelous Possessions: The Wonder of the New World* (New York: Oxford University Press, 1992), 26.

41 See Nussbaum, "Patriotism and Cosmopolitanism," *For Love of Country,* 3–17.

42 Martha C. Nussbaum, *Political Emotions: Why Love Matters for Justice* (Cambridge, MA: Harvard University Press, 2013), 380.

43 Ibid., 15.

44 David Grossman, "The Age of Genius: The Legend of Bruno Schulz," *The New Yorker,* June 8 & 15, 2009, 68.

45 Bruno Schulz, "The Age of Genius," *The Street of Crocodiles and Other Stories,* trans. Celina Wieniewska (New York: Penguin, 2008), 138.

46 Coetzee knows Schulz's stories, essays, and drawings well. See Coetzee, "Bruno Schulz," *Inner Workings: Literary Essays 2000–2005* (New York: Viking, 2007), 65–78.

47 Coetzee, "Jerusalem Prize," 97. In *White Writing: On the Culture of Letters in South Africa* (New Haven: Yale University Press, 1988), 9, Coetzee describes the history of South African pastoral writing in English as a "literature of failure," and specifically as a "failure to imagine a peopled landscape."

48 J. M. Coetzee, *The Master of Petersburg* (London: Vintage, 2004), 240.

49 Ibid., 242.

50 J. M. Coetzee, *Elizabeth Costello: Eight Lessons* (London: Vintage, 2004), 155.

51 Ibid., 149.

52 Ibid., 146–55. Costello distinguishes among *caritas, eros,* and *agape* and suggests that they denote quite different kinds of love. In "Grace," Marilynne Robinson blurs these distinctions, arguing that over the centuries English translators have translated each of these words as "love." See "Grace," *The Givenness of Things,* 47–8.

53 Coetzee, *Elizabeth Costello,* 155.

54 Ibid., 203.

55 J. C. clearly echoes both E. C. (Elizabeth Costello) and J. M. Coetzee. There are places in the novel when J. C. speaks directly as Coetzee, identifying himself as a former professor of literature and as the author of *Waiting for the Barbarians.* See, for example, *Diary of a Bad Year* (London: Vintage, 2008), 22, 171. Pages 183–5 seem to describe the character of Elizabeth Costello.

56 Ibid., 151.

57 Ibid., 167.

58 Ibid., 224.

59 Ibid., 225.

60 Coetzee, *Elizabeth Costello*, 127.

61 Ibid., 150.

62 Ibid., 151.

63 "The J. M. Coetzee Centre for Creative Practice," The University of Adelaide, accessed August 8, 2019, https://www.adelaide.edu.au/jmcoetzeecentre/about-the-centre

64 J. M. Coetzee, *Slow Man* (New York: Viking, 2005), 18. Interestingly, the writer Elizabeth Costello appears as a character in *Slow Man*, a novel about an elderly Australian man, Paul Rayment, who suffers a catastrophic injury that results in the amputation of a leg. Midway through the novel, Costello, who is a complete stranger to Rayment, arrives at his apartment and moves in. She is both unwanted guest, and metafictional author of Paul himself. In reference to his passion for his much younger nurse, she tells Paul that the purpose of her open-ended visit is to "find out what happens when a man of sixty engages his heart unsuitably." Ibid., 198–9. Of course, Costello is an expert is unsuitable movements of the heart, and she cannot persuade Paul to abandon his love for his nurse Marijana or his madcap desire to serve as godfather to her children. In *Slow Man*, Coetzee seems to return to his earlier experiments with metafiction that are most clearly visible in *Foe*, a novel published in the mid-1980s, in which Daniel Defoe and various other novelists appear alongside their own characters. See *Foe* (New York: Penguin, 1986).

65 Marilynne Robinson, *Gilead* (New York: HarperPerennial, 2004), 135.

66 Ibid., 52.

67 Ibid., 135.

68 Ibid., 136, 23. Italics in original.

69 See Coetzee, *Life & Times*, 89; Coetzee, *Waiting for the Barbarians*, 21; Coetzee, *The Master of Petersburg*, 53; Coetzee, *Foe*, 105.

70 Coetzee, *Life & Times*, 104.

71 Ibid., 117.

72 Coetzee, *Age of Iron*, 54.

73 Coetzee, *Life & Times*, 117.

74 Coetzee, *Elizabeth Costello*, 150.

75 J. M. Coetzee, *Disgrace* (New York: Penguin, 1999), 112.

76 Ibid., 49.

77 Ibid., 52.

78 Ibid., 161.

79 Ibid., 207.

80 Ibid., 208.

81 I make this argument and use similar language in Brittan, "Death and J. M. Coetzee's *Disgrace*," 494.

82 Matt. 6:3-4.

83 Coetzee, *Disgrace*, 143.

84 Ibid., 165.

85 Ibid., 173.

86 Jean-Luc Nancy, *Noli me tangere: On the Raising of the Body*, trans. Sarah Clift, Pascale-Anne Brault, and Michael Naas (New York: Fordham University Press, 2008).

87 Matt. 16:11, italics added.
88 Matt. 15:16.
89 John 4:32.
90 J. M. Coetzee, *The Childhood of Jesus* (New York: Random House, 2013), 6.
91 Ibid., 263.
92 David and Simón discuss numbers, words, and falling in many places in the novel. See for example, ibid., 166, 176–8. David's sense that the world is filled with gaps that he alone can see is linked to his desire to be a magician and lifesaver (terms that he uses interchangeably) who reverses death by pulling people out of the holes into which they have fallen.
93 Ibid., 172.
94 Ibid., 256. Jesus's relationship to religious law is at least as complex as Paul's. In Matthew, he says, "Do not think that I have come to abolish the Law or the Prophets; I have not come to abolish them but to fulfill them" (5:17). At the same time that he insists that his disciples match (or exceed) the righteousness of the Pharisees, Jesus is in constant conflict with these teachers of rabbinical law, whom he calls "blind guides" (Matt 15:14). In Matthew and John, the teachers and the members of the rabbinical court (the Sanhedrin) avenge the insult by plotting Jesus's death.
95 J. M. Coetzee, *The Schooldays of Jesus* (London: Harvill Secker, 2016), 246. Italics removed.

Chapter 3

1 Michel De Montaigne, *Essays*, trans. J. M. Cohen (London: Penguin, 1993), 23. Italics removed.
2 Wim Wenders, *Wings of Desire*, performed by Bruno Ganz and Otto Sander (1987; The Criterion Collection, 2009), DVD.
3 Many books written in the opening decades of the twenty-first century make a causal link among the decline of print literacy, loss of self-awareness, and future political dystopia. See, for example, David Mitchell, *Cloud Atlas* (2004); Gary Shteyngart, *Super Sad True Love Story* (2011); Jeanette Winterson, *The Stone Gods* (2010); and Michael Cunningham, *Specimen Days* (2005). Similar links are made in works of scholarship written for a general audience, including Sherry Turkle, *Alone Together: Why We Expect More from Technology and Less from Each Other* (2012) and Nicholas Carr, *The Shallows: What the Internet Is Doing to Our Brains* (2011). I thank my former graduate student Emily Corrie for her excellent M.A. thesis on this topic, "Post-literate Nostalgia in Speculative Visions of the Future" (M.A. diss., Dalhousie University, 2012).
4 On the economic origins of cuneiform, see N. K. Sandars, Introduction to *The Epic of Gilgamesh*, trans. N. K. Sandars (New York: Penguin, 1972), 11–12; Jean-Jacques Glassner, "The First Social Uses of Writing," *The Invention of Cuneiform: Writing in Sumer*, trans. and ed. Zainab Bahrani and Marc Van De Mieroop (Baltimore, MD: Johns Hopkins University Press, 2003),177–99; Jean Bottéro, *Mesopotamia: Writing, Reasoning, and the Gods*, trans. Zainab

Bahrani and Marc Van De Mieroop (Chicago: University of Chicago Press, 1992), 70; Samuel Noah Kramer, *History begins at Sumer: Thirty-Nine Firsts in Man's Recorded History* (Philadelphia: University of Pennsylvania Press, 1981), xxi.

5   *Gilgamesh*, 61. For a timeline of the *Epic*'s transition from speech to writing, see Sandars, Introduction, 8.

6   *Gilgamesh*, 61.

7   Ibid., 106.

8   Ibid., 107.

9   For an account of the conquest of Nineveh and its aftermath see Sandars, Introduction, 44–5. For the importance of libraries to ancient empires, including the Assyrian, Greek, and Roman, see Harold Innis, *Empire and Communications*, rev. Mary Q. Innis (Toronto: University of Toronto Press, 1972), 39, 91, 105. Also see Guglielmo Cavallo and Roger Chartier, Introduction to *The History of Reading in the West*, ed. Guglielmo Cavallo and Roger Chartier, trans. Lydia G. Cochrane (Amherst: The University of Massachusetts Press, 1999), 10.

10   Founded in 1753, the British Museum contained "a new form of library ... namely, one supported by the people as a whole, a collection of books that is accessible to every citizen, one that is a meaningful expression of popular will to collect the treasures of its own country." Karl Schottenloher, *Books and the Western World: A Cultural History*, trans. William D. Boyd and Irmgard H. Wolfe (Jefferson: McFarland & Company, Inc., 1989), 275. Under Napoleon, clerical book collections in France were confiscated by the state and transferred to the Bibliothèque Nationale in Paris, while during the same period Bavaria seized monastic holdings and attempted, despite the political splintering of Germany, to develop a library that would eventually "take in the entire country." Ibid., 300.

11   The piece became a gathering place for grieving New Yorkers. See MoMA. "Mourning 9/11 with Janet Cardiff's *The Forty Part Motet*," accessed May 18, 2021, https://www.moma.org/interactives/moma_through_time/2000/listening-together/

12   You can see and listen to the piece at National Gallery of Canada, "Forty-Part Motet: Janet Cardiff," accessed May 18, 2021, https://www.gallery.ca/whats-on/exhibitions-and-galleries/janet-cardiff-forty-part-motet-2

13   Patricia Hampl, *The Art of the Wasted Day* (New York: Viking, 2018), 97.

14   Michel de Montaigne, "On Experience," *Essays*, 396.

15   I'm thinking of Hampl, *Wasted Day*, but also Jenny Odell, *How to Do Nothing: Resisting the Attention Economy* (2019), Pico Iyer, *The Art of Stillness: Adventures in Going Nowhere* (2014), Brian O'Connor, *Idleness: A Philosophical Essay* (2018), Katherine May, *Wintering: The Power of Rest and Retreat in Difficult Times* (2020).

16   "Doris Lessing—Nobel Lecture: On Not Winning the Nobel Prize," *The Nobel Prize*, accessed May 18, 2021, http://www.nobelprize.org/nobel_prizes/literature/laureates/2007/lessing-lecture_en.html

17   George Orwell, *1984* (New York: Plume, 1983), 24.

18   Annie Dillard, *The Writing Life* (New York: HarperPerennial, 1990), 63–4.

19 Maurice Blanchot, "Literature and the Right to Death," *The Gaze of Orpheus and Other Literary Essays*, trans. Lydia Davis and ed. P. Adams Sitney (Barrytown, NY: Station Hill, 1981), 27.
20 Attridge, *The Singularity of Literature*, 78.
21 Hyde, *Trickster Makes This World*, 323.
22 Ibid., 326.
23 For a superb reading of the *Hymn* along these lines, see Hyde, "Hermes Slips the Trap," *Trickster Makes This World*, 203–25.
24 Plato, *The Cratylus, Phaedo, Parmenides, Timaeus and Critias of Plato*, trans. Thomas Taylor (Michigan: Wizards Bookshelf, 1976), 47.
25 Wilkins, *Mercury*. For a fuller account of John Wilkins's career and his interest in Hermes-Mercury, see Marina Warner, *Stranger Magic: Charmed States and the Arabian Nights* (London: Chatto & Windus, 2011), 339–43.
26 Philippe Petit, *Creativity: The Perfect Crime* (New York: Riverhead Books, 2014), 17–18.
27 Herodotus, *The Histories*, trans. Robin Waterfield (New York: Oxford University Press, 1998), 488.
28 Ibid., 316.
29 David Kahn, *The Codebreakers: The Comprehensive History of Secret Communication from Ancient Times to the Internet* (New York: Scribner, 1996), 126–30.
30 Jonathan Goldberg, *Writing Matter: From the Hands of the English Renaissance* (Stanford, CA: Stanford University Press, 1990), 95.
31 Ibid., 59–107.
32 Ibid., 171–2.
33 For a full account, see Kahn, *Codebreakers*, 157–88. Black Chambers only opened diplomatic mail sent from one embassy to another; the Post Office was entitled to open all the mail that it handled.
34 Marks describes the technical details of the poem-code in *Between Silk and Cyanide: A Codemaker's War, 1941–1945* (New York: Simon & Schuster, 2000), 11.
35 Kahn, *Codebreakers*, 514. Italics added.
36 For details of the technique of radio "fingerprinting" (or taking a "fist") which recorded samples of an agent's transmission style to make it harder to forge, see ibid., 527.
37 Alice Brittan, "War and the Book: The Diarist, the Cryptographer, and *The English Patient*," *PMLA* 121, no. 1 (2006): 203–5. Portions of this essay reprinted by permission of the copyright owner, The Modern Language Association of America (www.mla.org). "'*Funk* means 'radio,' while '*Spiel*' means 'play' or 'performance,' with secondary meanings of 'game,' 'sport,' and 'match.'" Qtd. in Kahn, *Codebreakers*, 531.
38 Karl Ove Knausgaard, *Some Rain Must Fall*, My Struggle: Book 5, trans. Don Bartlett (Toronto: Knopf, 2016), 583. Italics in original.
39 Knausgaard, *A Death in the Family*, My Struggle: Book 1, trans. Don Bartlett (London: Vintage, 2013), 172.
40 Marilynne Robinson, *When I Was a Child I Read Books* (Toronto: HarperPerennial, 2012), 7.

41 "President Obama & Marilynne Robinson: A Conversation in Iowa," *The New York Review*, November 5, 2015, accessed May 19, 2021, https://www.nybooks.com/articles/2015/11/05/president-obama-marilynne-robinson-conversation/?lp_txn_id=1249401

42 Jhumpa Lahiri, *In Other Words*, trans. Ann Goldstein (Toronto: Knopf, 2016), 55.

43 Ibid., 57.

44 Ibid., 55.

45 Ibid., 67.

46 Ibid., 69.

47 Ibid., 167.

48 "On Elena Ferrante: Jhumpa Lahiri and Ann Goldstein." *The Center for Fiction*, accessed May 19, 2021, http://www.centerforfiction.org/calendar/on-elena-ferrante-jhumpa-lahiri-and-ann-goldstein

49 Elena Ferrante, *The Days of Abandonment*, trans. Ann Goldstein (New York: Europa Editions, 2005), 127.

50 Ibid., 26, 86.

51 Ibid., 187.

52 Elena Ferrante, *Frantumaglia: A Writer's Journey*, trans. Ann Goldstein (New York: Europa Editions, 2016), 15.

53 Ibid., 261. Italics in original.

54 Elena Ferrante, "Odious Women," *Incidental Interventions*, trans. Ann Goldstein (New York: Europa Editions, 2019), 29, 30. This volume collects all of Ferrante's weekly articles for the *Guardian* published in 2018, at which point her column was closed by prior arrangement.

55 Elena Ferrante, *The Story of the Lost Child*, trans. Ann Goldstein (New York: Europa Editions, 2015), 472.

56 J. W. Goethe, *Faust*, trans. Walter Kaufmann, in *The Norton Anthology of World Literature: 1800–1900*, ed. Sarah Lawall and Maynard Mack (New York: Norton, 2002), 684, 693.

57 I also invite my students to redesign the front cover of the novel. Note to Europa Editions: if you'd like to see some alternatives to your current designs, I have a large file of options.

58 Elena Ferrante, *My Brilliant Friend*, trans. Ann Goldstein (New York: Europa Editions, 2012), 116.

59 Ibid., 90–1.

60 There are other, slightly less drastic examples, in which the threat of violence causes margins to dissolve, burst, or ignite: Marcello Solara threatens to kill Lila if she doesn't marry him, and a copper pot inexplicably explodes as she is washing the dishes. Ferrante, *Brilliant,* 228–9. The same thing happens to the photograph of Lila that the Solara brothers hang in their shoe store in *The Story of a New Name*, very much against her will. The image spontaneously bursts into flame and burns to ash. Ferrante, *The Story of a New Name*, trans. Ann Goldstein (New York: Europa Editions, 2013), 140.

61 Virgil, *The Aeneid*, trans. Robert Fitzgerald (New York: Vintage, 1990), 4.315.

62 Ibid., 4.457.

63 Ferrante, *Story of a New Name*, 433.

64 Elena Ferrante, *Those Who Leave and Those Who Stay*, trans. Ann Goldstein (New York: Europa Editions, 2014), 30.

65 Ibid., 53.

66 Ibid.

67 Ferrante, *Frantumaglia*, 277.

68 Ferrante, *The Story of the Lost Child*, 473.

69 Carlo Collodi, "The Adventures of Pinocchio," trans. M. A. Murray, in *Classics of Children's Literature*, ed. John W. Griffith and Charles H. Frey (New York: MacMillan, 1987), 245–328.

70 Ferrante, *Story of the Lost Child*, 403. Italics removed from "She stood out among so many because she, naturally, did not submit to any training, to any use, or to any purpose."

71 Medaya Ocher, "Karl Ove Knausgaard, Himself," *Los Angeles Review of Books*, June 15, 2014, https://lareviewofbooks.org/article/karl-ove-knausgaard/

72 Francesca Wilson, *Aftermath; France, Germany, Austria, Yugoslavia, 1945 and 1946* (London: Penguin, 1947). My account of Wilson's early life is drawn from Siân Lliwen Roberts, "Place, Life Histories and the Politics of Relief: Episodes in the Life of Francesca Wilson, Humanitarian Educator Activist." (Ph.D diss, University of Birmingham, 2010).

73 Jonathan Rose, *The Intellectual Life of the British Working Classes* (New Haven: Yale University Press, 2001), 88.

74 Hannah Arendt, Introduction to *Illuminations*, by Walter Benjamin, ed. Hannah Arendt, trans. Harry Zohn (New York: Schocken Books, 1968), 8.

75 David Constantine, "The Loss," *In Another Country* (Windsor, ON: Biblioasis, 2015), 50.

76 Ibid., 52.

77 Saikat Majumdar, "The Critic as Amateur," *New Literary History: A Journal of Theory and Interpretation* 48, no. 1 (2017): 7.

78 Ibid., 22.

79 Michel de Montaigne, "On Repentance," *Essays*, 236.

80 Montaigne, "On Experience," *Essays*, 353.

81 See, for example, Rita Felski, *Hooked: Art and Attachment* (Chicago: University of Chicago Press, 2020) and Deirdre Shauna Lynch, *Loving Literature: A Cultural History* (Chicago: University of Chicago Press, 2015). In a remarkable essay, Jennifer C. Nash traces the importance of the personal in Black American feminist writing, arguing for a kind of scholarship that is vulnerable, self-exposing, and beautiful. She identifies "the need for a new scholarly language—the beautiful—to capture loss" and an ongoing history of violence. She does not merely describe this new kind of language, but *performs* it in her own essay, blurring personal with intellectual history. See "Writing Black Beauty," *Signs: Journal of Women in Culture and Society* 45, no. 1 (2019): 104.

82 Saikat Majumdar and Aarthi Vadde, "Introduction: Criticism for the Whole Person," *The Critic as Amateur*, ed. Saikat Majumdar and Aarthi Vadde (New York: Bloomsbury, 2020), 3.

83 Ibid., 20.

Chapter 4

1   Simone Weil, "Forms of the Implicit Love of God," *Waiting for God*, trans. Emma Craufurd (New York: HarperPerennial, 2009), 92.
2   Michael Taussig, *Mimesis and Alterity: A Particular History of the Senses* (New York: Routledge 1993), 92.
3   Marcel Mauss, *The Gift: The Form and Reason for Exchange in Archaic Societies*, trans. W. D. Halls (New York: Norton, 1990), 66.
4   Greta Gerwig, *Lady Bird*, performed by Saoirse Ronan and Laurie Metcalf (2017; The Criterion Collection).
5   Ibid.
6   Ibid.
7   Christine Smallwood, "Greta Gerwig's Radical Confidence," *The New York Times Magazine*, November 1, 2017, https://www.nytimes.com/2017/11/01/magazine/greta-gerwigs-radical-confidence.html
8   Jenny Erpenbeck, *Go, Went, Gone*, trans. Susan Bernofsky (New York: New Directions, 2017), 117.
9   Ibid., 8.
10 Ibid., 14.
11 Ibid.
12 Ibid., 157.
13 Ibid., 179.
14 Ibid., 261.
15 Annette Weiner, *Inalienable Possessions: The Paradox of Keeping-While-Giving* (Berkeley, CA: University of California Press, 1992), 7.
16 William Pietz famously traces the history of the term fetish in a series of essays. See "The Problem of the Fetish, I," *Res: Anthropology and Aesthetics*, no. 9 (Spring 1985): 5–17; "The Problem of the Fetish, II," *Res: Anthropology and Aesthetics*, no. 13 (Spring 1987): 23–45; "The Problem of the Fetish, IIIa," *Res: Anthropology and Aesthetics*, no. 16 (Autumn 1988): 105–24.
17 Bernard Smith, "The First European Depictions," *Seeing the First Australians*, ed. Ian and Tamsin Donaldson (London: George Allen & Unwin, 1985), 21–34.
18 James Cook, *The Voyages of Captain James Cook Round the World, Vol. 1.* (London: John Tallis & Company, 1852), 208.
19 Ibid., 263; Joseph Banks, *The Endeavour Journal of Joseph Banks: 1768–1771*, Vol. II, ed. J. C. Beaglehole (London: Angus & Robertson, Ltd., 1962), 125.
20 Cook, *Voyages of Captain Cook*, 212.
21 Qtd. in Patricia Seed, *Ceremonies of Possession in Europe's Conquest of the New World, 1492–1640* (Cambridge: Cambridge University Press, 1995), 36.
22 Ibid., 179. For an overview of different national rituals of possession and the influences that shaped them, see ibid., 1–15.
23 See Banks, *Endeavour Journal*, 96 and Cook, *Voyages of Captain Cook*, 242. Such acts of reprisal were common throughout the late-eighteenth and early to late-nineteenth centuries as the frontier expanded and Aboriginal peoples repeatedly attempted to burn the settlers off the land by destroying their

homes, property, and cattle, the very objects which asserted the legitimacy of settlement against nomadism, private accrual against shared ownership, material "culture" against uncultivated "nature."

24 Cook, *Voyages of Captain Cook*, 255–6.

25 I write about Cook's and Banks's first arrival in Australia in Alice Brittan, "B-b-british Objects: Possession, Naming, and Translation in David Malouf's *Remembering Babylon*," *PMLA* 117, no. 5 (2002): 1158–71. Portions of this essay reprinted by permission of the copyright owner, The Modern Language Association of America (www.mla.org). On the deliberations of the Beauchamp Committee, see Robert Hughes, *The Fatal Shore: The Epic of Australia's Founding* (New York: Random House, 1988), 56–67. The status of Australia as *terra nullius* was reiterated in 1889 as the result of disputes over land ownership. See Heather Goodall, *Invasion to Embassy: Land in Aboriginal Politics in New South Wales, 1770–1972* (St. Leonards, NSW: Allen & Unwin, 1996), 106.

26 Lyndall Ryan, *The Aboriginal Tasmanians* (Vancouver, BC: University of British Columbia Press, 1981), 189.

27 M. F. Christie, *Aborigines in Colonial Victoria 1835–86* (Sydney, NSW: Sydney University Press, 1979), 132.

28 Geoffrey Gray, "From Nomadism to Citizenship: A. P. Elkin and Aboriginal Advancement," *Citizenship and Indigenous Australians: Changing Conceptions and Possibilities*, ed. Nicolas Peterson and Will Sanders (Cambridge: University of Cambridge Press, 1998), 56. In 1939, A. P. Elkin was the Chair of the Department of Anthropology at the University of Sydney; he was editor of the anthropological journal *Oceania* from 1933 to 1956, and John McEwen's advisor on Aboriginal cultures. In an essay called "Civilized Aborigines and Native Culture," *Oceania* 6, no. 2 (1935): 137 he writes about how important it is for Aboriginal peoples to learn to fold their clothes and store them in boxes or drawers.

29 David Livingstone, *Livingstone's Missionary Correspondence, 1841–1856*, ed. I. Schapera (Berkeley, CA: University of California Press, 1961), 301.

30 Anthony Trollope, *South Africa, Vol. 1* (1878; London: Dawson's of Pall Mall, 1968), 212.

31 Gary Hinkley, "Native Space in the City," *blank_____: Architecture, Apartheid and After*, ed. Hilton Judin and Ivan Vladislavic (Rotterdam: NAi Publishers, 1998), 209–12.

32 See for example Philip Bonner, "The Transvaal Native Congress, 1917–1920: The Radicalisation of the Black Petty Bourgeoisie on the Rand," *Industrialisation and Social Change in South Africa: African Class Formation, Culture, and Consciousness, 1870–1930*, ed. Shula Marks and Richard Rathbone (New York: Longman, 1982), 270–313.

33 See Nadine Gordimer, Introduction to *On the Mines*, ed. David Goldblatt (Cape Town: C. Struik Ltd., 1973), n.p. Also see Gavin Younge, *Art of the South African Townships* (New York: Rizzoli International Publications, Inc., 1988).

34 James Ferguson, *Global Shadows: Africa in the Neoliberal World Order* (Durham, NC: Duke University Press, 2006), 18.

35 Ibid., 19.

36 Ibid., 173.
37 Albert Luthuli, *Let My People Go* (New York: McGraw-Hill, 1962), 203.
38 See for example Laurine Platzky and Cherryl Walker, *The Surplus People: Forced Removals in South Africa* (Johannesburg: Ravan Press, 1985); Cosmas Desmond, *The Discarded People: An Account of African Resettlement* (Braamfontein: The Christian Institute of South Africa, 1970).
39 See the images in Desmond, *Discarded People.*
40 NoViolet Bulawayo, *We Need New Names* (New York: Back Bay Books, 2013), 60.
41 James Ferguson, "Declarations of Dependence: Labour, Personhood, and Welfare in Southern Africa," *Journal of the Royal Anthropological Institute* 19 (2013): 232.
42 Ibid., 233.
43 Ibid., 225–9.
44 Qtd. in Franco Barchiesi, "South African Debates on the Basic Income Grant: Wage Labour and the Post-Apartheid Social Policy," *Journal of Southern African Studies* 33, no. 3 (September 2007): 571.
45 Sally McGrane, "A Guaranteed Monthly Check Saved His Life. Now He Sends Out 650," *New York Times*, November 6, 2020, https://www.nytimes.com/2020/11/06/world/europe/bohmeyer-berlin-basic-income.html
46 Giorgio Agamben, "Identity without the Person," *Nudities*, trans. David Kishik and Stefan Pedatella (Stanford, CA: Stanford University Press, 2011), 52.
47 Ferguson, *Global Shadows*, 173.
48 Carolyn Kay Steedman, *Landscape for a Good Woman: A Story of Two Lives* (New Brunswick, NJ: Rutgers University Press, 1994), 109.
49 Ibid., 123. It is noteworthy that Steedman's mother joined the Conservative Party rather than the Labour Party, the party of the working classes. Rather than oppose the elite, she voted with them. This too seems a form of aspiration.
50 Bulawayo, *New Names*, 56.
51 Ibid., 270.
52 Ibid., 268.
53 Simone Weil, "Reflections on the Right Use of School Studies with a View to the Love of God," *Waiting for God*, 64.
54 Bulawayo often describes the conflicts among Darling, her friend Marina, who is from Nigeria, and Kristal, who is African-American. *New Names*, 222–6.
55 "Sandra Cisneros: A House of Her Own," *On Being with Krista Tippett*, February 13, 2020, https://onbeing.org/programs/sandra-cisneros-a-house-of-her-own/
56 Marilynne Robinson, "Grace and Beauty," *What Are We Doing Here?* (New York: McClelland & Stewart, 2018), 114.
57 Erpenbeck, *Go, Went, Gone*, 142.
58 Ibid., 209, 241.
59 In *In the Skin of a Lion*, set in Toronto during the 1920s and 1930s, David Caravaggio is an Italian-Canadian thief and saboteur. In *The English Patient*, set in Italy during and immediately after the Second World War, he is a spy; in *Divisadero*, set in later-twentieth-century America and France, he is an

unnamed Roma man. In *The Cat's Table*, set on board an ocean liner in the mid-twentieth century, he appears as a reference to his namesake, the early modern painter Michelangelo Caravaggio. See *The Cat's Table* (Toronto: McClelland & Stewart, 2011), 224–5.

60 Michael Ondaatje, *Anil's Ghost* (New York: Vintage, 2000), 303.

61 Michael Ondaatje, *Coming through Slaughter* (Toronto: Vintage Canada, 1998), 134, 135.

62 Ibid., 135.

63 Ibid.

64 Robinson, "Grace and Beauty," 114.

65 C. S. Lewis, *The Voyage of the Dawn Treader* (New York: HarperTrophy, 1994), 254, 260.

66 C. S. Lewis, *The Last Battle* (New York: HarperTrophy, 1994), 228.

67 Mohsin Hamid, *Exit West* (New York: Riverhead, 2017), 73. On *Charlotte's Web*, see "Mohsin Hamid's 6 Favorite Books," *The Week*, January 8, 2015, http://theweek.com/articles/463446/mohsin-hamids-6-favorite-books.

68 Hamid, *Exit West*, 56.

69 Ibid., 57.

70 Madeleine L'Engle, *A Wrinkle in Time* (New York: Square Fish, 2007), 179.

71 Hamid, *Exit West*, 72.

72 Ibid., 8.

73 Ibid.

74 Ibid., 9.

75 L'Engle, *Wrinkle in Time*, 26.

76 Hamid, *Exit West*, 146.

77 Ibid., 148.

78 Ibid., 156.

79 Ibid., 166.

80 Ibid., 169.

81 Ibid., 179.

82 Ibid., 184.

83 Ibid., 138.

84 Ibid., 110.

85 Alister McGrath, *C. S. Lewis: A Life* (Carol Stream, IL: Tyndale House, 2013), 288.

Chapter 5

1 Jenny Erpenbeck, *Go, Went, Gone*, trans. Susan Bernofsky (New York: New Directions, 2017), 210. *By Jenny Erpenbeck, from GO, WENT, GONE, copyright ©2015 by Albrecht Knaus Verlag, a division of Verlagsgruppe Random House GmbH, München, Germany. Translation copyright ©2017 by Susan Bernofsky. Reprinted by permission of New Directions Publishing Corp.

2 Antoine de Saint-Exupéry, *The Little Prince*, trans. Katherine Woods (Harmonsworth, England: Penguin, 1965), 88.

3   Ibid., 91.
4   Ibid., 107.
5   Lewis Hyde, *The Gift: Creativity and the Artist in the Modern World* (New York: Vintage, 2007), 29.
6   Mark Osborne, *The Little Prince*, performed by Jeff Bridges and Mackenzie Foy (2015; Paramount Pictures).
7   Euripides, "Herakles," *Grief Lessons: Four Plays by Euripides*, trans. Anne Carson (New York: New York Review of Books, 2006), 1147–51.
8   Ibid., 1374, 1373.
9   Ibid., 1200–2.
10 Ibid., 1312.
11 Lewis Hyde, *Trickster Makes This World: Mischief, Myth, and Art* (New York: North Point Press, 1998), 58.
12 Ibid., 58.
13 Richard Seaford, *Money and the Early Greek Mind: Homer, Philosophy, Tragedy* (New York: Cambridge University Press, 2004), 49.
14 Ibid.
15 Ibid., 109. For a general discussion of the transition from cooking spits to coinage, see ibid., 102–15. Leslie Kurke also describes the use of roasting spits, tripods, and bowls as forms of pre-monetary currency. See *Coins, Bodies, Games, and Gold: The Politics of Meaning in Archaic Greece* (Princeton, NJ: Princeton University Press, 1999), 11.
16 On the relationship among coinage, democracy, and distributive justice see ibid., 13–17.
17 Jeremy Trevett, "Coinage and Democracy at Athens," *Money and Its Uses in the Ancient Greek World*, ed. Andrew Meadows and Kirsty Shipton (Oxford: Oxford University Press, 2001), 33.
18 Kurke, *Coins, Bodies, Games, and Gold*, 305. Trevett quotes this sentence in "Coins and Democracy," 28, footnote 61.
19 Aristotle, *Aristotle's Nicomachean Ethics*, trans. Hippocrates G. Apostle (Grinnell: The Peripatetic Press, 1984), 87.
20 Ibid., 88.
21 Ibid.
22 Ibid., 87.
23 Ibid., 99.
24 Homer, *The Iliad*, trans. Robert Fagles (New York: Penguin, 1998), 9.386–8.
25 Seaford, *Money and the Early Greek Mind*, 51.
26 Kurke, *Coins, Bodies, Games, and Gold*, 288–95.
27 Ibid., 295.
28 Ibid., 292, footnote 92.
29 Marilynne Robinson, *Gilead* (New York: HarperPerennial, 2004), 197.
30 Marilynne Robinson, "Realism," *The Givenness of Things* (Toronto: HarperCollins, 2015), 273.
31 John 11:14.
32 Luke 22:51. This episode also appears at John 18:10, where the disciple is identified as Simon Peter and the servant as Malchus. In John's account, Jesus does not reattach the severed ear, although he does tell Peter to put his sword away.

33 Colm Tóibín, *Nora Webster* (New York: McClelland & Stewart, 2014), 344.
34 Ibid., 345.
35 Ibid.
36 Ibid.
37 Ibid., 359.
38 Homer, *The Odyssey*, trans. Emily Wilson (New York: Norton, 2018), 12.22–3.
39 Ibid., 11.104–5.
40 Ibid., 12.116–17.
41 Virgil, *Aeneid*, trans. Robert Fitzgerald (New York: Vintage, 1990), 5.911.
42 Ibid., 5.958–9.
43 Ibid., 6.1007.
44 Ibid., 6.1018.
45 Homer, *The Iliad*, 9.145. In Book 9 Achilles roughly rebuffs Agamemnon's ambassadors, Odysseus and Ajax, and scorns the gifts they offer. In Book 19, he accepts Agamemnon's apology, but dismisses the ransom for the second time. Ibid., 19.176–80.
46 Ibid., 9.789.
47 Ibid., 9.443.
48 Ibid., 9.413–15. Italics in original.
49 Ibid., 9.488.
50 Ibid., 9.741.
51 Ibid., 9.523.
52 Ibid., 18.266.
53 Ibid., 2.451.
54 Ibid., 18.588.
55 Ibid., 18.690.
56 Ibid., 19.229.
57 Ibid., 22.310–11.
58 Ibid., 24.388.
59 Simone Weil, *The Iliad or The Poem of Force*, trans. Mary McCarthy (Wallingford, PA: Pendle Hill, 1983), 29.
60 Bernard Knox, Introduction to *The Iliad*, trans. Robert Fagles (New York: Penguin, 1998), 59.
61 Homer, *Iliad*, 24.566.
62 Ibid., 24.590–1.
63 Ibid., 24.655.
64 Ibid., 2.451.
65 Anne Carson, "Every Exit Is an Entrance (A Praise of Sleep)," *Decreation: Poetry, Essays, Opera* (New York: Knopf, 2005), 38.
66 Ibid., 39. Italics in original. Carson discusses the strangeness of the way Achilles and Socrates understand their lives on 36–40.
67 Ibid., 20.
68 Ibid., 39. Italics removed from "*coming from somewhere else.*"
69 Simone Weil, "Letter II: Same Subject," *Waiting for God*, trans. Emma Craufurd (New York: HarperPerennial), 13.
70 Weil, "Letter IV: Spiritual Autobiography," *Waiting for God*, 30, 36.
71 Euripides, "Hekabe," *Grief Lessons*, 277.
72 Ibid., 751.

73   Ibid., 774.
74   Ibid., 802–3.
75   Ibid., 871.
76   Ibid., 1256–7.
77   Ibid., 1264–5.
78   The murder of Agamemnon by Clytemnestra is a mythic convention that Euripides cannot alter. The murder is described in Homer, *The Odyssey*, 11.404–62. In "Agamemnon," Aiskhylos attributes Clytemnestra's fury toward her husband to his sacrifice of Iphigenia. See "Agamemnon," *An Oresteia*, trans. Anne Carson (New York: FSG, 2009), 1062–75. In "Electra," Sophokles writes that Artemis stalled the winds and demanded the sacrifice to punish Agamemnon for boasting about his prowess as a hunter when he killed a stag in her bower. See "Electra," ibid., 749–72.
79   Héctor Tobar, "Sixty-Nine Days: How the Chilean Miners Survived," *The New Yorker*, July 7, 2014, 62.
80   Ibid., 71.
81   Helen Macdonald, "How to Stay Sane during a Solar Eclipse," *New York Times Magazine*, August 18, 2017, https://www.nytimes.com/2017/08/18/magazine/how-to-stay-sane-during-a-solar-eclipse.html
82   Annie Dillard, "Total Eclipse," *The Abundance: Narrative Essays Old and New* (New York: HarperCollins, 2016), 13–14.
83   Ibid., 14.
84   Robert Macfarlane, *Underland: A Deep Time Journey* (New York: Hamish Hamilton, 2019). Macfarlane writes about cataphiles, who explore the catacombs beneath Paris, in a chapter called "Invisible Cities," 127–73.
85   David Malouf, *Ransom* (New York: Pantheon, 2009), 213.
86   Qtd. in Jacques Derrida, *Adieu to Emmanuel Levinas*, trans. Pascale-Anne Brault and Michael Naas (Stanford, CA: Stanford University Press, 1999), 7.
87   Malouf, *Ransom*, 74.
88   Ibid., 69.
89   John 20:24-9.
90   Weil, *The Iliad or The Poem of Force*, 34.
91   Ibid.
92   Aleksandar Hemon, *The Lazarus Project* (New York: Riverhead, 2008), n.p. Italics removed
93   Ibid., 235.
94   Ibid.
95   Ibid., 251. Italics removed.
96   Ibid., 262.
97   Ibid., 281.
98   Ibid., 236.
99   Ibid., 262.
100 Ibid., 106.
101 Alice Oswald, *Memorial: A Version of Homer's Iliad* (New York: Norton, 2011), ix.
102 Ibid., 13, 69.
103 Ibid., 13.
104 Alice Oswald, "Alice Oswald on Poetry, Nature, and the Shedding of Identity," interview by Eleanor Wachtel, *Writers & Company*,

CBC, September 23, 2016, audio, 52:10, https://www.cbc.ca/radio/
writersandcompany/alice-oswald-on-poetry-nature-and-the-shedding-of-
identity-1.3769283
105   Oswald, *Memorial*, 80–1.

Conclusion

1   Italo Calvino, "Lightness," *Six Memos for the Next Millennium*, trans.
      Patrick Creagh (Cambridge, MA: Harvard University Press, 1988), 4.
2   Ibid.
3   Marina Warner, *Stranger Magic: Charmed States & the Arabian Nights*
      (London: Chatto & Windus, 2011), 23.
4   Calvino, *Six Memos*, 10.
5   Colum McCann, *Let the Great World Spin* (New York: HarperPerennial,
      2011), 239.
6   Teju Cole, *Open City* (New York: Random House, 2011), 194–7.
7   Kendrick Lamar, "Alright," *YouTube*, June 30, 2015, https://www.youtube.
      com/watch?v=Z-48u_uWMHY
8   Anne Carson, *Autobiography of Red* (New York: Vintage, 1998), 39. Italics
      removed from entire quote.
9   Ovid, *Metamorphoses*, trans. Rolfe Humphries (Bloomington: Indiana
      University Press, 1955), 4.781–2.
10   Ibid., 4.747; Calvino, *Six Memos*, 6.
11   Ovid, 4.749–50.
12   Ovid describes the slaughter of Medusa at 4.770–87, and the riot at
      Andromeda's house in Book 5.
13   Norman Bryson, *Looking at the Overlooked: Four Essays on Still Life
      Painting* (London: Reaktion Books, 1990), 140.

BIBLIOGRAPHY

Agamben, Giorgio. *The Highest Poverty: Monastic Rules and Form-of-Life*. Translated by Adam Kotsko. Stanford, CA: Stanford University Press, 2013.

Agamben, Giorgio. *Homo Sacer: Sovereign Power and Bare Life*. Translated by Daniel Heller-Roazen. Stanford, CA: Stanford University Press, 1998.

Agamben, Giorgio. "Identity without the Person." In *Nudities*. Translated by David Kishik and Stefan Pedatella, 46–54. Stanford, CA: Stanford University Press, 2011.

Agamben, Giorgio. *The Kingdom and the Glory: For a Theological Genealogy of Economy and Government*. Translated by Lorenzo Chiesa with Matteo Mandarini. Stanford, CA: Stanford University Press, 2011.

Agamben, Giorgio. *The Time That Remains: A Commentary on the Letter to the Romans*. Translated by Patricia Dailey. Stanford, CA: Stanford University Press, 2005.

Aiskhylos. "Agamemnon." In *An Oresteia*. Translated by Anne Carson, 11–74. New York: FSG, 2009.

Arendt, Hannah. Introduction to *Illuminations*, by Walter Benjamin, edited by Hannah Arendt. Translated by Harry Zohn, 1–55. New York: Schocken Books, 1968.

Aristotle. *Aristotle's Nicomachean Ethics*. Translated by Hippocrates G. Apostle. Grinnell: The Peripatetic Press, 1984.

Armstrong, Karen. *St Paul: The Misunderstood Apostle*. London: Atlantic Books, 2015.

Aslan, Reza. *Zealot: The Life and Times of Jesus of Nazareth*. New York: Random House, 2013.

Attridge, Derek. "Age of Bronze, State of Grace: Music and Dogs in Coetzee's *Disgrace*." *Novel* 34, no. 1 (2000): 98–121.

Attridge, Derek. *J. M. Coetzee and the Ethics of Reading: Literature in the Event*. Chicago: University of Chicago Press, 2004.

Attridge, Derek. *The Singularity of Literature*. New York: Routledge, 2004.

Badiou, Alain. *Saint Paul: The Foundation of Universalism*. Translated by Ray Brassier. Stanford, CA: Stanford University Press, 2003.

Banks, Joseph. *The Endeavour Journal of Joseph Banks: 1768–1771, Vol. I*, edited by J. C. Beaglehole. London: Angus & Robertson, 1962.

Barchiesi, Franco. "South African Debates on the Basic Income Grant: Wage Labour and the Post-Apartheid Social Policy." *Journal of Southern African Studies* 33, no. 3 (September 2007): 561–75.

Barnard, Rita. *Apartheid and beyond: South African Writers and the Politics of Place*. New York: Oxford University Press, 2007.

Bennett, Jane. *Vibrant Matter: A Political Ecology of Things*. Durham, NC: Duke University Press, 2010.

Black, Shameem. *Fiction across Borders: Imagining the Lives of Others in Late Twentieth-Century Novels*. New York: Columbia University Press, 2010.

Blanchot, Maurice. "Literature and the Right to Death." In *The Gaze of Orpheus and Other Literary Essays*, translated by Lydia Davis and edited by P. Adams Sitney, 21–62. Barrytown, NY: Station Hill, 1981.

Boehmer, Elleke. "Not Saying Sorry, Not Speaking Pain: Gender Implications in *Disgrace*." *Interventions* 4, no. 3 (2002): 342–51.

Bonner, Philip. "The Transvaal Native Congress, 1917–1920: The Radicalisation of the Black Petty Bourgeoisie on the Rand." In *Industrialisation and Social Change in South Africa: African Class Formation, Culture, and Consciousness, 1870–1930*, edited by Shula Marks and Richard Rathbone, 270–313. New York: Longman, 1982.

Bornkamm, Günther. *Paul*. Translated by D. M. G. Stalker. New York: Harper & Row, 1969.

Bottéro, Jean. *Mesopotamia: Writing, Reasoning, and the Gods*. Translated by Zainab Bahrani and Marc Van De Mieroop. Chicago: University of Chicago Press, 1992.

Breton, Stanislas. *A Radical Philosophy of Saint Paul*. Translated by Joseph N. Ballan. New York: Columbia University Press, 2011.

Brittan, Alice. "B-b-british Objects: Possession, Naming, and Translation in David Malouf's *Remembering Babylon*." *PMLA* 117, no. 5 (2002): 1158–71.

Brittan, Alice. "Death and J. M. Coetzee's *Disgrace*." *Contemporary Literature* 51, no. 3 (2010): 477–502.

Brittan, Alice. "War and the Book: The Diarist, the Cryptographer, and *The English Patient*." *PMLA* 121, no. 1 (2006): 200–13.

The Brothers Grimm. "The Sleeping Beauty." In *Classics of Children's Literature*, edited by John W. Griffith and Charles H. Frey, 89–91. New York: MacMillan, 1987.

Bryson, Norman. *Looking at the Overlooked: Four Essays on Still Life Painting*. London: Reaktion Books, 1990.

Bulawayo, NoViolet. *We Need New Names*. New York: Back Bay Books, 2013.

Calvino, Italo. *Six Memos for the Next Millennium*. Translated by Patrick Creagh. Cambridge, MA: Harvard University Press, 1988.

Carr, Nicholas. *The Shallows: What the Internet Is Doing to Our Brains*. New York: Norton, 2011.

Carson, Anne. *Autobiography of Red*. New York: Vintage, 1998.

Carson, Anne. *Decreation: Poetry, Essays, Opera*. New York: Knopf, 2005.

Carson, Anne. *Economy of the Unlost*. Princeton, NJ: Princeton University Press, 1999.

Cary, Phillip. *Inner Grace: Augustine in the Traditions of Plato and Paul*. Oxford: Oxford University Press, 2008.

Cassirer, Heinz W. *Grace & Law: St. Paul, Kant, and the Hebrew Prophets*. Grand Rapids, MI: Eerdmans/Handsel, 1988.

Cavallo, Guglielmo and Roger Chartier. Introduction to *The History of Reading in the West*, translated by Lydia G. Cochrane and edited by Guglielmo Cavallo and Roger Chartier, 1–36. Amherst, MA: The University of Massachusetts Press, 1999.

Celan, Paul. *Collected Prose*. Translated by Rosemarie Waldrop. Manchester: Carcanet Press, 1986.

The Center for Fiction. "On Elena Ferrante: Jhumpa Lahiri and Ann Goldstein." Accessed May 19, 2021. http://www.centerforfiction.org/calendar/on-elena-ferrante-jhumpa-lahiri-and-ann-goldstein ·

Christie, M. F. *Aborigines in Colonial Victoria 1835–86*. Sydney: Sydney University Press, 1979.

Coetzee, J. M. *Age of Iron*. New York: Penguin, 1990.

Coetzee, J. M. *The Childhood of Jesus*. New York: Random House, 2013.

Coetzee, J. M. *The Death of Jesus*. London: Harvill Secker, 2019.

Coetzee, J. M. *Diary of a Bad Year*. London: Vintage, 2008.

Coetzee, J. M. *Disgrace*. New York: Penguin, 1999.

Coetzee, J. M. *Doubling the Point: Essays and Interviews*. Edited by David Attwell. Cambridge, MA: Harvard University Press, 1992.

Coetzee, J. M. *Elizabeth Costello: Eight Lessons*. London: Vintage, 2004.

Coetzee, J. M. *Foe*. New York: Penguin, 1986.

Coetzee, J. M. *Giving Offense: Essays on Censorship*. Chicago: Chicago University Press, 1996.

Coetzee, J. M. *Inner Workings: Literary Essays 2000–2005*. New York: Viking, 2007.

Coetzee, J. M. *Life & Times of Michael K*. London: Vintage, 2004.

Coetzee, J. M. *The Master of Petersburg*. London: Vintage, 2004.

Coetzee, J. M. *The Schooldays of Jesus*. London: Harvill Secker, 2016.

Coetzee, J. M. *Slow Man*. New York: Viking, 2005.

Coetzee, J. M. *Waiting for the Barbarians*. London: Vintage, 2004.

Coetzee, J. M. *White Writing: On the Culture of Letters in South Africa*. New Haven: Yale University Press, 1988.

Cole, Teju. *Known and Strange Things: Essays*. New York: Random House, 2016.

Cole, Teju. *Open City*. New York: Random House, 2011.

Collodi, Carlo. "The Adventures of Pinocchio." In *Classics of Children's Literature*, translated by M. A. Murray. edited by John W. Griffith and Charles H. Frey, 245–328. New York: MacMillan, 1987.

Constantine, David. *In Another Country*. Windsor, ON: Biblioasis, 2015.

Cook, James. *The Voyages of Captain James Cook Round the World*, Vol. 1. London: John Tallis & Company, 1852.

Corrie, Emily. "Post-literate Nostalgia in Speculative Visions of the Future." M.A. diss., Dalhousie University, 2012.

Cunningham, Michael. *Specimen Days*. New York: HarperCollins, 2005.

Derrida, Jacques. *Adieu to Emmanuel Levinas*. Translated by Pascale-Anne Brault and Michael Naas. Stanford, CA: Stanford University Press, 1999.

Derrida, Jacques. *The Gift of Death*. Translated by David Wills. Chicago: University of Chicago Press, 1995.

Derrida, Jacques. *Given Time: I. Counterfeit Money*. Translated by Peggy Kamuf. Chicago: University of Chicago Press, 1994.

Derrida, Jacques. "Psyche: Invention of the Other." In *Acts of Literature*, edited by Derek Attridge, 310–43. New York: Routledge, 1992.

Derrida, Jacques. *On Cosmopolitanism and Forgiveness*. Translated by Mark Dooley and Michael Hughes. New York: Routledge, 2007.

Desmond, Cosmas. *The Discarded People: An Account of African Resettlement*. Braamfontein: The Christian Institute of South Africa, 1970.

Dillard, Annie. *The Abundance: Narrative Essays Old and New*. New York: HarperCollins, 2016.

Dillard, Annie. *Pilgrim at Tinker Creek*. New York: HarperPerennial, 2007.

Dillard, Annie. *The Writing Life*. New York: HarperPerennial, 1990.

Douglas, Mary. Foreword to *The Gift: The Form and Reason for Exchange in Archaic Societies*, by Marcel Mauss. Translated by W. D. Halls, vii–xviii. New York: Norton, 1990.

Durrant, Sam. "J. M. Coetzee, Elizabeth Costello, and the Limits of the Sympathetic Imagination." In *J. M. Coetzee and the Idea of the Public Intellectual*, edited by Jane Poyner, 118–34. Athens, OH: Ohio University Press, 2006.

Ehrenreich, Barbara. *Living With a Wild God: A Nonbeliever's Search for the Truth about Everything*. New York: Twelve, 2014.

Elie, Paul. "The Velvet Reformation." *The Atlantic*, March 1, 2009.

Elkin, A. P. "Civilized Aborigines and Native Culture." *Oceania* 6, no. 2 (1935): 117–46.

The Epic of Gilgamesh. Translated by N. K. Sandars. New York: Penguin, 1972.

Erpenbeck, Jenny. *Go, Went, Gone*. Translated by Susan Bernofsky. New York: New Directions, 2017.

Euripides. *Grief Lessons: Four Plays by Euripides*. Translated by Anne Carson. New York: New York Review of Books, 2006.

Felski, Rita. *Hooked: Art and Attachment*. Chicago: University of Chicago Press, 2020.

Ferguson, James. "Declarations of Dependence: Labour, Personhood, and Welfare in Southern Africa." *Journal of the Royal Anthropological Institute*, no. 19 (2013): 223–42.

Ferguson, James. *Global Shadows: Africa in the Neoliberal World Order*. Durham, NC: Duke University Press, 2006.

Ferrante, Elena. *The Days of Abandonment*. Translated by Ann Goldstein. New York: Europa Editions, 2005.

Ferrante, Elena. *Frantumaglia: A Writer's Journey*. Translated by Ann Goldstein. New York: Europa Editions, 2016.

Ferrante, Elena. *Incidental Interventions*. Translated by Ann Goldstein. New York: Europa Editions, 2019.

Ferrante, Elena. *My Brilliant Friend*. Translated by Ann Goldstein. New York: Europa Editions, 2012.

Ferrante, Elena. *The Story of the Lost Child*. Translated by Ann Goldstein. New York: Europa Editions, 2015.

Ferrante, Elena. *The Story of a New Name*. Translated by Ann Goldstein. New York: Europa Editions, 2013.

Ferrante, Elena. *Those Who Leave and Those Who Stay*. Translated by Ann Goldstein. New York: Europa Editions, 2014.

Gerwig, Greta. *Lady Bird*. Performed by Saoirse Ronan and Laurie Metcalf. 2017; The Criterion Collection.

Gilroy, Paul. *After Empire: Melancholia or Convivial Culture?* New York: Routledge, 2006.

Glassner, Jean-Jacques. "The First Social Uses of Writing." In *The Invention of Cuneiform: Writing in Sumer*. Translated and edited by Zainab Bahrani and Marc Van De Mieroop, 177–99. Baltimore, MD: Johns Hopkins University Press, 2003.

Gobodo-Madikizela, Pumla. *A Human Being Died That Night: A South African Story of Forgiveness*. New York: Houghton Mifflin, 2003.

Goethe, J. W. *Faust*. Translated by Walter Kaufmann. *The Norton Anthology of World Literature: 1800–1900*, edited by Sarah Lawall and Maynard Mack, 678–780. New York: Norton, 2002.

Goldberg, Jonathan. *Writing Matter: From the Hands of the English Renaissance*. Stanford, CA: Stanford University Press, 1990.

Goodall, Heather. *Invasion to Embassy: Land in Aboriginal Politics in New South Wales, 1770–1972*. St. Leonards, NSW: Allen & Unwin, 1996.

Gordimer, Nadine. Introduction to *On the Mines*, edited by David Goldblatt, n.p. Cape Town: C. Struik Ltd., 1973.

Grant, Adam. *Give and Take: Why Helping Others Drives Our Success*. New York: Penguin, 2013.

Gray, Geoffrey. "From Nomadism to Citizenship: A. P. Elkin and Aboriginal Advancement." In *Citizenship and Indigenous Australians: Changing Conceptions and Possibilities*, edited by Nicolas Peterson and Will Sanders, 55–76. Cambridge: University of Cambridge Press, 1998.

Greenblatt, Stephen. *Marvelous Possessions: The Wonder of the New World*. New York: Oxford University Press, 1992.

Grossman, David. "The Age of Genius: The Legend of Bruno Schulz." *New Yorker*, June 8 & 15, 2009.

Hamid, Mohsin. *Exit West*. New York: Riverhead, 2017.

Hampl, Patricia. *The Art of the Wasted Day*. New York: Viking, 2018.

Heidegger, Martin. *Poetry, Language, Thought*. Translated by Albert Hofstadter. New York: Perennial Classics, 2001.

Hemon, Aleksandar. *The Lazarus Project*. New York: Riverhead, 2008.

Herman, Gabriel. *Ritualised Friendship and the Greek City*. Cambridge: Cambridge University Press, 1987.

Herodotus. *The Histories*. Translated by Robin Waterfield. New York: Oxford University Press, 1998.

Hinkley, Gary. "Native Space in the City." In *blank____: Architecture, Apartheid and After*, edited by Hilton Judin and Ivan Vladislavic, 209–12. Rotterdam: NAi Publishers, 1998.

Homer. *The Iliad*. Translated by Robert Fagles. New York: Penguin, 1998.

Homer. *The Odyssey*. Translated by Emily Wilson. New York: Norton, 2018.

Hughes, Robert. *The Fatal Shore: The Epic of Australia's Founding*. New York: Random House, 1988.

Hyde, Lewis. *The Gift: Creativity and the Artist in the Modern World*. New York: Vintage, 2007.

Hyde, Lewis. *Trickster Makes This World: Mischief, Myth, and Art*. New York: North Point Press, 1998.

Innis, Harold. *Empire and Communications*. Revised by Mary Q. Innis. Toronto: University of Toronto Press, 1972.

Iyer, Pico. *The Art of Stillness: Adventures in Going Nowhere*. New York: Simon & Schuster, 2014.

Kafka, Franz. *The Basic Kafka*. Translated by Willa and Edwin Muir. New York: Schocken Books, 1977.

Kahn, David. *The Codebreakers: The Comprehensive History of Secret Communication from Ancient Times to the Internet*. New York: Scribner, 1996.

Keen, Suzanne. *Empathy and the Novel*. New York: Oxford University Press, 2007.

Klein, Terrance W. *Wittgenstein and the Metaphysics of Grace*. Oxford: Oxford University Press, 2007.

Knausgaard, Karl Ove. *A Death in the Family*, My Struggle: Book 1. Translated by Don Bartlett. London: Vintage, 2013.

Knausgaard, Karl Ove. *A Man in Love*, My Struggle: Book 2. Translated by Don Bartlett. New York: Vintage, 2013.

Knausgaard, Karl Ove. "My Struggle with Autobiographer Karl Ove Knausgaard." Interview by Eleanor Wachtel. *Writers & Company*, CBC, June 29, 2014. Audio, 52: 55. https://www.cbc.ca/radio/writersandcompany/karl-ove-knausgaard-interview-1.2790787

Knausgaard, Karl Ove. *Some Rain Must Fall*, My Struggle: Book 5. Translated by Don Bartlett. Toronto: Knopf, 2016.

Knausgaard, Karl Ove. *A Time for Everything*. Translated by James Anderson. New York: Archipelago Books, 2009.

Knox, Bernard. Introduction to *The Iliad*, by Homer. Translated by Robert Fagles, 3–64. New York: Penguin, 1998.

Kramer, Samuel Noah. *History Begins at Sumer: Thirty-Nine Firsts in Man's Recorded History*. Philadelphia: University of Pennsylvania Press, 1981.

Krog, Antjie. *Country of My Skull: Guilt, Sorrow, and the Limits of Forgiveness in the New South Africa*. New York: Three Rivers Press, 2000.

Kundera, Milan. *The Unbearable Lightness of Being*. Translated by Michael Henry Heim. New York: HarperPerennial, 1999.

Kurke, Leslie. *Coins, Bodies, Games, and Gold: The Politics of Meaning in Archaic Greece*. Princeton, NJ: Princeton University Press, 1999.

LaCapra, Dominick. *History and Its Limits: Human, Animal, Violence*. Ithaca, NY: Cornell University Press, 2009.

Lahiri, Jhumpa. *In Other Words*. Translated by Ann Goldstein. New York: Knopf, 2016.

Lamar, Kendrick. "Alright." *YouTube*. June 30, 2015, https://www.youtube.com/watch?v=Z-48u_uWMHY

L'Engle, Madeleine. *A Wrinkle in Time*. New York: Square Fish, 2007.

Lessing, Doris. "Doris Lessing—Nobel Lecture: On Not Winning the Nobel Prize." *The Nobel Prize*. Accessed May 18, 2021. http://www.nobelprize.org/nobel_prizes/literature/laureates/2007/lessing-lecture_en.html

Levinas, Emmanuel. *Of God Who Comes to Mind*. Translated by Bettina Bergo. Stanford, CA: Stanford University Press, 1998.

Levinas, Emmanuel. *Totality and Infinity: An Essay on Exteriority*. Translated by Alphonso Lingis. Pittsburgh, PA: Duquesne University Press, 1969.

Lewis, C. S. *The Last Battle*. New York: HarperTrophy, 1994.

Lewis, C. S. *The Voyage of the Dawn Treader*. New York: HarperTrophy, 1994.

Livingstone, David. *Livingstone's Missionary Correspondence, 1841–1856*. Edited by I. Schapera. Berkeley, CA: University of California Press, 1961.

Luthuli, Albert. *Let My People Go*. New York: McGraw-Hill, 1962.

Lynch, Deirdre Shauna. *Loving Literature: A Cultural History*. Chicago: University of Chicago Press, 2015.

Macdonald, Helen. *H Is for Hawk*. New York: Penguin, 2014.

Macdonald, Helen. "How to Stay Sane During a Solar Eclipse." *New York Times Magazine*. August 18, 2017. https://www.nytimes.com/2017/08/18/magazine/how-to-stay-sane-during-a-solar-eclipse.html

Macfarlane, Robert. *Underland: A Deep Time Journey*. New York: Hamish Hamilton, 2019.

MacLachlan, Bonnie. *The Age of Grace: Charis in Early Greek Poetry*. Princeton, NJ: Princeton University Press, 1993.

Majumdar, Saikat. "The Critic as Amateur." *New Literary History: A Journal of Theory and Interpretation* 48, no. 1 (2017): 1–25.

Majumdar, Saikat and Aarthi Vadde. Introduction to *The Critic as Amateur*, edited by Saikat Majumdar and Aarthi Vadde, 1–28. New York: Bloomsbury, 2020.

Malouf, David. *Ransom*. New York: Pantheon, 2009.

Marais, Michael. "J. M. Coetzee's *Disgrace* and the Task of the Imagination." *Journal of Modern Literature* 29, no. 2 (2006): 75–93.

Marais, Michael. "Violence, Postcolonial Fiction, and the Limits of Sympathy." *Studies in the Novel* 43, no. 1 (2011): 94–114.

Marks, Leo. *Between Silk and Cyanide: A Codemaker's War, 1941–1945*. New York: Simon & Schuster, 2000.

Márquez, Gabriel García. "The Handsomest Drowned Man in the World: A Tale for Children." In *Major Writers of Short Fiction*, edited by Ann Charters and translated by Gregory Rabassa. 448–52. New York: Bedford /St. Martin's, 1993.

Marsh, James. *Man on Wire*. Performed by Philippe Petit. 2008; Magnolia Pictures. DVD.

Mauss, Marcel. *The Gift: The Form and Reason for Exchange in Archaic Societies*. Translated by W. D. Halls. New York: Norton, 1990.

May, Katherine. *Wintering: The Power of Rest and Retreat in Difficult Times*. New York: Riverhead, 2020.

McCann, Colum. *Let the Great World Spin*. New York: HarperPerennial, 2011.

McDonald, Peter D. *The Literature Police: Apartheid Censorship and Its Cultural Consequences*. Oxford: Oxford University Press, 2009.

McGrane, Sally. "A Guaranteed Monthly Check Saved His Life. Now He Sends Out 650." *New York Times*. November 6, 2020. https://www.nytimes.com/2020/11/06/world/europe/bohmeyer-berlin-basic-income.html

McGrath, Alister. *C. S. Lewis: A Life*. Carol Stream, IL: Tyndale House, 2013.

Mitchell, David. *Cloud Atlas*. Toronto: Vintage, 2004.

"Mohsin Hamid's 6 Favorite Books." *The Week*. January 8, 2015. http://theweek.com/articles/463446/mohsin-hamids-6-favorite-books.

MoMA. "Mourning 9/11 with Janet Cardiff's *The Forty Part Motet*." Accessed May 18, 2021, https://www.moma.org/interactives/moma_through_time/2000/listening-together/

Montaigne, Michel de. *Essays*. Translated by J. M. Cohen. London: Penguin, 1993.

Morris, Errol. "The Fog of War: Transcript." *The Fog of War: Eleven Lessons from the Life of Robert S. McNamara*. September 21, 2012. http://www.errolmorris.com/film/fow_transcript.html

Morrison, Toni. *Beloved*. New York: Vintage, 2004.

Nancy, Jean-Luc. *God, Justice, Love, Beauty: Four Little Dialogues*. Translated by Sarah Clift. New York: Fordham University Press, 2011.

Nancy, Jean-Luc. *Noli me tangere: On the Raising of the Body*. Translated by Sarah Clift, Pascale-Anne Brault, and Michael Naas. New York: Fordham University Press, 2008.

Nash, Jennifer C. "Writing Black Beauty." *Signs: Journal of Women in Culture and Society* 45, no. 1 (2019): 101–22.

National Gallery of Canada. "Forty-Part Motet: Janet Cardiff." Accessed May 18, 2021. https://www.gallery.ca/whats-on/exhibitions-and-galleries/janet-cardiff-forty-part-motet-2

Nussbaum, Martha C. "Patriotism and Cosmopolitanism." In *For Love of Country: Debating the Limits of Patriotism*, edited by Joshua Cohen, 3–17. Boston: Beacon Press, 1996.

Nussbaum, Martha C. *Political Emotions: Why Love Matters for Justice*. Cambridge, MA: Harvard University Press, 2013.

Ocher, Medaya. "Karl Ove Knausgaard, Himself." *Los Angeles Review of Books*. June 15, 2014. https://lareviewofbooks.org/article/karl-ove-knausgaard/

O'Connor, Brian. *Idleness: A Philosophical Essay*. Princeton, NJ: Princeton University Press, 2018.

Odell, Jenny. *How to Do Nothing: Resisting the Attention Economy*. New York: Melville House, 2019.

Ondaatje, Michael. *Anil's Ghost*. New York: Knopf, 2000.

Ondaatje, Michael. *The Cat's Table*. Toronto: McClelland & Stewart, 2011.

Ondaatje, Michael. *Coming through Slaughter*. Toronto: Vintage Canada, 1998.

Ondaatje, Michael. *Divisadero*. Toronto: McClelland & Stewart, 2007.

Ondaatje, Michael. *The English Patient*. New York: Vintage, 1993.

Ondaatje, Michael. *In the Skin of a Lion*. New York: Vintage, 1997.

Orwell, George. *1984*. New York: Plume, 1983.

Osborne, Mark. *The Little Prince*. Performed by Jeff Bridges and Mackenzie Foy. 2015; Paramount Pictures.

Oswald, Alice. *Memorial: A Version of Homer's Iliad*. New York: Norton, 2011.

Oswald, Alice. "Alice Oswald on Poetry, Nature, and the Shedding of Identity." Interview by Eleanor Wachtel. *Writers & Company*, CBC. September 23, 2016. Audio, 52: 10. https://www.cbc.ca/radio/writersandcompany/alice-oswald-on-poetry-nature-and-the-shedding-of-identity-1.3769283

Otto, Walter F. *The Homeric Gods: The Spiritual Significance of Greek Religion*. Translated by Moses Hadas. New York: Pantheon, 1954.

Ovid. *The Metamorphoses*. Translated by Rolfe Humphries. Bloomington: Indiana University Press, 1955.

Petit, Philippe. *Creativity: The Perfect Crime*. New York: Riverhead Books, 2014.

Pietz, William. "The Problem of the Fetish, I." *Res: Anthropology and Aesthetics*, no. 9 (Spring 1985): 5–17.

Pietz, William. "The Problem of the Fetish, II." *Res: Anthropology and Aesthetics*, no. 13 (Spring 1987): 23–45.

Pietz, William. "The Problem of the Fetish, IIIa." *Res: Anthropology and Aesthetics*, no. 16 (Autumn 1988): 105–24.

Plato. *The Cratylus, Phaedo, Parmenides, Timaeus and Critias of Plato*. Translated by Thomas Taylor. Michigan: Wizards Bookshelf, 1976.

Platzky, Laurine and Cherryl Walker. *The Surplus People: Forced Removals in South Africa*. Johannesburg: Ravan Press, 1985.

"President Obama & Marilynne Robinson: A Conversation in Iowa." *The New York Review*. November 5, 2015, https://www.nybooks.com/articles/2015/11/05/president-obama-marilynne-robinson-conversation/?lp_txn_id=1249401

Rancière, Jacques. *Dissensus: On Politics and Aesthetics*. Edited and translated by Steven Corcoran. New York: Continuum, 2010.

Rankine, Claudia. "The Condition of Black Life Is One of Mourning." *The New York Times Magazine*. June 22, 2015. https://www.nytimes.com/2015/06/22/magazine/the-condition-of-black-life-is-one-of-mourning.html

Roberts, Siân Lliwen. "Place, Life Histories and the Politics of Relief: Episodes in the Life of Francesca Wilson, Humanitarian Educator Activist." Ph.D diss., University of Birmingham, 2010.

Robinson, Marilynne. *Gilead*. New York: HarperPerennial, 2004.

Robinson, Marilynne. *The Givenness of Things: Essays*. New York: HarperCollins, 2015.

Robinson, Marilynne. *Housekeeping*. New York: HarperPerennial, 2005.

Robinson, Marilynne. *What Are We Doing Here?* New York: McClelland & Stewart, 2018.

Robinson, Marilynne. *When I Was a Child I Read Books*. New York: HarperPerennial, 2012.

Rose, Jonathan. *The Intellectual Life of the British Working Classes*. New Haven: Yale University Press, 2001.

Ryan, Lyndall. *The Aboriginal Tasmanians*. Vancouver, BC: University of British Columbia Press, 1981.

Sacks, Oliver. "Altered States: Self-Experiments in Chemistry." *New Yorker*. August 27, 2012.

Saint-Exupéry, Antoine de. *The Little Prince*. Translated by Katherine Woods. Harmonsworth, England: Penguin, 1965.

Sandars, N. K. Introduction to *The Epic of Gilgamesh*. Translated by N. K. Sanders, 7–60. New York: Penguin, 1972.

"Sandra Cisneros: A House of Her Own." Interview by Krista Tippett, *On Being with Krista Tippett*. February 13, 2020. https://onbeing.org/programs/sandra-cisneros-a-house-of-her-own/

Schottenloher, Karl. *Books and the Western World: A Cultural History*. Translated by William D. Boyd and Irmgard H. Wolfe. Jefferson: McFarland & Company, Inc., 1989.

Schulz, Bruno. *The Street of Crocodiles and Other Stories*. Translated by Celina Wieniewska. New York: Penguin Books, 2008.

Seaford, Richard. *Money and the Early Greek Mind: Homer, Philosophy, Tragedy*. Cambridge: Cambridge University Press, 2004.

Seed, Patricia. *Ceremonies of Possession in Europe's Conquest of the New World, 1492–1640*. Cambridge: Cambridge University Press, 1995.

Serres, Michel. *Hermes: Literature, Science, Philosophy*. Edited by Josué V. Harari and David F. Bell. Baltimore, MD: Johns Hopkins University Press, 1983.

Seuss, Dr. *On Beyond Zebra!* New York: Random House, 1983.

Shakespeare, William. *Measure for Measure*. Edited by S. Nagarajan. New York: Signet, 1988.

Shteyngart, Gary. *Super Sad True Love Story*. New York: Random House, 2011.

Smallwood, Christine. "Greta Gerwig's Radical Confidence." *New York Times Magazine*. November 1, 2017. https://www.nytimes.com/2017/11/01/magazine/greta-gerwigs-radical-confidence.html

Smith, Bernard. "The First European Depictions." In *Seeing the First Australians*, edited by Ian and Tamsin Donaldson, 21–34. London: George Allen & Unwin, 1985.

Sophokles. "Electra." In *An Oresteia*, translated by Anne Carson, 87–172. New York: FSG, 2009.

St. Aubyn, Edward. *The Complete Patrick Melrose Novels*. New York: Picador, 2015.

Steedman, Carolyn Kay. *Landscape for a Good Woman: A Story of Two Lives*. New Brunswick, NJ: Rutgers University Press, 1994.

Strauss Clay, Jenny. *The Politics of Olympus: Form and Meaning in the Major Homeric Hymns*. Princeton, NJ: Princeton University Press, 1989.

Stueber, Karsten R. *Rediscovering Empathy: Agency, Folk Psychology, and the Human Sciences*. Cambridge, MA: MIT Press, 2006.

Su, John J. *Imagination and the Contemporary Novel*. Cambridge: Cambridge University Press, 2011.

Taussig, Michael. *Mimesis and Alterity: A Particular History of the Senses*. New York: Routledge 1993.

Thoreau, Henry D. *Walden*. Edited by J. Lyndon Shanley. Princeton, NJ: Princeton University Press, 2016.

Thoreau, Henry D. *Walden and Other Writings of Henry David Thoreau*. Edited by Brooks Atkinson. New York: The Modern Library, 1965.

Tobar, Héctor. "Sixty-Nine Days: How the Chilean Miners Survived." *New Yorker*, July 7, 2014.

Todorov, Tzvetan. *The Conquest of America: The Question of the Other*. Translated by Richard Howard. New York: HarperPerennial, 1984.

Tóibín, Colm. *Nora Webster*. New York: McClelland & Stewart, 2014.

Trevett, Jeremy. "Coinage and Democracy at Athens." In *Money and Its Uses in the Ancient Greek World*, edited by Andrew Meadows and Kirsty Shipton, 23–34. Oxford: Oxford University Press, 2001.

Trollope, Anthony. *South Africa, Vol. 1*. 1878; London: Dawson's of Pall Mall, 1968.

Turkle, Sherry. *Alone Together: Why We Expect More from Technology and Less from Each Other*. New York: Basic Books, 2012.

The University of Adelaide. "The J. M. Coetzee Centre for Creative Practice." Accessed August 8, 2019. https://www.adelaide.edu.au/jmcoetzeecentre/about-the-centre

Virgil. *The Aeneid*. Translated by Robert Fitzgerald. New York: Vintage, 1990.

Warner, Marina. *Stranger Magic: Charmed States and the Arabian Nights*. London: Chatto & Windus, 2011.

Weil, Simone. *The Iliad or The Poem of Force*. Translated by Mary McCarthy. Wallingford, PA: Pendle Hill, 1983.

Weil, Simone. *Waiting for God*. Translated by Emma Craufurd. New York: HarperPerennial, 2009.

Weiner, Annette. *Inalienable Possessions: The Paradox of Keeping-While-Giving*. Berkeley, CA: University of California Press, 1992.

Wenders, Wim. *Wings of Desire*. Performed by Bruno Ganz and Otto Sander. 1987; The Criterion Collection, 2009.

White, E. B. *Charlotte's Web*. New York: Scholastic, 1952.

Wilkins, John. *Mercury: Or the Secret and Swift Messenger*. Amsterdam: John Benjamins Publishing Co, 1984.

Williams, Rowan D. "The Body's Grace." In *Theology and Sexuality: Classic and Contemporary Readings*, edited by Eugene F. Rogers, Jr., 309–32. Massachusetts: Blackwell, 2002.

Wilson, Francesca. *Aftermath: France, Germany, Austria, Yugoslavia, 1945 and 1946*. London: Penguin, 1947.

Wiman, Christian. *My Bright Abyss: Meditation of a Modern Believer*. New York: FSG, 2013.

Winterson, Jeanette. *The Stone Gods*. New York: Houghton Mifflin Harcourt, 2010.

Younge, Gavin. *Art of the South African Townships*. New York: Rizzoli International Publications, 1988.

Žižek, Slavoj, Eric L. Santner and Kenneth Reinhard. *The Neighbor: Three Inquiries in Political Theology*. Chicago: University of Chicago Press, 2005.

INDEX